"A Pernicious Sort of Woman"

Studies in Medieval and Early Modern Canon Law

Kenneth Pennington, General Editor

Editorial Advisory Board

Studies in Medieval and Early Modern Canon Law

VOLUME 6

"A Pernicious Sort of Woman"

Quasi-Religious Women and Canon Lawyers in the Later Middle Ages

Elizabeth Makowski

The Catholic University of America Press
Washington, D.C.

The paper used in this publication meets the minimum requirements of
American National Standards for Information Science—Permanence of Paper
for Printed Library Materials, ANSI Z39.48-1984.
∞

Library of Congress Cataloging-in-Publication Data

Makowski, Elizabeth M., 1951–
    A pernicious sort of woman : quasi-religious women and canon
lawyers in the later Middle Ages / Elizabeth Makowski.— 1st ed.
        p. cm. — (Studies in medieval and early modern canon law ; v. 6)
    Includes bibliographical references.
    ISBN 0-8132-1392-4 (alk. paper)
    1. Monasticism and religious orders for women (Canon law)—
History—To 1500. 2. Third orders—History—To 1500. I. Title. II. Series.
BX4212.M12 2005
262.9′2—dc22
                                        2004001570

In memory of my sister, Dorothy Bertz, whose achievements I have always tried to equal and shall always fail to surpass.

Contents

Preface

Originality may be the hallmark of a good scholarly monograph, but it seldom distinguishes its preface. Time and again we learn that the book we are about to read began as a response to an issue raised and, of necessity, left unexplored in a preceding study. This work is no exception.

I began writing my last book, *Canon Law and Cloistered Women: Periculoso and Its Commentators 1298–1545*, because of the gap that seemed to exist between scholarly assertions about the importance of Boniface VIII's decree, *Periculoso*, and the evidence upon which those assertions rested. Traditional ecclesiastical historians all regarded the pope's attempt to impose strict cloister regulations on nuns as a watershed in the history of religious women, since by mandating both active and passive enclosure—that is, by limiting exit from as well as entrance (by unauthorized persons) into monastery precincts—it effectively cut them off from secular associations and the public life in general. These assessments of *Periculoso* presumed that the decree had effectively altered long-established practice; that its normative requirements translated with relative ease into action. Yet when I began my own research on the subject, for no close study of the decree's content and history existed, I found little evidence to support this assumption.

Academic lawyers of the period had indeed endorsed the cloistered ideal that *Periculoso* embodied by strictly interpreting the words of the decree. But their endorsement had merely helped to keep the ideal alive until it could be more successfully implemented in the era of Tridentine reform. *Periculoso's* immediate impact was far less impressive. Efforts to enforce it had met with stiff resistance by nuns who saw that it would dramatically affect the manner in which they attracted pious bequests, conducted monastic business, and dealt with patrons and family members. In addition, communities of unenclosed female religious had continued to exist, and even to be founded, long after Boniface VIII's efforts could have been expected to bear fruit.

Periculoso had not been successfully implemented, and it appeared that the increasing popularity of alternatives to conventional monasticism helped to explain that failure. The twelfth century had seen a groundswell of female piety that resulted in a proliferation of quasi-religious roles for women, and by the time *Periculoso* was promulgated unprecedented numbers of women were espousing an ideal of spiritual perfection quite at odds with that of the cloistered nun. Convinced that complete separation from the world enjoined upon conventional religious was not a prerequisite for sanctity, these women joined informal religious communities whose members were bound neither by solemn vows nor by an approved monastic rule.

In issuing *Periculoso*, Boniface VIII had hoped to draw a clear line of demarcation between nuns, those who were religious women in strictly canonical terms, and quasi-religious women, those who were neither professed nor cloistered but who were still popularly referred to as *mulieres religiosae*. But because women continued to swell the ranks of unenclosed monasteries and unofficial, unauthorized, religious communities for the next two hundred years, that exclusionary principle proved impossible to effect. Quasi-religious women continued to be regarded as "religious women" by the people among whom they lived, even though they fell short of the formal requirements for that designation. Nevertheless—and this is the crucial issue—all of those legal requirements were in place by the end of the thirteenth century and their existence had implications for all devout lay women who did not meet them. To the eminent canonist Henry of Susa, or Hostiensis (d. 1274), a beguine was "a pernicious sort of woman" whose uncloistered living arrangements reflected her easy morals. Nearly a century later, academic jurists were still quoting him as they all but unanimously condemned such women. Nor were beguines the only ones to be maligned. Secular canonesses, Sisters of the Common Life, and tertiaries all lived their lives against a backdrop of struggle and insecurity resulting, in large measure, from their ambivalent legal status. Because they lacked one or more of the canonical earmarks of religious women strictly speaking, they had to justify their unauthorized way of life and to defend themselves against association with those of their number who had been branded unorthodox, unruly, or even heretical. Ambiguous legal status within the organized Church, and the contests to which it gave rise is, in fact, a constant theme in the historiography of quasi-religious women, yet there has been no full-scale study of what it meant, at law, to be a *mulier religiosa*.

This book attempts to provide such a study. It surveys the writings of canon lawyers in the late Middle Ages as they come to terms, both in their academic work and also in their roles as judges and advisors, with women who were not, strictly speaking, religious, but who were popularly thought of as such. It looks at the ways in which jurists strove to categorize these women and to clarify the sometimes ambivalent canons relating to their lives in community. It uncovers the sometimes profound differences that existed between legal theory and practical application of the law, and assesses some of the reasons for those differences.

I hope this study of the legal status of quasi-religious women at large will be a useful supplement to monographs devoted to individual women or to specific manifestations of female lay piety. I also hope that I have dealt with all technical material in such a way that not only historians of law and religion, but also anyone with a genuine interest in the history of religious women, will be able to read it with some pleasure, and with full comprehension.

Acknowledgments

The technological miracles of the last decades notwithstanding, libraries continue to be essential to the historian's task. I wish to thank the librarians at the following institutions for their generous help and support and to acknowledge the permission of these libraries to quote from portions of manuscripts and rare books from their collections: The Harry Ransom Humanities Research Center of the University of Texas, Austin; The Library of Congress Law Library, Rare Books Division; The Bibliothèque Nationale, Manuscrits Division Occidentale; The Biblioteca del Cabildo, Toledo; The Law Library, Robbins Collection, of the University of California at Berkeley; the University of Pennsylvania Library; and the Biblioteca Apostolica Vaticana. Thanks as well to the staff of the Hill Monastic Manuscript Library, the Vatican Film Library, the Perry Castañeda and Law Libraries of the University of Texas, and to the obliging librarians in the Reference and Inter-Library Loan Departments of Alkek Library at Texas State University, San Marcos—Margaret Vaverek and Jerry Weathers in particular.

An article entitled *"Mulieres Religiosae*, Strictly Speaking: Some Fourteenth-Century Canonical Opinions,"* summarized some of the findings that I explore in further detail in this book. It appeared in the *Catholic Historical Review* LXXXV (January, 1999): 1–14, and I acknowledge permission to reproduce some portions.

Financial support for this book was provided by three faculty research grants from Texas State, which allowed me to work in libraries in Washington D.C. and in Paris and to purchase microfilmed manuscripts. A semester of developmental leave in Spring, 1998, gave me concentrated time to write.

Of the many colleagues who have given of their talents and time over the course of the long years spanned by this project I want to especially thank Constance Berman, F. Donald Logan, James A. Brundage, Sabrina Corbellini, Hildo Van Engen, Cordelia Warr, John Van Engen, Maiju Lehmijoki-Gardner, Thomas M. Izbicki, and Kenneth Pennington. I am also most grateful to David J. McGonagle, Director of the Catholic University of America Press, and to those who responded with useful criticism and thoughtful questions after hearing parts of this work, presented in the form of conference papers at meetings of the Texas Medieval Association; the IMC, Leeds, U.K.; and the International Congress on Medieval Studies, Kalamazoo. The anonymous reviewers who read an earlier, less focused, draft of this book manuscript also deserve to be acknowledged for their thoroughness, attention to detail and extremely helpful suggestions for revision.

My colleagues in the history department at Texas State have been, and remain, a group as dedicated to their own scholarship as they are supportive of that of their fellows. Through the years, I have benefited from their generosity of spirit. Special thanks to Carol Bargeron, Kenneth Margerison, and Jesús F. de la Teja. I owe a debt as well to the many fine students that I have had the pleasure of teaching, and, in particular to my former graduate student and research assistant, Beth Fuchs.

Less easily articulated, but fully as important, are the contributions that my daughter, Margaret Mary Boylan, and my husband, Roger Boylan, made to the completion of this project.

Abbreviations

BMCL	*Bulletin of Medieval Canon Law,* Berkeley, 1971– .
BN	Bibliothèque Nationale, Paris
Coing, Handbuch	*Handbuch der Quellen und Literatur der neuren europäischen Privatrechtsgeschichte,* ed. Helmut Coing. 3 vols. Munich: C. H. Beck, 1973.
DCB	*Dictionary of Catholic Biography,* ed. J.Delaney. New York: Doubleday, 1961.
DDC	*Dictionnaire de droit canonique,* ed. R. Naz. 7 vols. Paris: Letouzey et Ané, 1935–65.
DHGE	*Dictionnaire D'Histoire et de Géographie Ecclésiastiques.* Paris: Letouzey et Ané, 1977.
DIP	*Dizionario degli Istituti di Perfezione,* ed. G.Pelliccia and G. Rocca. Rome: Edizioni Paoline, 1974– .
DMA	*Dictionary of the Middle Ages,* ed. Joseph Strayer. 13 vols. New York: Scribner's, 1982–89.
Fredericq, *Corpus*	P. Fredericq, *Corpus documentorum inquistionis haereticae pravitatis Neerlandicae.* 3 vols. Ghent: J. Vuylsteke, 1889–1906.

xv

Friedberg, *Corpus*	*Corpus iuris canonici*, ed. Emil Friedberg. 2 vols. Leipzig: B. Tauchnitz, 1879–81. Rpt. Graz: Akademische Druck-u. Verlagsanstalt, 1959.
Hefele/Leclercq	K. J. von Hefele, *Histoire des counciles d'après les documents originaux*, ed. H. Leclercq. 11 vols. in 22. Paris: Letouzey et Ané, 1907–52.
LMA	*Lexikon des Mittelalters*. 10 vols. München und Zürich: Artemis Verlag, 1977–80.
Mansi	*Sanctorum conciliorum nova et amplissima collecto*, ed. Giovanni Domenico Mansi. 31 vols. Florence-Venice, 1759–98.
MIC	*Monumenta iuris canonici*. Vatican City: Biblioteca Apostolica Vaticana, 1965–. *Corpus collectionum*, 1973–. *Corpus glossatorum*, 1969–. *Subsidia*, 1965–.
NCE	*The New Catholic Encyclopedia*. 15 vols. New York: McGraw Hill, 1967.
Niermeyer	*Mediae Latinitatis Lexicon Minus*, ed. J. F. Niermeyer. Leiden: Brill, 1976.
Potthast	*Regesta Pontificum Romanorum*, ed. August Potthast. 2 vols. Berlin: Rudolf de Decker, 1874–79.
Schulte, *QL*	J. Friedrich von Schulte. *Die Geschichte der Quellen und Literatur des canonischen Rechts von Gratian bis auf die Gegenwart*.
Schulte, QL	J. Friedrich von Schulte. *Die Geschichte der Quellen und Literatur des canonischen Rechts von Gratian bis auf die Gegenwart*. 3 vols. Stuttgart: F. Enke, 1875–77; Rpt. Graz: Akademische Druck-u. Verlagsanstalt, 1956.
Van Hove	A. Van Hove. *Prolegomena*. 2nd. ed. Malines-Rome: Dessain, 1945.

Introduction

How did late-medieval canon lawyers deal with a legally suspect, yet irrepressible, phenomenon of their age: the formation of quasi-religious women's communities? How did they respond to the demands of colleagues, judges, and litigants to clarify the legal status of those pious women whose way of life lacked one or more of the attributes necessary to qualify them as 'true religious'? How did legal theory mesh with practice?

These are questions which historians of medieval religious women have rarely asked, and then only with reference to specific quasi-religious groups: Charles de Miramon's study of the *donati/ conversi*, which incorporates a sampling of significant canonical commentary and *consilia*, some of it relating to *conversae*, is a case in point.[1] Yet recent scholarship suggests that we should ask, and attempt to answer, these questions as they relate to quasi-religious women generally.

1. Charles de Miramon, *Les <<donnés>> au Moyen Âge: Une forme de vie religieuse laïque v. 1180–v. 1500*, (Paris: Cerf, 1999). Note also that Gerhard Rehm, *Die Schwestern vom Gemeinsamen Leben im nordwestlichen Deutschland*, (Berlin: Duncker & Humblot, 1985) discusses the legal status of the Sisters of the Common Life, with reference to some legal commentary, in chapter VI.

Women's religious culture in the later Middle Ages is certainly not a new topic of historical inquiry; nor did an earlier generation of historians fail to recognize the marked increase in quasi-religious manifestations of female piety in the period.[2] But it is also true that quasi-religious women have become the focus of an unprecedented number of books and articles, many written by North American academics, in the last few decades. One of the books which helped to create this upsurge of interest is Herbert Grundmann's groundbreaking study, *Religious Movements in the Middle Ages*.[3]

Published in 1935, revised in 1961, and translated into English in 1995, Grundmann's book stimulated research with its argument that women were prominent in all aspects of the religious revival of the twelfth and thirteenth centuries, and that their piety expressed itself in the great variety of orthodox as well as heretical movements of the time. It also drew special attention to the beguines of northern Europe, devout lay women who lived chastely and in common but who refused to be bound by formal monastic vows, classifying them as a unique instance of female-inspired and self-regulated piety.[4]

2. Classic studies such as Karl Bücher, *Die Frauenfrage im Mittelalter*, 2nd ed., (Tübingen: Laupp, 1910) are still cited with regularity in modern scholarship, and the richness of nineteenth-century scholarship with particular reference to beguines has been pointed out especially by Joanna Ziegler, "The *Curtis* Beguinages in the Southern Low Countries: Interpretation and Historiography," *Bulletin van het Belgisch Historisch Instituut te Rome/Bulletin de l'Institut Historique Belge de Rome* 57 (1987): 31–70.

3. Herbert Grundmann, *Religiöse Bewegungen im Mittelalter: Untersuchugen über die geschichtlichen Zusammenhängen zwischen der Ketzerei, den Bettelorden, und der religösen Frauenbewegung im 12 und 13 Jahrhundert und über die geschichtlichen Grundlagen der Deutschen Mystik* (Berlin: E. Ebering, 1935; rev. ed., Hildesheim: Georg Olms Verlagsbuchhandlung, 1961), trans. Steven Rowan as *Religious Movements in the Middle Ages* (Notre Dame, IN: University of Notre Dame Press, 1995). This work had a profound impact on earlier scholarship, and continues to influence modern historians, as demonstrated by recent translation of his work. For a good survey of the impact of Grundmann's work on modern beguine scholarship see Juliette Dor, et al., eds., *New Trends in Feminine Spirituality: The Holy Women of Liège and their Impact* (Turnhout: Brepols, 1999), pp. 1–4.

4. There are a remarkable number of recent books and articles written about the beguines, and although many titles will be mentioned and discussed in this introduction, those who require a concise introduction to

The beguines were among the first to figure prominently in twentieth-century historiography of quasi-religious women, and with the 1954 publication of Ernest McDonnell's *The Beguines and Beghards in Medieval Culture* many more English-speaking historians began to take an interest in a topic which had been the preserve of their Dutch, German, and French counterparts.[5] McDonnell's work had the double merit of being unconventional—his was not a standard topic for an American medievalist to undertake at the time—and exhaustive. The author made use of the vast eighteenth- and nineteenth-century compendia of church records relative to beguines, inquisition reports, and episcopal legislation, as well as archival material. He also examined evidence from chronicles, polemical treatises, and even satirical poetry.

McDonnell's book centered on Belgium, and the strikingly large and numerous beguine communities peculiar to the southern Low Countries were to attract the most scholarly attention in the next decades. A new generation of scholars used notarial protocols (especially of wills), hagiographical literature, canonization proceedings, and works of art, all with considerable success, as sources for fresh insights about the existence, individual and collective, of these 'holy women.'[6] Older theories about the connections between beguines

the topic, with appended bibliography, might consult Robert Lerner, "Beguines and Beghards," *DMA*, 2:158–62; K. Elm, R. Sprandel, and R. Manselli, "Beg(h)inen," *LMA*, 1:1799–1803.

5. Ernest W. McDonnell, *The Beguines and Beghards in Medieval Culture* (New Brunswick, NJ: Rutgers University Press, 1954). The tremendous amount of information in McDonnell's work has helped to make it extremely influential in recent decades. It should be noted here, however, that even McDonnell ignored canon law commentary and *consilia*.

6. For example, see: Walter Simons, "The Beguine movement in the southern Low Countries: a reassessment," *Bulletin de l'Institut Historique Belge de Rome* 59 (1989): 63–105; and Penelope Galloway, "'Discreet and Devout Maidens': Women's Involvement in Beguine Communities in Northern France, 1200–1500," in *Medieval Women in their Communities*, ed. Diane Watt (Toronto: University of Toronto Press, 1997). Joanna Ziegler, "The *Curtis* Beguinages," 31–70, investigates community organization, and *Sculpture of Compassion: The Pieta and the Beguines in the Southern Low Countries, 1300–1600* (Brussels/Rome: Institut historique belge de Rome, 1992), examines beguine piety. There are many recent explorations of beguine

xx   Introduction

and the venerable institution of secular canonesses were reasserted.[7] And, importantly, because Gundmann's vision had been given
new currency by McDonnell, many scholars also adopted a more
synthetic approach to the study of quasi-religious women.
"The Belgian extraregular was but one manifestation of a Euro-
pean-wide movement," opined McDonnell, and his view that quasi-
religious movements parallel to that of the beguines arose simultaneously throughout continental Europe was soon shared by others.[8]
The *beatas* of Spain began to be cited as counterparts to the beguines, and pronounced similarities were noted between Italian
quasi-religious women—referred to variously as *bizzoche, pinzochere,
mantelle* and *sorores de poenitentia*—and their northern sisters.[9] Links

devotional practices, including Judith Oliver, "Devotional psalters and the
study of beguine sprituality, with reference to beguines in the diocese of
Liège in the 13th century," *Vox Benedictina* 9:2 (1992): 199–225; Miri Rubin, *Corpus Christi: Eucharist in Late Medieval Culture* (Cambridge: Cambridge
University Press, 1992); and Dor, *New Trends.* Beguines as victims of persecution for heresy are treated in several modern works, and with special
thoroughness in Gordon Leff, *Heresy in the Later Middle Ages* (New York:
Manchester University Press, 1967); and Robert Lerner, *The Heresy of the
Free Spirit in the Late Middle Ages* (Berkeley: University of California Press,
1972).
  7. Joanna Ziegler, "Secular Canonesses as Antecedent of the Beguines
in the Low Countries: An Introduction to Some Older Views," *Studies in
Medieval and Renaissance History* 13 (1991): 117–35.
  8. McDonnell, *Beguines,* p. 7. Also note that Grundmann, *Religious
Movements,* chapters four and five, has much to say about the similarities
among pious lay women throughout medieval Europe.
  9. For example, see: Romana Guarnieri, "Beghinismo d'Oltralpe e bizzochismo Italiana tra il secolo XIV e il secolo XV," *La Beata Angelina Da
Montegiove e il Movimento del Terz'Ordine Regolare Francescano Feminile,* ed. R.
Pazzelli and M. Sensi, (Roma: TOR, 1984) and her entry: '*Pinzochere,*' *DIP,*
1:1721–49; Joyce Pennings, "Semi-Religious Women in 15th century
Rome," *Mededelingen van het Nederlands Historisch Instituut te Rome* 47:12
(1987): 115–45; Katherine Gill, "Open Monasteries in Late Medieval
Italy," in *The Crannied Wall: Women, Religion and the Arts in Early Modern Europe* (Ann Arbor: University of Michigan Press, 1992), pp. 15–47; and the
variety of articles in *Women and Religion in Medieval and Renaissance Italy,*
ed. Daniel Bornstein and Roberto Rusconi (Chicago: University of Chicago
Press, 1996); Maiju Lehmijoki-Gardner, *Worldly Saints, Social Interaction of
Dominican Penitent Women in Italy, 1200–1500* (Helsinki: Suomen Historiallinen Seura, 1999).

were observed between beguines, tertiaries, and the Sisters of the Common Life as well.[10] Amid the diversity of nomenclature and specific institutional forms, scholars consistently recognized a uniformity of devotional purpose among these *mulieres religiosae*, as they were popularly called, and that recognition began to make its way into standard reference works. The entry *'Beg(h)inen'* in the *Lexikon des Mittelalters*, for instance, includes two sections: I. 'Gebiete nördlich der Alpen' and II. 'Südfrankreich, Italien,' and trans-alpine similarities are highlighted in essays on the *pinzochere* and *beghini* in the *Dizionario degli Istituti di Perfezione.*[11]

Recent research then, has made it quite clear that late medieval quasi-religious women throughout Europe shared the belief that a life lived outside the monastic cloister, without vows or a formal monastic rule, could be sanctified. Manual labor, charity to neighbors, and pious practice in the world, not cut off from it, were their means to this end. Recent research has also revealed that to a greater or lesser extent all quasi-religious women lived out these ideals in an atmosphere of insecurity.

The persecution of beguines, especially after the publication of the decrees of the Council of Vienne (1311–12), which cast suspicion on their orthodoxy, is by far the best-studied example of female quasi-religious vulnerability. The story of attempts by both secular and ecclesiastical forces to disband communities and to harass individual beguines has been well documented and often repeated, if

10. Florence Koorn, "Women without Vows," in *Women and Men in Spiritual Culture XIV–XVII Centuries*, ed. E. Schulte van Kessel (The Hague: Netherlands Government Publications Office, 1986), pp. 135–47; and Rehm, *Die Schwestern*, chapter II, for beguines and the Sisters of the Common Life. Jean-Claude Schmitt, *Mort d'une hérésie: L'église et les clercs face aux béguines et aux beghards du Rhin supérieur du XIVe au XVe siècle* (Paris: Ecole des Hautes Etudes en Sciences, 1978), especially chapter V, discusses the similarities between tertiaries and beguines in a somewhat controversial context, but scholars such as McDonnell and Lerner have clearly drawn associations as well that continued to be discussed in the scholarship.

11. K. Elm, 'Beg(h)inen,' *LMA*, 1:1799–1803; Romana Guarnieri, 'Pinzochere,' *DIP*, 6:1721–49; A. Mens, 'Behini, begardi, beghinaggi,' *DIP*, 1:1165–80.

only in summary.[12] But historians have also illustrated the ways in which both female tertiaries and Sisters of the Common Life, because they resembled beguines, found themselves subjects of inquisitorial investigation on charges ranging from hypocrisy and immorality to heresy. The ways in which ecclesiastical suspicion and censure affected even the most socially privileged of quasi-religious women, secular canonesses, has been described as well.

United by a spiritual ideal, but also by an ambivalent or marginal status within the institutional church and society at large, the *mulieres religiosae* of late medieval Europe could be, and often were, praised for their humility, asceticism and chastity. Their informal, unconstrained devotion might even be lauded as more admirable than that of the nun who was bound to her religious practices by irrevocable vows. Yet the vows that a nun took had more than spiritual significance. Vows constrained, but they also protected; they defined individual obligation but also rewarded the one so bound by recognizing societal responsibility to her. A professed nun could not marry and she lost all claims to her inheritance. But she was immune to the jurisdiction of secular courts, and her very person was protected from violence by threat of excommunication.

Lacking formal ecclesiastical status, quasi-religious women lacked safeguards against arbitrary action. A female tertiary might be allowed to inherit property in one Italian town, but be forbidden to do so by the laws of another. Rhenish Beguines might be required to pay taxes and to appear before secular magistrates during the lifetime of one bishop, and find themselves exempt from both obligations by his successor. Lacking a definite legal status, quasi-religious women might be protected from inquisitors by their patrons and might even enjoy many of the same privileges that were accorded religious women. But they enjoyed those privileges, when they did, on an *ad hoc* basis since, unlike nuns, they possessed no canonical bulwark against the vicissitudes of popular and ecclesiastical opinion.

12. References to secondary scholarship which describes the vulnerability of beguines, tertiaries, Sisters of the Common Life and secular canonesses, can be found in the relevant chapters that follow.

The ways in which jurists interpreted those canons and pronouncements that touched on the relationship between quasi-religious women, the Church, and Christian society at large, deeply affected the day-to-day lives of these women. Canon lawyers did not make the law but they shaped the way that law was understood, and they might do so in ways that differed significantly from the apparent purpose of the lawmakers. Why then has there been so little written on the legal literature related to late medieval quasi-religious women? The nature of that literature, I think, accounts in part for the neglect.

Medieval canon law cannot be studied without the vast body of commentary generated by that law. As Richard Helmholz points out, it is the commentary that "shows how the law was taught in the medieval schools. It provided an essential means by which the law itself was moved forward, and it provides the modern student with an understanding of the inner nature of canonistic thought."[13] Yet for all its importance and erudition, this literature is extremely difficult to make sense of. It contains innumerable and not always legible abbreviations, and equally numerous technical citations to obscure sources. Moreover, the style in which commentators present their arguments is both repetitive and sophistic. This is particularly true for "those vast elephantine commentaries" of the later canonists which even legal scholars have traditionally avoided in favor of the more elegant products of the classical period (1140–1375) of canon law development.[14]

A broad historiographical shift, now some decades old, may also be partly responsible for the reluctance of historians to treat the subject. That shift, characterized by a strongly populist bent, has

13. Richard Helmholz, *The Spirit of Classical Canon Law* (Athens/London: University of Georgia Press, 1996), p. 22.

14. Brian Tierney, "Canon law and Church Institutions in the late Middle Ages," in *Proceedings of the Seventh International Congress of Medieval Canon Law*, ed. Peter Linehan, *MCI*, Series C: Subsidia vol.8 (Vatican City: Biblioteca Apostolica Vaticana, 1988), pp. 49–69. Tierney notes that the preeminent historian of the canon law, Gabriel Le Bras, once declared that "the epoch of the Great Schism . . . provides no material for a historian of the canon law."

spawned research into non-institutional piety, enthusiastic religion, and other expressions of popular devotion, rather than studies of doctrine and abstract theory—the erstwhile mainstay of medieval religious history.[15] Profound disjunctions between normative literature and popular religious practice, particularly women's pious practice, began to appear. The dominant paradigms were shown to be partial at best: The content of female devotion, for instance, could no longer be described merely in terms of motifs and images constructed by men.[16]

Given these new directions in the historiography, the examination of prescriptive, male-biased canonical literature would hardly have been given top priority. Yet, just as the devotional life of medieval women cannot be studied in isolation from the men who guided, criticized, or interfered with it, neither can the social realities of quasi-religious life be understood without reference to the men who interpreted the law under which it was lived. More generally, the trans-national focus of canonical literature recommends it as a source particularly germane to the study of phenomena which possess distinctive, and in the case of quasi-religious women almost limitless, regional variations, along with fundamental similarities.

The decrees of councils and synods, the material routinely interpreted by academic canonists, were binding in theory if not always

15. Fredric Cheyette and Marcia Colish "Medieval Europe," *AHA Guide to Historcal Literature*, 3rd ed., vol. 1 (New York: Oxford University Press, 1995), p. 622. And see John Van Engen, "The Future of Medieval Church History," *Church History* 71 (2002): 492–522. This shift of scholarly attention to the non-elite is certainly not confined to medieval religious history. See, for example, David Foote, "How the Past Becomes a Rumor: The Notarialization of Historical Consciousness in Medieval Orvieto," *Speculum* 75 (2000): 794.

16. See, for example, Caroline Walker Bynum, *Holy Feast and Holy Fast* (Berkeley: University of California Press, 1987), p. 29 and chapter 10, and *Fragmentation and Redemption: Essays on Gender and the Human Body in Medieval Religion* (New York: Zone Books, 1991), especially the Introduction–chapter II. Bynum has noted that male and female saints had different self-conceptions and that these differences emerge when we look at the way in which male biographers record and reflect upon the deeds of their female subjects. Note as well, observations in Jane Schulenburg, *Forgetful of Their Sex* (Chicago: University of Chicago Press, 1998).

in fact on all Christians regardless of national or regional identities. At the level of practice, laity and clergy, men and women alike, routinely encountered the canon law in the courtroom, which makes the *consilium*, or legal opinion, rendered at the request of a litigant or sitting judge a link between medieval legal theory and its application.[17] And although the practice of using *consilia* as sources for legal and social history is a relatively recent one, legal historians working on topics that range from medieval marriage and sexual mores to the rights of princes, paupers, and Jews, have proven its value.[18]

Finally, investigating the work of canon lawyers sheds some much-needed light on the jurists themselves. Close scrutiny of their writings and decisions reveals a range and variety of legal opinion too often obscured by the assumption that elite status *ipso facto* implied cultural conservatism; that upon admittance to that chimerical monolith, "the ecclesiastical hierarchy," jurists lost all vestiges of individuality and assumed instead a uniform and invariably repressive point of view.

Having established the need for this study of the law as it relates to quasi-religious women, we must now look at how medieval lawyers themselves used the terms we have been employing less technically. What did they mean when they talked of pious women who were not fully religious or those who were religious in the

17. See the introduction to Peter R. Pazzaglini and Catherine Hawks, *Consilia: A Bibliography of Holdings in the Library of Congress and Certain Other Collections in the United States* (Washington, DC: The Library of Congress, 1990) for a useful overview of the genre, and relevant bibliography of secondary literature.

18. Many examples might be given but the trend is well illustrated by studies such as Brian Tierney, *Medieval Poor Law. A sketch of canonical theory and its application in England* (Berkeley: University of California Press, 1959); Norman Zacour, *Jews and Saracens in the Consilia of Oldradus de Ponte* (Toronto: University of Toronto Press, 1990); Kenneth Pennington, *The Prince and the Law 1200–1600* (Berkeley: University of California Press, 1993); John T. Noonan, *Power to Dissolve: Lawyers and Marriages in the Courts of the Roman Curia* (Cambridge, Harvard University Press, 1972); James A. Brundage, *Law, Sex and Christian Society in Medieval Europe* (Chicago: University of Chicago Pres, 1987) for the use of *consilia*, see especially chapter 10.

broad sense of the term only? Was the designation quasi-religious (a term which they used) and if so, did it have negative implications?

Questions of terminology are always important in historical research but they are especially significant, and significantly troublesome, for students of medieval religious experience. In his book *The Reformation of the Twelfth Century*, Giles Constable illustrates the complex and elusive nature of the technical vocabulary of medieval religious life. The term *clericus*, for instance, although commonly used to refer to anyone who had been ordained, could also mean someone who was literate; *conversus* usually designated an adult entrant into religious life (as distinct from the child oblate) but was also used to refer to a variety of lay monastic affiliates; the term *canon* had accrued eight distinct meanings by the start of the High Middle Ages and parallel overlapping usages were anything but uncommon—inconsistencies which, Constable wryly observes, "seem on the whole to have disturbed contemporaries less than they do scholars who try to understand and impose order on the developments at that time. . . ."[19]

Ideas about what a devout life entailed were as much subject to reinterpretation as technical terminology. In the early Middle Ages, monasticism, with its emphasis on community, had been the favored model for representing the *vita apostolica*. From about the middle of the twelfth century, however, itinerant preachers and quasi-religious fraternities also claimed to better represent that species of primitive Christian life, engaged as they were in the sort of preaching and pastoral work that had been enjoined upon the first apostles.[20]

In a development not unrelated to the reassessment of what it

19. Giles Constable, *The Reformation of the Twelfth Century* (Cambridge: Cambridge University Press, 1996), p. 13. See all of the Introduction for a sampling of multiple meanings which words could and did have.

20. Constable, *The Reformation*, pp. 156–160. Changing notions regarding the apostolic ideal are also central to the arguments advanced by Herbert Grundmann, *Religious Movements*. See also Clarissa Atkinson, "'Precious Balsam in a Fragile Glass': The Ideology of Virginity in the Later Middle Ages," *Journal of Family History* 8 (1983): 131–43, which deals with shifts in religious feeling that led to the reinterpretation of an ideal which we normally think of as unequivocal.

meant to live the apostolic life, the term *religio* itself became increasingly elastic in the thirteenth century. The word continued to denote monastic observance, the life lived by the 'regular' monk or nun, but it also began to be employed to designate any person who lived a life of dedication to God—the latter meaning in no way driving out the former.[21]

Writing early in the thirteenth century, that redoubtable defender of the beguines Jacques de Vitry (d. 1240) said, "We do not consider religious only those who renounce the world and go over to a religious life, but we can also call religious all the faithful of Christ who serve the Lord under the one highest and supreme Abbot."[22] And this definition was not restricted to use by spiritual directors and advocates for the various manifestations of a more interiorized form of religious life.

In 1253 the famous canon lawyer Hostiensis, also known as Henry of Susa, wrote that "Someone who lives in a holy and religious way in his own house, although not professed, is also called religious in a broad sense (*in largo modo*) not because that sort of person is bound to any precise rule but rather because he leads a stricter and holier life than other secular people."[23]

Like Hostientsis, the late medieval canonists with whom we are

21. Grundmann, *Religious Movements*, p. 1; Peter Biller, "Words and the Medieval Notion of 'Religion'," *Journal of Ecclesiastical History* 36:3 (1985): 351–69.

22. As quoted from Jacques de Vitry's *Historia occidentalis*, in Constable, *The Reformation*, p. 293. See also the references to de Vitry in Miramon, *Les <<donnés>>*, pp. 196–99.

23. Hostiensis (Henricus de Segusio), *Summa aurea*, III, *De regularibus transeuntibus ad religionem, ii, Religiosus largo modo quis dicatur* (Venice, 1574). His comment has been often mentioned in the context of later medieval thought on the topic. See for example: Biller, "Words," p. 358 n.24; André Vauchez, *The Laity in the Middle Ages*, trans. Margery Schneider (Notre Dame: University of Notre Dame Press, 1993), p. 113; John Van Engen, "Friar Johannes Nyder on Laypeople Living as Religious in the World," in *Vita Religiosa im Mittelalter, Festschrift für Kaspar Elm zum 70.Geburtstag*, ed. F. Felten und N. Jaspert (Berlin: Duncker & Humblot, 1999), p. 591–92; Swanson, *Religion and Devotion*, p. 104; Constable, *The Reformation*, pp. 7–8; and Miramon, *Les <<donnés>>*, pp. 164–65, and with reference to privileges entailed by his designation, pp. 178–83.

concerned were well aware of the broad sense in which the term *religio* could be used; they could and did employ the term *largo modo*, when writing about individuals and groups less interested in external forms than in the personal expression of their devotion. They used the term *religio* in its strict sense too, but when they did so the canonists of the fourteenth and fifteenth centuries referred to something even more precise, even more bristling with juridical requirements than that alluded to by Hostiensis.

Even as late as the twelfth century, it could be said that entry into religion "implied a way of life more than a legal status; it was not entirely clear how someone became a monk or nun."[24] By the fourteenth century, all such ambiguity had been removed. Since the Fourth Lateran Council (1215) had forbidden the founding of new religious orders with the decree *Ne nimia religionum,* anyone who subsequently wished to become a religious, strictly speaking, had to enter one of the already approved orders.[25] A decree of the Second Council of Lyon (1274), *Religionum diversitatem,* repeated the Lateran ban, adding that any new order which had arisen since 1215 without express papal confirmation was to be suppressed.[26] *Ne nimia* was incorporated into the collection of canon law known as the *Decretals* of Gregory IX, or *Liber Extra* (*X* 3.36.9) and *Religionum diversitatem* found its way into the *Liber Sextus* (*VI* 3.17.1); medieval canonists would cite both decrees from these collections.[27]

Pope Boniface VIII subsequently removed any ambiguity about

24. Constable, *The Reformation*, p. 16.
25. Mansi, XX, 1002. Note that the critical edition of the canons of the Fourth Lateran Council is that of Antonio García y García, *MIC, Corpus glossatorum*, vol. 1 (Vatican City: Biblioteca Apostolica Vaticana, 1981). An English facing-text of the council's decree can be found in Norman Tanner, ed., *Decrees of the Ecumenical Councils* (Washington, DC: [[publisher name]], 1990), p. 242. The Latin text in this edition is a reprint from the *Decreta oecumenicorum conciliorum*, 3rd ed., Giuseppe Aiberigo, et al. (Bologna, 1972).
26. Tanner, *Decrees*, pp. 326–27.
27. The Latin texts can be found in the standard modern edition of the body of medieval canon law, Emil Friedberg, ed., *Corpus iuris canonici* (Leipzig: B. Tauchnitz, 1879; rpt. Graz: Akademische Druck-u. Verlagsanstalt, 1959) at 2:607 and 2:1042–43 respectively.

the way in which an approved community could admit new members. The candidate for religious life would not only pronounce the traditional vows of poverty, chastity, and obedience, but also make formal profession. The public act of profession, signified by the assumption of a distinctive habit, was considered the action by which the vows of religion were made solemn.[28]

By the start of the fourteenth century, a person defined by canon law as religious was one who had not only taken vows but who had also made solemn profession in an already existing order. For women, although not for their male counterparts, solemn profession involved a commitment to strict claustration.[29] In prevailing juridical terms, women's religious communities which were organized in such a way that they lacked one or more of the above legal requirements were "not fully religious" and the *mulieres religiosae* who lived in those communities were not "strictly speaking" religious although their lifestyles were distinctly imitative of "true religious." They were, in short, quasi-religious women.[30]

28. *VI 3.15.1* Friedberg, *Corpus*, 2:1054–55.

29. The 1298 decree of Pope Boniface VIII, *Periculoso* (*VI 3.16.1*; Friedberg, *Corpus*, 2:1053–54) stipulated that all professed nuns observe cloister regulations. Claustration rules strictly limited the occasions on which outsiders, even members of the clergy, could enter a women's monastery, and they forbade unauthorized exits save for emergencies. For a detailed discussion of this decree see Elizabeth Makowski, *Canon Law and Cloistered Women: Periculoso and its Commentators 1298–1545* (Washington, DC: The Catholic University of America Press, 1997).

30. This is the sense in which older studies of the canon law use the term. See, for instance, Bernard Joseph Ristuccia, *Quasi-Religious Societies* (Washington, DC: The Catholic University of America Press, 1949). Another legal summary of the evolution of the canon law with regard to informal religious groups refers to them as societies, but requires a considerable subheading W. A. Stanton, *De Societatibus, Sive Virorum sive Mulierum in Communi Viventium Sine Votis* (Halifaxiae: Apud Custodiam Librariam Maioris Seminarii A Sanctissimo Corde B.M.V., 1936). The term *semi-religious* has also been employed in outstanding modern treatments of beguines and other quasi-religious, for instance, Kaspar Elm, *"Vita regularis sine regula: Bedeutung,Rechtsstellung und Selbstverstänis des mittelalterlichen und frühneuzeitlichen Semireligiosentums," Häresie und vorzeitige Reformation im Spätmittelalter*, ed. F. Smahel (München: R. Oldenbourg, 1998), 239–73.

As Charles de Miramon has noted, the term "quasi-religious" denotes a relationship; it is less a descriptive than a comparative term.[31] To be quasi-religious means to exist outside, but not too far outside, an institutionalized and legally recognized model for religious life. The late medieval canonists used words like "almost" or "nearly" *(pene)* religious to designate those who were not merely laity *(non mere sunt personae seculares; non mere laice)* but who could still not be called truly religious *(non sunt veri religiosi; non proprie regulares nec est proprie et stricte religiosi).* And while some historians have used the term "semi-religious" to succinctly refer to these same people, I chose to use the term "quasi-religious" throughout this book because it seems to capture the sense of medieval canonical usage rather than suggesting a more pronounced and clearer demarcation between lay and religious than was actually made in the late Middle Ages.

Before leaving the topic of terminology it should be noted that the classification "quasi-religious" was a legal, not a moral one. The judgment that an individual had omitted some act or word that was legally required of the "true" religious had other legal ramifications: for testamentary rights, for instance, or for the legality of a marriage subsequent to leaving an informally constituted community. Of course the canonists did consider questions of morality as well as law in their commentaries, and they generally concurred that members of informal religious groups might fall prey to heresy more easily than their more closely regulated, not to mention cloistered, counterparts. Mere classification as "quasi-religious," however, did not imply heterodox belief. In short, to belong to a group that lacked full religious status was not *ipso iure* bad. As will become apparent, the jurists themselves recognized just how common such communities were, and how much support they received from patrons and pious benefactors. It was the very popularity of quasi-religious communities, in fact, that made their legal status something with which the working jurist could not fail to become conversant.

It is also worth mentioning that for the canonists the question of

31. Miramon, *Les <<donnés>>*, p. 9. The entire Introduction is a valuable contribution to the discussion of terminology and methodology.

community organization among quasi-religious was a crucial one. It was group organization similar to, but departing in some essential way from, full-fledged religious communities that so often resulted in confusion among the faithful; and commentators allude again and again to such a blurring of distinctions. Women whose vocations were essentially individual or solitary—the anchoress, hermit, or vowess for example—are dealt with much less frequently. Consequently, the reader will find few references to these women in the pages that follow.

Some concluding comments about the organization and chronology of this book are also in order. Medieval canon law was self-referential, and this characteristic affects the way I have organized this study. The canonists constructed their glosses on a particular enactment or decree by securing each element in the logical chain of argument with proof texts or authoritative statements. These supporting authorities in turn could be drawn from the Roman law of antiquity, from early church councils, or from the teachings of the fathers of the church, but they might also be drawn from the lecture notes *(lectura)*, from the *summae*, or from commentaries of distinguished contemporary jurists. Therefore, while both major parts of this book have a roughly chronological framework, that structure gives way as needed to a synchronous approach.

Part I deals with specific enactments which found their way into the law books and which consequently generated academic commentary for decades after their promulgation. This commentary is presented alongside the decree which gave rise to it not only to illustrate the course taken by canonical reasoning, but also to acquaint the reader with allusions and authoritative texts that will reappear in subsequent glosses.

Part II examines instances in which the canonists applied the law in actual cases involving quasi-religious women. This section includes evidence drawn from *consilia*, as well as from *decisiones* of the Roman Rota. It also contains a discussion of the discrepancies that exist between academic commentary and case law, and some explanations for the less than perfect correspondence between legal theory and practice.

Since the content of academic commentary on laws relating to quasi-religious women bears directly on issues raised by modern scholarship, Part III contains a chapter summarizing what medieval lawyers had to say and assessing the implications of their opinions for present-day researchers.

Finally, this book focuses on the fourteenth and fifteenth centuries because these last medieval centuries present historians of religious women with a paradox. On the one hand, scholars point to the repressive character of the era ushered in by the condemnation of the beguines at the Council of Vienne (1311–12).[32] Historians who are inclined to equate the promulgation of condemnatory legislation with effective suppression of those targeted have not only posited the extinction of beguine communities during this time, but have also maintained that with few exceptions "women living outside the traditional institutional authority of the Church found themselves numbered with the heretics, vulnerable to persecution and to death."[33]

On the other hand, recent studies show that during this same two-hundred-year period, quasi-religious women's groups not only survived, but even proliferated. "In general, a high degree of tolerance for varieties among women's religious communities prevailed in the fourteenth and fifteenth centuries," writes Katherine Gill, and Craig Harline finds proof of late medieval support of quasi-religious women in the founding of the Grey Sisters and other unenclosed female communities in the Low Countries.[34]

32. This characterization of the fourteenth century is a commonplace. See for example: Lerner, *The Heresy of the Free Spirit;* Kate Galea, "Unhappy Choices: Factors that Contributed to the Decline and Condemnation of the Beguines," *Vox Benedictina* 10 (1993): 56–73; Jean-Claude Schmitt, *Mort d'une hérésie.*

33. Bonnie Anderson and Judith Zinsser, *A History of Their Own*, vol. I (New York: Harper and Row, 1988), p. 226. Carol Neel, "The Origins of the Beguines," *Signs* 14:2 (1989): 321–41, states: ". . . communities [of beguines] all but disappeared, forced out of existence by ecclesiastical reprobation . . .", p. 325. All older studies of the canon law, such as Ristuccia, *Quasi-Religious Societies*, and Stanton, *De Societatibus*, leave the impression that papal condemnation meant instant oblivion for beguines.

34. Katherine Gill, "Scandala: controversies concerning *clausura* and

This apparent paradox, which features repressive legislative intent and its incomplete realization, invites further investigation. Looking at the ways in which fourteenth- and fifteenth-century canonists interpreted and implemented the canon law regarding quasi-religious women will improve our understanding of the mechanisms which sustained this discrepancy.

---

women's religious communities in late medieval Italy," *Christendom and Its Discontents*, ed. Scott Waugh and Peter Diehl (Cambridge: Cambridge University Press, 1996), pp. 177–203, 198; Craig Harline, "Actives and Contemplatives: The Female Religious of the Low Countries before and after Trent," *Catholic Historical Review* LXXXI:4 (1995): 541–67. See also, Hildo van Engen, "The canonical status of the tertiaries of the Utrecht Chapter," a paper delivered as part of the round-table discussion of semi-religious women in the urban environment during the later Middle Ages, International Medieval Congress, Leeds, U.K., July, 2001. Van Engen shows that from the start of the 15th century, tertiaries in the Utrecht diocese were given unconditional support by the bishop of Utrecht, who granted them full ecclesiastical immunity, in spite of the fact that they did not yet take solemn vows. Mario Sensi, "Anchoresses and Penitents in Thirteenth- and Fourteenth-Century Umbria," in *Women and Religion*, pp. 56–83, describes the variety of ways in which fourteenth-century *bizzoche* successfully avoided claustration while continuing to enjoy communal semi-religious life as pious women supported popularly and politically in Italian cities.

Part I

Academic Commentary:
Lawyers Interpret the Law

O N E

Attendentes and Secular Canonesses

P ope Clement V published his new collection of canon law on March 21, 1314. He called it *Liber Septimus* since it was a compilation of papal constitutions and conciliar legislation that had come into existence subsequent to the promulgation of the *Liber Sextus* by Pope Boniface VIII in 1298.[1] Less than a month later Clement V died and both the name and, to some extent, the content of his collection changed.

Formal promulgation or circulation of copies of a new legal collection to the universities, especially to the preeminent law school at the university of Bologna, was fundamental to medieval practice. Clement V's death postponed promulgation of his book, and it was not until October, 1317, that the new pope, John XXII, completed that process. In the intervening years the collection had been renamed the *Clementinae* or *Constitutiones Clementinae*, and John had also felt free to make modifications in the text itself.

The *Clementinae* was the last official collection of medieval canon

---

1. A. Van Hove, *Prolegomena*, Commentaria Lovaniense in Codicem iuris canonici I.1, 2nd. ed. (Malines-Rome, 1945), p. 366; *NCE*, 3:945–46; Sophie Menache, *Clement V* (Cambridge: Cambridge University Press, 1998), p. 289.

law and, as such, its content and the circumstances surrounding its publication have interested legal historians for some time.[2] But for historians of women religious, Clement's collection of laws is known principally because it contains two decrees, referred to by their opening words *Cum de quibusdam* and *Ad nostrum.* Both deal, although from very different perspectives, with the beguines, and given the popularity of beguine scholarship it is not surprising that these two constitutions are routinely cited to illustrate Clement V's attitude toward quasi-religious women. But the *Clementinae* contains legislation dealing with a much more venerable quasi-religious group as well. A canon of the Council of Vienne (1311–12) published in Book III of the *Clementinae,* pertains to a group of aristocratic quasi-religious known as secular canonesses, women whose claim on the religious life of the church was as ancient as it was contested.

The beguines originated in the late twelfth century, but some historians, and medieval canonesses themselves, traced the roots of the canonical way of life back to the fourth century. They found evidence that in the Eastern Church at that time, the term *canonica,* along with several others such as *mulier religiosa, ancilla Dei,* and *femina Deo devota,* designated women whose pious services for a church were recorded in its canon or register.[3] Even if we confine ourselves

2. The debate about content and circumstances of publication will be dealt with in the next chapter, along with questions regarding the number of canons actually issued by the council of Vienne and included in the Clementines.

3. N. Backmund, "Canonesses," *NCE,* 3:53; Jo Ann Kay McNamara, *Sisters in Arms* (Cambridge, MA: Harvard University Press, 1996), p. 177. Karl Heinrich Schäfer, *Die Kanonissenstifter in deutschen Mittelalter* (Stutt-gart: F. Enke, 1907, rpt. Amsterdam: P. Schippers, 1965) is a classic monographic study. For good historical overviews of the institution see: M. Parisse, "Kanonissen," *LMA,* 5:907–8; "Canonichesse Secolari," *DIP,* 2:42–45; and P. Torquebiau, "Chanoinesses," *DDC,* 3:488–530, which places emphasis on ancient origins as well as citing some of the proof texts we deal with in this chapter. For early medieval developments consult Suzanne Fonay Wemple, "Monastic Life of Women from the Merovingians to the Ottonians," in *Hrotsvit of Gandersheim—Rara Avis in Saxonia?* ed. Katharina M. Wilson (Ann Arbor, MI: MARC Publishing, 1987), pp. 35–54.

to Western prototypes, however, it becomes clear that secular canonesses had provided a quasi-religious alternative to convent life for aristocratic women in Germany, France, and the Low Countries at least since the eighth century. In 742 the *Concilium Germanicum* drew the distinction between *virgines velatae,* or nuns, and *virgines non velatae,* canonesses. The term *canonicae* was then applied to virgins and widows who did not enter a convent but rather lived according to the synodal canons of the local bishop, *"sub ordine canonica."* In an attempt to regularize practice in Frankish territories, various councils ordered that pious women choose between profession as a Benedictine nun or a life guided by canonical regulation. Those regulations remained inconsistent and largely unavailable to women until the Council of Chalons in 813 published rules for canonesses *(sanctimoniales qui canonicas vocant).* In 816, when the Council of Aachen met, these rules were expanded into the *Institutio sanctimonialium,* and the institution of canonesses was officially recognized.

As the Latin terminology cited above suggests, the distinction between nuns and canonesses was not always clear-cut. Both nuns and canonesses were ruled by abbesses, and even the regulations issued by the Council of Aachen address canonesses as *sanctimoniales,* the term generally used to mean nuns.[4] Modern historians forced to rely on evidence from foundation documents and chronicles with imprecise terminology have had considerable difficulty differentiating between nuns and canonesses.[5] Medieval canonesses, however, frequently insisted upon such a distinction, especially when resisting reformist attempts to turn institutes of canonesses into Benedictine nunneries.

Canonesses consistently claimed to be distinct from nuns in that they were not bound by strict cloister regulations and made no formal profession, hence taking no permanent vows. The rejection of strict claustration stemmed from the fact that canonesses had traditionally performed public liturgical functions, ranging from ringing

4. McNamara, *Sisters,* pp. 178–79.
5. Wemple, "Monastic Life," p. 40; McNamara, *Sisters,* pp. 178–79.

church bells and leading processions to participating in provincial synods, and that such functions made enclosure impractical, if not impossible. The absence of permanent vows had even greater ramifications. Since they did not vow chastity, they could leave the canonical life to marry; since they took no vow of poverty, secular canonesses retained rights to private property, and they lived in their own houses or apartments within the monastery walls, built around the abbey church.[6]

Throughout the Middle Ages, secular canonesses were highly regarded. Their patrons were kings, queens, popes, and local nobility. Emperors freed these communities of noble women, some founded by their mothers or sisters, from local jurisdiction; some even obtained exemption from episcopal tithes. The greatest houses, such as Gandersheim, Quedlinburg, and Essen, possessed tremendous wealth and became centers of learning and culture. The abbesses in such houses wielded power commensurate with their titles of *metropolitana* and *diaconissa*.

Money and powerful patronage protected secular canonesses even from reforming churchmen whose sense of order was offended by the 'irregularity' of their institution. As noted, Carolingian legislation sought to regularize religious practice among Frankish women. Efforts were also made at that time to impose strict, or at least stricter, claustration among canonesses and to restrict their quasi-sacerdotal liturgical activities. Both reform programs were resisted, and there are many examples from the tenth century of powerful abbesses living unrestricted lives amid considerable personal and communal wealth.[7]

Nevertheless, with the renewed reform efforts of the late eleventh century, the quasi-religious character of secular canonesses once again became an issue among some of the church hierarchy.

6. See Ziegler, "Secular Canonesses," on the importance of recognizing fundamental similarities between quasi-religious canonesses and Beguines. Suzanne Fonay Wemple, *Women in Frankish Society: Marriage and the Cloister 500 to 900* (Philadelphia: University of Pennsylvania Press, 1981), pp. 168–74, provides an introduction to the subject of secular canonesses.

7. McNamara, *Sisters*, pp. 196–97.

In 1059 a Roman synod required canonesses to opt for either the Benedictine or Augustinian rule and, as we shall see, a decree from the Second Lateran Council of 1139 was even more pointed in its denunciations of alleged abuses.[8]

It is within this context of renewed clerical criticism of certain features of female canonical life—criticism that stopped short of becoming blanket condemnation of an aristocratic tradition—that we must place the Clementine decree *Attendentes*. Along with several other canons of the Council of Vienne, this constitution reflects continuing efforts to renew and reform monastic life. Indeed, almost all of the text is devoted to procedures to be followed in the visitation of nuns:[9]

"Visitors, be they bishops or others responsible for the oversight of *monasteria monialium*, are enjoined to regulate the dress and comportment of nuns, to dissuade them from wearing the latest fashions and from attending banquets and dances." Provisions regarding the office of abbess are followed by instructions about the number and nature of the visitor's entourage, and the decree concludes with a warning directed at those who would dare to interfere with any aspect of ordinary visitation. Shortly before this conclusion, however, there occurs a cryptic insertion pointedly subjecting secular canonesses to visitation:

> We also order, by our apostolic authority, that those women who are commonly called secular canonesses and who lead a life like that of secular canons, making no renunciation of private property and no profession, should be visited by the local ordinaries, who are to visit the non-exempt on their own authority and the exempt on the authority of the apostolic see. By this, however, we are not intending to approve the status, rule or order of secular canonesses.[10]

8. McNamara, *Sisters,* p. 191 for mention of the Roman synod; consideration of the Lateran decree follows in my discussion of Johannes Andreae's gloss.

9. *Clem.3.10.2.* The full Latin text can be found in Friedberg, *Corpus,* 2:1168–69.

10. This English translation is provided, with facing Latin, in Norman Tanner, ed., *Decrees of the Ecumenical Councils,* vol. I (Washington, DC: Sheed and Ward,1990), p. 373.

Within two years of its formal presentation to the law schools of the major medieval universities, canonists began to produce commentaries on the *Clementinae* and so on *Attendentes*. Their written analyses could assume several forms, but despite differences in arrangement and depth of treatment, all were intended to explicate legal texts for teaching purposes. One popular form, the *Lectura* for instance, was nothing more than the compiled lecture notes of a medieval law student or professor.[11]

Commonly, the text to be examined, or glossed, filled the center of a manuscript page and the marginal notes of the commentator bordered that text. Certain words or phrases were singled out for comment and references to other laws, canon or civil, were appended to prove (hence the term 'proof text') or reinforce the glossator's points. While tradition and professional practice constrained them, jurists did have a certain amount of leeway when composing their commentaries. They might choose not to comment on some of the legislation included in a compilation such as the *Clementines*, or they might reserve detailed analysis for those laws or the portions thereof that most interested them.

Furthermore, commentary produced at an opportune time by a well-regarded jurist might become the *glossa ordinaria*, or standard gloss to a major legal compilation. The ordinary gloss would then have profound influence on legal scholarship and practice since it would be reproduced alongside the original legislation in each new copy of a compilation in manuscript or, by the close of the fifteenth century, in print. Once a standard gloss on a given body of law existed, subsequent commentators would be heavily influenced by it, as would law faculty and working lawyers consulting those books contained in the *corpus* of canon law.

Canonical comment on *Attendentes* will illustrate most, if not all, of the above generalizations about the production of academic commentary. Reviewing the factors that routinely influenced the style

11. Stephan Kuttner, "The Revival of Jurisprudence," in *Renaissance and Renewal in the Twelfth Century,* ed. Benson and Constable (Cambridge: Cambridge University Press, 1982), pp. 299–323 discusses legal literary forms and methodology. See also Brundage, *Medieval Canon Law,* chapter 3.

and content of academic glosses also enables us to understand juristic elaborations that might otherwise appear inapposite, or even bizarre, to the modern reader.

The earliest surviving commentary on the *Clementine Constitutions*, the *Lectura super Clementinis*, was the work of the French canonist Guilelmus de Monte Laudano.[12] Guilelmus, a Cluniac monk who received his doctorate in canon law from the University of Paris, taught at the University of Toulouse, and completed his commentary only two years after the formal promulgation of the *Clementines*. He chose to gloss the decree *Attendentes*, and when he reached the statement concerning secular canonesses, singled out the word *approbare* (to approve) in the context: ". . . By this, however, we are not intending to approve the status rule or order of secular canonesses."[13] His comment is then limited to one statement: "We cannot entirely prohibit the evil inclinations (choices) of mankind."[14]

Guilelmus' reference comes directly from a statement attributed to Saint John Chrysostom and included in the standard medieval textbook of canon law, Gratian's *Decretum* (C. 31 q.1 c.9).[15] Chrysos-

---

12. Stephan Kuttner, "The Apostillae of Johannes Andreae on the Clementines," *Etudes D'Histoire Du Droit Canonique* (Paris: Sirey, 1965), pp. 197–98; Ibid., "Professeurs de droit canon à Toulouse," *L'Eglise et le droit dans le Midi (XIIIᵉ–XIVᵉ S.)*, Cahiers de Fanjeaux, vol. 29, (Toulouse: Editions Privat, 1994), p. 285. For further biographical details see Schulte, pp. 197–98; G. Mollat, *DDC*, 5:1078–79. This canonist's name, along with those of many of his contemporaries, is spelled variously.

13. Guilelmus de Monte Laudano, *Apparatus in Clementinas*, Paris, BN lat 14331, folo 102v.

14. Guilelmus de Monte Laudano, *Apparatus: ad verbum approbare: malas hominum voluntates ad plenum prohibere non possumus.*

15. Officially entitled *Concordia discordantium canonum*, this attempt to systematize the law of the church using scholastic methodology was commonly referred to simply as the *Decretum*. Written by a Bolognese monk named Gratian, it was once generally believed to have been completed in 1140 but there is now considerable scholarly doubt about the accuracy of that dating, on which see Anders Winroth, *The Making of Gratian's Decretum* (Cambridge: Cambridge University Press, 2000). Because it sought to order and make logical sense of diverse authoritative texts, including the canons of ancient and contemporary church councils, scripture, and writings of the church fathers, it soon became indispensable to students and teachers of canon law. It became the first book in the *corpus iuris canonici*, a

tom had used the words to conclude his discussion of second marriages: "Some things are ordained and some things are merely permitted. Following St.Paul, it is permitted to contract a second marriage [a technically undesirable, if not quite 'evil' choice] rather than risk falling into the sin of fornication."

While we might quibble about the appropriateness of Guilelmus' proof text—we can only speculate about the parallel to fornication which he might have had in mind—it is clear that Guilelmus applied St. Chrysostom's reasoning to explain the fact that the enduring, yet suspect, institution of canonesses was still permitted to exist.

In 1322 the brevity characteristic of Guilelmus de Monte Laudano gave way to much fuller analysis, complete with citations to some important medieval legislation concerning secular canonesses.[16] It was in that year that Johannes Andreae (1270–1348), one of the most renowned canonists of the later Middle Ages, finished his lengthy *Apparatus* to the *Clementines*.[17]

Johannes received his doctorate from the University of Bologna between 1296 and 1300, and held a chair of canon law in 1303. He numbered influential canonists like Johannes Calderinus and Paulus de Liazariis among his students, and no less a luminary than Petrarch among his friends. When he was not teaching, practicing law, or engaged in diplomatic service to the city fathers of Bologna and to Pope John XXII, Johannes wrote prolifically. The esteem

---

designation meant to parallel the name given to the body of Roman law learned by civilians. Modern citation forms direct the reader to one of the three major divisions of the *Decretum*.

16. Mattheus Romanus' *Lectura super Clementinis* may also have been written before the publication of the *glossa ordinaria*, according to Kuttner, "Apostillae," p. 198. I have not been able to study this work, which only exists in manuscript (Halle, Universitätsbibl. Ye 29), but later canonists' citations of Romanus' work will be mentioned as they occur.

17. This is the date given by Kuttner, "Apostillae," p. 196, correcting the date of 1326 given by Schulte, QL, 2:217. For details of his life and work see: James A. Brundage, *Medieval Canon Law* (London: Longman, 1995), pp. 58–59, 216–17; S. Stelling-Michaud, "Jean d'André," *DDC*, 6:89–92. For the most extensive introduction in English, both to his work and that of other canonists of the period 1140–1500, see the forthcoming volume in the "History of Medieval Canon Law" series, published by The Catholic University of America Press, Washington, D.C.

with which he was regarded by contemporaries, who referred to him as *iuris canonici fons et tuba* (roughly, *source and trumpet/transmitter of canon law*), is reflected in the fact that both his commentary on the *Liber Sextus* and his *Apparatus* to the *Clementines* were quickly accepted as the standard glosses to these important collections. As the author of the *glossa ordinaria*, Johannes would profoundly influence the way in which the reference to secular canonesses in *Attendentes* was to be interpreted.

Glossing the words *canonicae seculares*, Johannes cites three separate pieces of previous ecclesiastical legislation in order to identify these women.[18] The oldest of these laws is a canon issued at the Council of Tribur (895) and included as C.12 q.5 c.7 in Gratian's *Decretum*.[19] A brief and clear-cut directive, this canon mandates that the estate of any cleric *(quicumque ex gradu ecclesiastico)* who died without having drawn up a will, and without surviving cognate relatives, devolve to the church that cleric served during his lifetime. And the same is to apply to women referred to simply as *sanctimoniales*.[20]

A second proof text, Pope Honorius III's response to a petition from the abbess of Quedlinburg, is best known by its opening word *Dilecta*.[21] This reply was not sent directly to the abbess but rather to the abbot of Saint Michael's, diocese of Halberstadt—a peculiarity

18. Johannes Andreae, *Glos.ord.* to *Clem.3.10.2, ad verbum: canonicae seculares,* in *Corpus Iuris Canonici* (Venice, 1584), p. 216.

19. Tribur is an ancient German town near Darmstadt, site of a Carolingian palace. The Council of Tribur issued fifty-eight canons. See Edward H. Landon, *A Manual of Councils*, vol. II (Edinburgh: John Grant, 1909). The Latin text of the canon in question can be found in Friedberg, *Corpus*, 1:717.

20. This declaration *ex concilio Triburiensi* is cited by Johannes as 12 q.ult. c.ult.[C.12. q.5 .c.7]. As previously mentioned, the term *sanctimoniales* (holy nuns) is not used with consistency in medieval ecclesiastical sources. Here, with the addition of some details regarding the possession of private property, Johannes clearly believes that it designates secular canonesses. Note that the rule of life devised by the Council of Aachen for secular canonesses was entitled the *Institutio Sanctimonialium*.

21. *de maio. & obe., Dilecta* [X 1.33.12]. This petition is included in the *Decretals of Gregory IX*, more commonly known as the *Liber Extra*, hence the abbreviation, X. See Friedberg, *Corpus*, 2:202. See K. Blaschke, "Quedlinburg," *LMA*, 7:359–60, for an overview of this house of canonesses.

which the context of the decretal helps to explain.[22] Apparently the abbess had complained to the pope that, because she lacked the power to excommunicate, disobedient canonesses and clerics under her authority refused to abide by her decisions to suspend them from office and/or to confiscate their livings; therefore, these subordinates remained uncorrected.

Having rehearsed her complaint, Honorius charges the abbot of Saint Michael's, *discretioni tuae*, to be sure that the disobedient clerks and canonesses in question abide by the warnings and admonitions of the abbess *(eius salubria monita et mandata observent)*. The pope adds that the abbot might use ecclesiastical censures to that end if needed *(monitione praemissa ecclesiastica censura appellatione remota compellas)*.

By involving a third party, a male third party, in this affair, Honorius implicitly confirmed the fact that excommunication could not be included as a weapon in the arsenal of a canoness, even when that canoness was the abbess of so prestigious a house as Quedlinburg. Yet the pope forthrightly admitted that the abbess was owed the obedience of a superior by both the clerics and canonesses under her jurisdiction. To coerce that obedience, if need be, he enlisted the aid of an abbot who *did* have the power to impose the ultimate ecclesiastical sanction.

Johannes' third proof text is the decree *Indemnitatibus* of Pope Boniface VIII.[23] Like *Attendentes*, this decree set down guidelines for nuns (in this case rules by which elections were to be governed) which Boniface VIII wished to have applied equally to secular canonesses. Unlike *Attendentes*, however, *Indemnitatibus* granted secular canonesses a concession made necessary by the particular circumstances of their quasi-religious life: This decree applies to all nuns living under any approved rule, says Boniface, and even to those who live, as is customary in some places, without renouncing property or making profession as regulars. But since secular canonesses never make religious profession, they are naturally exempt from the re-

22. The same entry occurs as #7732 in Potthast and is dated 1222.
23. *de elect. c.Indemnitatibus, penul lib. 6* [VI 1.6.43]; Friedberg, *Corpus* 2:967–69.

quirement [set forth in *Indemnitatibus*] that candidates for the office of abbess be fully professed members of their communities. "By this concession, however," Boniface immediately adds "we do not wish nor intend to approve their status, order, or rule."[24]

Of the three proof texts chosen by Johannes Andreae, two of them, the decree of the Council of Tribur and *Dilecta*, betray no animus whatsoever toward the institution of secular canonesses. And even *Indemnitatibus* treats these women as familiar, if not particularly desirable, elements of ecclesiastical life. Johannes might have adduced these authorities merely to establish the fact that secular canonesses had been the subject of canonical regulation for a very long time.

Yet while these three texts are not in and of themselves hostile to the institution of secular canonesses, they could be, and would be, used to provide evidence of its irregularity. The Council of Tribur had ruled on an issue—inheritance of personal property—that could only have arisen in the absence of a monastic vow of poverty; *Dilecta* featured the unedifying spectacle of male clergy subordinated to female jurisdiction; and *Indemnitatibus* highlighted the fact that secular canonesses disregarded solemn religious profession, with all that entailed for religious women.

Johannes saw all three of these authorities as pointing out the "irregularity" of the life of a secular canoness in relation to that prescribed for a nun, a *mulier religiosa*, strictly speaking. And his intended readers, his fellow lawyers, would not have had to arrive at this interpretation unassisted, since Johannes himself had already drawn those inferences for them.

In 1312, years before he wrote his commentary on *Clementines*, Johannes had written a commentary on the *Decretals* of Gregory IX, in which he included a gloss of *Dilecta*.[25] Cited often by later generations of canonists, Johannes' gloss of *Dilecta* betrays the ambivalence

24. Friedberg, *Corpus* 2:969.
25. See Schulte, *QL*, 2:214 and 220 for the dates of Johannes' glosses to the *Sext* as well as *Extra*. Both glosses appeared earlier (1304–5 and 1312, respectively) than his commentary on the *Clementines* and hence it can be reasonably assumed that many of his colleagues would have read them before encountering his gloss on *Attendentes*. Although Johannes did gloss

that he felt about the continued existence of secular canonesses; it also anticipates the conclusions he draws from *Attendentes*.

He begins this gloss of *Dilecta* by stating that in certain churches there are canons as well as canonesses and, although they have separate choir arrangements, the men and women come together for public processions, albeit not (one trusts) in private: *In aliquibus talibus ecclesiis habent etiam canonicos, qui licet a mulieribus habeant chorum divisum, simul tamen conveniunt in processionibus et utinam non in latebris.* Johannes points up the irregularity of this behavior by citing two authorities that speak directly to it. The first is Boniface VIII's decree *Periculoso* (*VI* 3.16.1) which we have encountered previously.[26] Since *Periculoso* had mandated strict active and passive enclosure for religious women, the behavior of secular canonesses sets them well outside the pale, both because they leave their monasteries for a public function and because they associate, or are suspected of associating, with male clerics within the walls of those monasteries.

Violation of the norms set for *mulieres religiosae* is also the chief concern of Johannes' second citation, the decree *Perniciosam*. Promulgated by the Second Lateran Council of 1139, *Perniciosam* was much cited by late medieval canonists because of the importance that Johannes Andreae attached to it and, for that reason, it bears full quotation:

> We decree that the pernicious and detestable custom which has spread among some women who, although they live neither according to the rule of blessed Benedict, nor Basil, nor Augustine, *yet wish to be thought of by everyone as nuns*, is to be abolished. For when, living according to

Indemnitatibus in his commentary on the *Liber Sextus*, (see *Glos.ord* to VI 1.6.43 *Corpus iuris canonici* (Venice, 1584), p. 187), he makes only one interesting aside with reference to secular canonesses: *ad verbum provinciarum: ut Theutonia*. Aside from this reference to the Germanic nature of the institute Johannes merely refers readers to apposite proof texts. His gloss of *Dilecta*, often and interestingly cited for generations, is much richer. I shall use the gloss as it is contained in Johannes Andreae, *In primum-quintum decretalilum librum novella comentaria. . . .* 5 vols. in 4 (Venetiis: *Franciscum Franciscium, Senensem*, 1581) gloss to X 1.33.12, p. 267.

26. See the Preface for a summary of this legislation and the Introduction for comments on its relevance to the definition of the term quasi-religious.

the rule in monasteries, they ought to be in church, or in the refectory, or dormitory in common, they build for themselves their own retreats and private dwelling places where, under the guise of hospitality, indiscriminately and without any shame they receive guests and secular persons contrary to the sacred canons and good morals. Because everyone who does evil hates the light, these women think that, *hidden in the tabernacle of the just, they can conceal themselves from the eyes of the Judge who sees everything;* so we prohibit in every way this unrighteous, hateful, and disgraceful conduct and forbid it to continue under pain of anathema. In the same way we prohibit canonesses *(sanctimoniales)* to come together with canons or monks in choir for the singing of the office.[27]

Perniciosam is more harshly worded than previous reform legislation, but it still fits squarely within that tradition. Since Carolingian times, reformers had been trying to diminish the differences between canonesses and nuns, and this is what *Perniciosam* attempts as well. Like earlier legislation, it is couched in terms of 'alleged abuses,' seeks to end those abuses, yet stops short of condemning the whole institution. At this point in his gloss (but not, as we shall see, when he adduces the same text in his commentary on *Attendentes*), Johannes follows suit. Abandoning description and critique of the institution *per se*, he turns instead to the central issue of *Dilecta:* the jurisdictional powers of the abbess of Quedlinburg.

At the beginning of *Dilecta*, Pope Honorius III had mentioned that in an attempt to achieve control over her subordinates, the abbess had used tactics such as suspension from office. While the pope had not commented one way or the other on these suspensions, Johannes wants his readers to recognize that the pope's silence on the issue does not suggest his approval. The pope had offered to support her "salubrious warnings," says Johannes, but had in no way recognized the validity of her *de facto* suspension.[28]

27. This English translation (emphases mine) is found in Tanner, *Decrees*, p. 203. I have, however, taken the liberty of translating "sanctimoniales" as canonesses rather than nuns, as does Tanner, since the context requires it. This decree is included in the *Decretum* at C.28 q.2 c.25 and the Latin text can be found in Friedberg, *Corpus*, 1:836.

28. Johannes Andreae, *In primum-quintum decretalium* . . . X 1.33.12, p.

Johannes gives a variety reasons why the abbess could not legitimately compel obedience via suspension—reasons which stress both the legal and the theological incapacity of women.[29] Unlike Honorius III, who had upheld the rights of the abbess of Quedlingburg to exercise jurisdiction over her subordinates, albeit implicitly denying her the right to excommunicate recalcitrants, Johannes explicitly rejects the notion that she can coerce obedience by any means other than *salubria monita*.

Finally, as if to end his gloss on the same note on which it began, Johannes draws the distinction between those *conversa ecclesiae secularis* who are allowed to marry, and those 'converts to religion' *(in conversis religiosorum)* who may not. To the latter he accords *privilegium canonis* while denying it to the former. The privilege in question, which warned that anyone who physically attacked a member of the clergy would be excommunicated, had been extended to *deo devota* in the past, but it is a precedent which Johannes chooses to ignore.[30]

With Johannes Andreae's gloss of *Dilecta* before our eyes it is easier to see how he arrives at his conclusions in his commentary on *Attendentes. Dilecta* might logically have been read as, and used as proof of, the papally recognized jurisdictional rights of a secular canoness and abbess. Johannes had chosen to undercut that positive interpretation at every turn. He substituted a restrictive reading

---

267, *ad verbum: Monita, non dicit suspensionem nunquid illam ergo servare tenentur.*

29. *Ibid. tenendum est igitur secundum Hostiensis quod saltem ab offici suspendere non potest, ut in gl. cum enim excommunicatio, suspensio, et interdictum contineantur sub censura,uno prohibitio iure connexioni prohibentur et reliqua et satis est istud mulieribus non esse expresse permissum . . . ad verbum: compellas, quasi dicat abbatissa habet monere et mandare, tu habes coercere. . . .* As ultimate support for his position, Johannes has recourse to the creation story attesting to the inferior status of woman *qua* woman: *Eva processerit ab Adam et sic ipsa non est imago Dei in creatione.*

30. *Ibid. idem de quolibet converso vel conversa ecclesiae secularis scilicet quod contrahere potest, nec gaudet immunitate canonis, si quis suadente, secus in conversis religiosorum.* For further discussion of this clerical immunity, and the use of Johannes' gloss in two very different curial decicions, see Chapter 5. Johannes also mentions that houses of secular canonesses, like monasteries of nuns, must be visited annually, citing *Attendentes* for support.

which diminished the legitimate governing powers of an abbess and backed up his denial of the *privelegium canonis* to secular canonesses generally.

Hardly surprising, then, when glossing the word *approbare* (to approve) as it appears in *Attendentes*, Johannes writes cryptically: "rather it [the status or order of secular canonesses] seems to be condemned."[31] To support his terse conclusion, Johannes appends the proof text *Perniciosam*.

For Johannes, *Perniciosam* was acerbic enough in tone and sufficiently suggestive of moral danger to warrant being used to support a conclusion which the legislation itself—all previous reforming legislation in fact—had resisted drawing. Johannes used it to support his contention that the status of secular canonesses—the institution *per se* and not just some abuses within it—merited condemnation. Certainly, he was predisposed to do so and he had predisposed his readers to do the same by providing them with accumulated evidence of behavior "unbecoming" religious women, especially religious women subject to the recent restrictions of *Periculoso*. Then he used *Perniciosam* to add the final touch: the suggestion that corruption hid behind a mask of goodness.

Perniciosam characterizes the way of life of the secular canoness as much more than a quaint vestige of a less closely regulated church: These women pose as nuns, they live *as if* nuns, thus threatening not only good order, but the virtue of the unwary. Simple folk who are taken in by mere appearances are scandalized by behavior which departs from that demanded of professed religious. This behavior may range from marriage of a canoness to participation in public liturgical functions. It is the appearance of canoness as nun, the deception alluded to in *Perniciosam*, that rankles, and it is a theme that will emerge again with reference to a group of quasi-religious women whom many glossators would see as intimately related to secular canonesses, the beguines.

"Immo reprobari videtur," Johannes had opined, and that opinion would not go unnoticed. Contained in the ordinary gloss on the

31. Johannes Andreae, *Glos.ord.* to *Clem. 3.10.2*, p. 216, *ad verbum approbare*. "*immo reprobari videtur* [18. q.2]. *perniciosam* [C.28 q.2 c.25]."

Clementines, Johannes Andreae's assessment of the status of secular canonesses would become the point of departure for some of the most prominent canonists of the subsequent generation. The comments of the renowned teacher and churchman Cardinal Franciscus Zabarella (1360–1417) well illustrate this point.[32]

Having received the doctorate *utriusque iuris* (in canon and civil law) in 1385, Franciscus Zabarella taught law in Padua until 1410, numbering among his students the man commonly referred to as the last great canonist of the Middle Ages, Nicolaus de Tudeschis (better known as Panormitanus). Perhaps best remembered as an articulate advocate of conciliarism and as a major player at the Council of Constance, Cardinal Zabarella also wrote an extensive and influential commentary on the *Clementines.*

When glossing the relevant section of *Attendentes* the cardinal begins by restating Johannes Andreae's words: *immo reprobari videtur,* adding that this is also the opinion of Guilelmus de Monte Laudano.[33] To buttress this opinion, he cites the decree *Periculoso* of Pope Boniface VIII, which mandated strict enclosure of all *nuns* throughout Christendom; by doing so he identifies canonesses *as* nuns.[34] It is now just a short step to his next assertion that since secular canonesses do not observe the cloister regulations set down for nuns, they subvert those rules.

No doubt the time-honored association of canonesses with public liturgical functions explains his choice of proof text: Pope Innocent III's denunciation of clerical participation in popular theatricals performed on major feast days.[35] The cardinal also adds a citation from the *Liber Sextus* reminding judges that religious women were not to be compelled to make personal appearances in a court of law.[36]

---

32. For a biographical details see *NCE,*14:1101; On his work see Schulte, *QL,* 2:283–85. Several articles, as well as portions of books dealing with the Great Schism, treat of Zabaralla's role in the conciliar movement. For example, Brian Tierney, *Foundations of the Conciliar Theory* (Cambridge: Cambridge University Press, 1955), pp. 220–37.
33. Franciscus Zabarella, *Lectura super Clementinis* (Venice, 1499), gloss to Clem. 3.10.2 *ad verbum: ipsas,* p. 137.
34. See the preface to this book for details regarding this decree.
35. X 3.1.12.
36. VI 2.1.2.

Following Guilelmus of Monte Laudano, Zabarella continues, the status of secular canoness is a dangerous one and for that reason the pope permits rather than approves it; nor should it be assumed that because it *is* permitted that the status of secular canoness is without fault since it is of itself evil *(cum sit de se malus)*. Supporting this view we find not only the reference, earlier employed by Guilelmus, that "we are not able to completely prohibit the evil inclinations of mankind" (C.31 q.1 c.9), but also two authorities of his own choosing.

The first comes from the *Moralia* of Pope Gregory the Great, included as D.13 c.2 in Gratian's *Decretum*.[37] It is an exegesis of *Job 40:17–20* and concerns the choice of the lesser of two evils. "Many commit sins," says Gregory, "when, because they want to avoid one sin, they cannot escape the snare of another, and thus they commit one fault to avoid another. They find no way to escape one sin without consenting to the other." The second supporting text, drawn once again from the *Liber Sextus* of Boniface VIII, is a rule of law: "He who is silent does not openly confess [to something], but neither does he undoubtedly deny it."[38]

There can be no doubt about Cardinal Zabarella's position regarding the institution of secular canonesses. His opinion, ornamented by a few ingenious cross-references and the addition of Guilelmus of Monte Landauno's gloss, perpetuates the negative assessment found in the *glossa ordinaria*. Given his high profile in church government and his legacy as a teacher, his work helped to

37. Found in Friedberg, *Corpus*, 1:30–31, the entire text, with its ordinary gloss, is translated in Gratian, *The Treatise on Laws (Decretum DD. 1–20)*, trans. Augustine Thompson, Studies in Medieval and Early Modern Canon Law, vol. 2 (Washington, DC: The Catholic University of America Press, 1993).

38. Zabarella, *Lectura*, p. 137 ad.v. Illas: "*. . . propterea papa non approbat sed permittit nec propter talem permissionem est earum status sine vicio cum sit de se malus.*" The cardinal uses proof texts such as Saint John Chrysostom on the permissibility of second marriages (C.31 q.1 c.9) to illustrate that the pope might unwillingly permit something that is not in itself good, since "it is impossible to completely prohibit mankind's evil inclinations." The rule of law cited is *regula XIV: Is, qui tacet, non fatetur; sed nec utique negare videtur.*

ensure the durability of this point of view. And although other canonists who commented on *Attendentes* after the publication of the *glossa ordinaria* were less expansive than Cardinal Zabarella, they seldom failed to reproduce the by-now standard opinion about secular canonesses.

Stephanus Hugonetti (1280–1332), also known as Stephanus Provincialis, provides an example.[39] Having achieved prominence as a judge in the papal court known as the Rota, Stephanus served as chancellor to the papal legate to Lombardy from 1320 to 1330. He became bishop of Bologna two years before his death. Stephanus wrote his commentary on the *Clementines* between 1324 and 1330, and included a few notes on secular canonesses when he glossed *Attendentes*.[40] Stephanus begins with a paraphrase of the text of the decree, saying that although papal directives about the visitation of monasteries of nuns are to extend to canonesses, their order is not thereby approved. Toward the end of his commentary, he adduces *Indemnitatibus* at the word *approbare*.[41]

An important canonist and influential teacher of the next generation, Johannes de Imola (1372–1436) was nearly as terse as Stephanus and just as wedded to tradition.[42] Johannes wrote his commentary *in Clementinis* at the start of the fifteenth century, yet his assessment of the institution of secular canonesses differed not at all from that made decades earlier. *Et nota quod per hoc non approbatur status predictarum*, he cautions, and, at the word *approbare*, refers the reader to the sternly worded *Perniciosam*.[43]

---

39. Biographical information on Stephanus Hugonetti can be found in Schulte, *QL* 2:200–201.

40. His gloss on *Attendentes* can be found in fols. 42–43v, *Apparatus in Clementinis*, MS Lat. 95, Philadelphia, University of Pennsylvania Library. See Norman Zacour, "Stephanus Hugoneti and his 'Apparatus' on the Clementines," *Traditio* 17 (1961), pp. 527–30, for more biographical details and information on the dating of his work.

41. VI 1.6.43.

42. Johannes de Imola, *In Clementinis* (Venice: Andreas Toressanus, de Asula, 1492–93), fol. 136v–137v. For biographical details about Johannes, see, Schulte, *QL* 2:296–98.

43. Johannes de Imola, *In Clementinis*, fol. 136v and fol. 137v, *ad verbum: approbare*.

Of course in both the fourteenth and fifteenth centuries there were some canonists who chose not to comment at all on *Attendentes*, and others, such as Lapus Tactus (fl. mid-fourteenth century) and Petrus de Ancharano (1333–1416), who made no mention of secular canonesses in their glosses of the decree.[44] But no matter how briefly or with what apparent lack of zest some canonists glossed *Attendentes*, we must not assume that those jurists were either unaware of, or out of sympathy with, the opinions expressed by Johannes Andreae.[45]

Neither the Avignonese canonist Bonifacius Ammannati, nor the renowned jurist Panormitanus, for instance, made any mention of secular canonesses when they glossed *Attendentes*.[46] Yet, as we shall see, Bonifacius reproduced the standard (negative) observations about them in his gloss of *Cum de quibusdam*, and Panormitanus too showed himself to be completely conversant with these arguments (although he makes somewhat different use of them) in one of his *consilia*.[47]

To judge from the academic commentary on *Attendentes*, fourteenth- and fifteenth-century canonists overwhelmingly accepted the notion that secular canonesses were troublesome adjuncts to in-

44. See Lapus Tactus, *Super Libro Sexto decretalium et Clementinus*, (Rome, 1589), pp. 224–25. Petrus de Ancharano,*Lectura super Clementinas* (Venice, 1493), fol.77v–78r.

45. Jesselin de Cassagnes (d. 1334), whose work we will deal with in the next chapter, is a possible exception. His commentary on the *Clementines* appeared only a year after that of Johannes Andreae. At any rate, when glossing *Attendentes*, Jesselin simply noted that secular canonesses were not exempt from visitation: *Commentaria super Clementinis*, Paris BN lat.14331 fol. 137v.

46. Bonifacius Ammannati (Pseudo Bonifacio de Vitalinis), *Lectura Clementinarum*, Toledo: Biblioteca del Cabildo, Codex 23-1. Nicolaus de Tudeschis (Panormitanus), *Lectura in Clementinas* (Venice, 1490). The work of Bonifacius will be dealt with at length in Chapter 2. See Chapter 4 for details on the life and work of Panormitanus.

47. Bonifacius Ammannati, *Lectura Clementinarum*, fol. 87v; Panormitanus, *Consilia* (Strasbourg: Heinrich Eggestein, 1474), c.lv fol.xxxv. Note that Panormitanus also wrote a gloss on *Dilecta* that was somewhat less sour than that of Johannes Andreae: Niccolo de Tudeschi, *Prima-ultima pars Abb. Panor. Super primo-quartoet quinto Decre . . .* (Lugdini: Jehan Petit, 1521–22) gloss to X 1.33.12, p. 125.

stitutionalized religious life. For some they appeared to be little more than irksome reminders of a less "well-regulated" era. For others, like Johannes Andreae and Cardinal Zabarella, they posed a threat to virtue and even subverted the good order of monastic life. For all who chose to comment on them in the context provided by *Attendentes*, the murky legal status of these quasi-religious women was of paramount concern.

Secular canonesses lacked papal approbation and official approval of a religious community was first and foremost a hallmark of orthodoxy. But apostolic approval also brought with it privileges and immunities relevant to the community as a corporate entity, and to the individual members of that community as well as to their families, patrons, and benefactors. Arguments about inheritance, feudal obligations, and even the legal venue for a court case could and did hinge on this legal technicality. Ecclesiastical approbation was a concern of the commentators not only because it signaled orthodox belief, but because confusion was wrought in its absence. Secular canonesses *appeared to be* nuns, but *de iure* were not. The discrepancy was noted and deplored as deceptive, sometimes in the harshest terms, despite both the antiquity of the institution of secular canonesses and the wealth that institution represented. In their dealings with beguines, a newer and far less socially privileged group of quasi-religious women, the lawyers would employ even more pointed allegations of subversion and subterfuge than they had marshaled against secular canonesses.

T W O

Cum de quibusdam, Ratio recta, and Beguines

*T*he *Constitutions* of Pope Clement V, the last official compilation of medieval canon law to become part of the *Corpus
Iuris Canonici,* contained what is arguably the most famous
decree concerning the beguines. Known by its opening words, *Cum
de quibusdam,* this enactment has been translated, in whole or in
part, quite often, McDonnell's rendering, albeit without the canon's
final clause, being the most often quoted in the secondary literature.[1]

Nevertheless, because of the questions surrounding its composi-
tion, the confusion to which its publication gave rise, and the work
habits of the canonists who commented on it, there follows a rather
literal translation of *Cum de quibusdam* with commonly glossed
words italicized:

> Since certain women *(mulieribus)* commonly known *(vulgariter nuncu-
> patis)* as beguines *(beguinabus)* neither promise obedience *(obedientiam)*
> to anyone, nor renounce personal property, nor profess any approved
> rule, they are by no means considered religious, although they wear a
> so-called beguine habit and attach themselves to *(adhaereant)* certain
> religious to whom they are drawn by special affection *(affectio).* Reports

1. McDonnell, *Beguines and Beghards,* p. 524. Cited as *Clem. 3.11.1.*

have come to us from trustworthy sources that some of them, as if having been led into insanity *(insaniam)*, dispute and preach *(disputent/praedicent)* about the highest Trinity and the divine essence and introduce *(introducant)* opinions contrary to the catholic faith concerning the articles of the faith and the sacraments of the church. They lead many simple people who are deceived in such things into various errors, and they do and commit much else under the veil of sanctity *(sanctitatis)* which occasions danger to souls. Having frequently heard from these and from others about their perverse opinions, on account of which they have merited suspicion, we, with the approval of the sacred council, declare that their status ought to be perpetually prohibited and completely abolished *(abolendum)* from the church of God. We expressly enjoin upon these and all other women under pain of excommunication, which we wish those who do otherwise to incur automatically *(ipso facto)*, that they no longer follow *(sectentur)* this way of life in any way whatsoever, regardless of whether they adopted it some time ago *(dudum)* or whether, having once lived it, they take it up anew. Moreover, we strictly forbid under the penalty of similar excommunication, which they shall immediately incur *(incursuros)* if they act otherwise, those previously mentioned religious *(religiosis)*, who are said to have favored these women and to have induced them to take up this way of life in the beguinage, to admit any women who formerly adopted the status in question or who perhaps wish to take it up again, or to give to these sectarians any counsel, aid, or favor; no privilege availing against the above. Of course by the preceding we in no way intend to forbid any faithful women, whether or not they promise chastity, from living honestly in their dwellings *(in suis hospitiis)*, doing penance, and serving the Lord in a spirit of humility *(humilitatis)*, this being allowed to them as the Lord inspires them.[2]

While the phrase "with the approval of the sacred council" occurs in this decree, it is doubtful whether *Cum de quibusdam*, in the form translated above, was actually the work of the Council of Vienne (1311–12). As we have seen, the death of Pope Clement V in 1314 delayed the process of sending out copies of the *Clementine* to

---

2. The Latin text of this decree can be found in Friedberg, *Corpus*, 2:1169–70. See also the Latin- and English-facing text of *Cum de quibusdam* in Tanner, *Decrees*, 1:374; the difficulties involved in ascribing the decree, in its present form, to the Council of Vienne will be discussed shortly.

the universities, and his successor, Pope John XXII, did not formally promulgate the law collection until 1317. Johannes Andreae tells us that John XXII was responsible for some textual "changes and corrections" in the intervening period.[3] Even more telling, however, is the fact that in 1312 Clement V himself ordered all copies of the Vienne canons then in circulation to be destroyed or recalled in anticipation of revised versions.[4]

For some time, historians of the beguines have had recourse to these facts about time lapse and revision of conciliar texts to explain the apparently self-contradictory message of *Cum de quibusdam* (Clem. 3.11.1)—the existence of the so-called escape clause at the end that seems to nullify the blanket condemnation with which the decree begins.[5] With this internal contradiction, *Cum de quibusdam* stands in uneasy relationship to *Ad nostrum* (Clem. 5.3.3), a simultaneously published decree which condemned German beguines and their male counterparts (beghards) as heretical sectarians subscribing to no fewer than eight doctrinal errors.[6] The beguines of *Ad nostrum* are part of a geographically localized, heretical group consisting

3. Jacqueline Tarrant, "The Clementine Decrees on the Beguines: Conciliar and Papal Versions," *Archivum historiae pontificae* 12 (1974): 300, n.5.

4. Tarrant, "Clementine Decrees," p. 301.

5. McDonnell, *Beguines and Beghards,* for one, refers to this delay and reworking of the decrees when he states: "The contradictory character of the provisions concerning beghards and beguines is perhaps attributable to these repeated revisions." p. 529.

6. For the Latin text see Friedberg, *Corpus,* 2:1183–84. For a discussion of the content of *Ad Nostram* and its relationship to beguines see: Leff, *Heresy,* pp. 314–15; Lerner, *Heresy,* pp. 81–84; McDonnell, *Beguines and Beghards,* pp. 497, 527. While late medieval canon lawyers did write academic commentary on *Ad nostrum,* they confined themselves to an explication of the list of doctrinal errors that it contained. In this way they confirm the distinction that modern scholars like Leff and Lerner have made between the two decrees, *Ad Nostrum* being the "doctrinal accompaniment" to *Cum de quibusdam,* which concerned itself chiefly with questions of institutional organization. Unlike the commentary generated by *Cum de quibusdam,* medieval glosses on *Ad nostrum* shed no light on the central issue of this book: canonical opinions about quasi-religious status or way of life. Thus, although *Ad Nostrum* will be mentioned in the broad context of heretical opinions often ascribed to female semi-religious, I shall not provide in-depth analysis of commentary on it. For the problems which arise

of both men *and* women, a sect whose members subscribe to specifically listed errors having to do with the perfection of human nature, and whose conduct merits inquisitorial action. They appear to bear little relationship to those beguines mentioned in *Cum de quibusdam*—women (exclusively, no mention of beghards is made) whose quasi-religious way of life (a *status* and not a *secta quadedam abominabilis*) might have given *some* of them the "insane" idea that they could discuss matters of theology and so spread confusion (of an ill-defined sort, in an unspecified locale).

In an important article, "The Clementine Decrees on the Beguines: Conciliar and Papal Versions," Jacqueline Tarrant proposes a strategy for resolving the apparent contradictions both within and between these two decrees. She contends that a close reading of *Cum de quibusdam* reveals qualifications throughout the decree, long before the oft-cited escape clause with which it concludes. The use of the words "some of them" and "certain women" imply from the outset the existence of a group of beguines whose way of life was above suspicion. The escape clause, Tarrant explains, "is not unrelated to the rest of the decree but is intended to be the safeguard for those orthodox beguines who are otherwise not treated in the decree. It does not contradict the rest of the decree because no comprehensive accusation of beguines has been made nor have all beguines been forbidden to continue their way of life."[7]

Tarrant provides an even simpler solution for the problem of inconsistency between *Cum de quibusdam* and *Ad nostrum:* The two decrees refer to two completely different groups; "the decrees have little more in common than the occurrence of the name *beguine* in each."[8] That name, like the very structure of beguine life at the time, lacked rigorous definition, and so could be, and was, used to refer to different quasi-religious groups that bore a resemblance to one another.[9]

---

when distinctions between the purport of these two very different decrees are obscured see Robert Lerner's review of Jean-Claude Schmitt's *Mort d'une hérésie* in *Speculum* 54 (1979): 842–44.

7. Tarrant, "The Clementine Decrees," p. 306.
8. Ibid.
9. Note that Grundmann, *Religious Movements*, drew attention to the

In sum, two issues, one a question of church discipline (the unauthorized preaching and quasi-religious organization referred to in *Cum de quibusdam*), and the other a question of doctrinal deviation (the specified theological errors in *Ad nostrum*) appear in two different directives, addressed to two different groups. In his revision of the Vienne decrees, Pope Clement V recognized that there was considerable diversity among beguines and endeavored to distinguish among them. It had never been Clement's intention to include orthodox beguines in his condemnation.

While intentionality is always a problematic concept for historians to deal with, Tarrant's analysis of Clementine legislation relating to begines has much to recommend it. But, as the author herself points out, it is not the sort of analysis engaged in by contemporaries. Certainly the bishops directed to implement papal policy proved unwilling or unable to engage in it.

Almost as soon as it was published, *Cum de quibusdam* gave rise not to reasoned examination of its content, but to confusion. Generally interpreted as a blanket condemnation of beguines, it was used to authorize cycles of indiscriminate persecution. "Good" as well as "bad" beguines, along with those quasi-religious women who resembled them, would be caught up in these cycles, which lasted for over a century. John of Dürbheim, bishop of Strasbourg (1306–28), provides us with an early indication of the difficulties to which the decree could give rise. In a letter dated 1318 and written to Clement V's successor, John XXII, the bishop describes the harassment suffered by orthodox beguines and tertiaries in dioceses throughout Germany and requests clarification of the Vienne decrees as a means to end it.[10]

In his introductory comments on *Cum de quibusdam*, the author of the ordinary gloss to the *Clementines*, Johannes Andreae, mentions having seen a part of this correspondence between the pope

---

shifting meaning of the name *beguine*, as well as to the organizational variety among beguines from the time of their first appearance in the historical record.

10. Tarrant, "The Clementine Decrees," p. 307 n.22; See also Lerner, *Heresy,* p. 94 and Leff, *Heresy,* pp. 337–38.

and the bishop of Strasbourg.[11] He also says that he has heard of, but does not have at hand, another curial document concerning the disputed constitution, although he cannot vouch for its authenticity.[12] These statements attesting to the author's familiarity with the practical problems surrounding the enforcement of *Cum de quibusdam*, particularly the use of the decree to justify the persecution of tertiaries, help to explain a preceding (and otherwise rather oddly placed) excursus. After a few notations pointing out the highlights of the gloss, there occurs a summary of the distinctions among the three Franciscan orders:

> The first order of St. Francis, the masculine branch, possesses all of the essentials of a religious order, and it is the strictest; the second order, of the sisters of St. Clare, also has the substantial elements of the religious life (that is, the three vows of poverty, chastity, and obedience), but it differs from the first order in that communal property is permitted; the third order, with both male and female members who promise obedience and have a rule, is nevertheless not a religious order but rather a way of life *(modus vivendi)* approved by the holy see. Members of the third order may be married but in following the regulations of their way of life abstain from conjugal relations on certain days of the week.

Elements of this rather detailed explanation of the distinctions among the three orders of the friars minor are repeated later in the gloss proper and constitute Johannes Andreae's single attempt to limit the reach of *Cum de quibusdam*. Although they are not techni-

11. Johannes Andreae, *Glos.ord.* to *Clem. 3.11.1* in *Corpus iuris canonici* (Venice, 1584), p. 216: "*Vidi autem duas contrarias & ut puto in Alemania compositas, quarum altera videbantur edita ad consultationem episcopi Argentinensis.*" As Tarrant notes (p. 308 n. 26), Johannes refers here to the bishop of Strasbourg, John of Dürbheim. I have found this same prologue in manuscript versions of the ordinary gloss, including Paris BN lat. 4136, *Apparatus Johannis Andree super clementinis*, and Paris BN lat. 14331 fol. 29r, but in printed versions a lengthy summary of the whole of the gloss, highlighting Johannes' exemption of tertiaries from condemnation, precedes the author's own introductory remarks. See Johannes Andreae above, p. 216, as well as *Constitutiones Clementis Quinti* (Venice, 1572), p. 111, and (Venice, 1511), fol. 48.

12. Johannes Andreae, *Glos.ord.*, p. 216: "*Dicitur quaedam declaratoria super hac constitutione emanasse, quam de curia habere non potui, et a quibusdam audivi quod a curia non manavit.*"

cally speaking members of a religious order, Franciscan tertiaries, unlike beguines, promise obedience and follow a way of life approved by the papacy. Tertiaries may look like beguines, but can be distinguished from them, and so they are exempt from Clement V's condemnation. Neither at this juncture nor when glossing the decree's saving clause, however, does Johannes extend similar protection to orthodox or "good" beguines. Instead of parsing *Cum de quibusdam* as it applies to these women, he chooses to reinforce its negative connotations by demonstrating that Clement V's suspicions were well grounded in the canon law.

Johannes makes his case by compiling a *florilegium* of supporting comments from the glosses of Cardinal Hostiensis (also known as Henricus de Segusio, or Henry of Susa, *circa* 1200–1271), possibly the most eminent canonist of the previous generation.[13] For instance, when writing of the proper deportment of alms collectors, Hostiensis had warned such men not to take up lodgings in unsuitable places *(in locis incongruis).*[14] Although Hostiensis had not actually used the words "in houses of prostitution," Johannes opines he certainly would have classed those houses, along with beguinages *(quasi prostibulis, sicut sunt hospitia beguinarum),* as "unsuitable." After all, according to Hostiensis, a beguine was "a pernicious sort of woman" *(perniciosum genus est mulierum)* who easily allowed men other than religious to enter her house.[15]

13. For biographical background on Hostiensis see Brundage, *Medieval Canon Law,* p. 214, and Kenneth Pennington, "Henricus de Segusio (Hostiensis)," in *Dizionario biografico degli Italiani,* vol.42, (Rome: Istituto della Enciclopedia Italiana, 1960–2001).

14. Hostiensis (Henricus de Segusio), *In primum [-sextum] decretalium librum commentaria* (Venice: 1581; rpt. Turin: Bottega D'Erasmo, 1965), gloss to X 5.38.14 *de poenitentiis et remissionibus,* p. 104a, *ad verbum: incongruis.* Johannes Andreae quoted almost, but not quite, the whole of Hostiensis' statement, which appears in the next endnote. Those words found only in Hostiensis' commentary have been placed in square brackets.

15. Johannes Andreae, *Glos.ord.* p. 216: *"Hostiensis : parcit, quod non dicit, prostibulis [quae omnino prohibitur] sed cavendum est a quasi prostibulis, sicut sunt hospitia [quorundam] beguinarum [sectarum] quod perniciosum genus est mulierum [nec] quae de facili alios quam religiosos admittunt [a quibus modis omnibus est cavendum.]"*

Johannes supports his reading of Hostiensis with a citation to *Perniciosam*, the decree which he brandished with such enthusiasm in his commentary on secular canonesses.[16] He then lists other instances in which Hostiensis himself had warned against beguine immorality; when, for example, the cardinal had admonished clerics to avoid having anything to do with beguines who "under the pretext of holiness and hospitality, allow scandalous lovers to come and go among them."[17]

In Hostiensis then, Johannes finds support for a stereotype of beguines that had been part of popular culture for some time. As that staunch defender of the group, Jacques de Vitry, reported in the early thirteenth century: "The Preachers . . . rashly suspected that . . . such congregations of holy virgins were brothels rather than religious convents, and attributing the faults of a few women to all, so far as defaming the order approved by God and God-fearing persons, they shocked many."[18] And satirical poets and polemicists like Gautier de Coincy (d.1236), Rutebeuf, and Jean de Meun, helped to perpetuate the image of sexually lax beguines well into the next century.[19]

Because he was a canonist, however, and a most respected one at that, Hostiensis' articulation of this vulgar image allows Johannes to use it in his legal explication of *Cum de quibusdam*. Johannes also follows Hostiensis in construing the "feigned" piety of secular canonesses, as they are characterized in *Perniciosam*, as analogous to that of beguines.[20]

16. Found in the *Decretum* at C 18.q 2.c 25. See Chapter 1 for Johannes' use of the decree when dealing with canonesses.

17. Johannes locates this reference at X 3.1.8 *de vita et honestate clericorum ad verbum monasteria*, but I have also found it in the *Summa aurea* (Venice, 1574), at X 3 *de cohabitatione clericorum et mulierum, ad verbum utrum cohabitatio*, p 856: "*et a beguinis, sive beguinabus, que praetextu sanctitatis es hospitalitatis turpes amatores admittunt, cavendum est.*" Note that in this instance Hostiensis adduces the decree "*Perniciosam.*"

18. McDonnell, *Beguines and Beghards*, p. 190.

19. Renate Blumenfeld-Kosinski, "Satirical Views of the Beguines in Northern French Literature," in *New Trends in Feminine Spirituality*, pp. 237–49.

20. See above, footnote 17. As Grundmann, *Religious Movements*, p. 23,

The main features of Johannes' *prolegomena:* a concern to distinguish between beguines and tertiaries, an unqualified distrust of the former, and the suggestion that beguines and secular canonesses represent related problems, continue to appear in his gloss proper— that is, the portion of his work which contains his definition of or elaboration upon particular words (those in bold print in the translation given above) in Clement's decree.

At the word *beguinabus,* for example, Johannes refers his readers to the Clementine rubric *de haereticis* (Clem. 5.2), and so to the decree *Ad nostrum,* for details "about the errors of the German beguines and beghards."[21] This ambiguous citation makes it possible to argue that Johannes Andreae distinguished between the beguines of *Cum de quibudam* and those of *Ad nostrum.* Yet even if he intended to point out that the beguines *"Alemaniae"* constituted a group separate from those discussed in *Cum de quibusdam,* his citation of a piece of legislation which expressly deals with beguine heretical errors implies guilt by association, at the very least.

When glossing the word *obediantiam* Johannes asserts again, and this time with no ambiguity, that *sorores minorum quae dicitur tertii ordinis,* Franciscan tertiaries, are not included in Clement V's condemnation. This is the case for two reasons: first, unlike beguines, they promise obedience; second, they have a rule which, although lacking in the three things essential to religious life strictly speaking (*tria substantialia,* that is, vows of poverty, chastity, and obedience), outlines a certain way of life *(modus vivendi)* which has been approved by the apostolic see.[22]

Johannes supports this argument by citing another Clementine

---

mentions, the words *religionis speciem simulantes,* "simulating the appearance of religion," was a formula "that had always proved useful to the Church when stripping heresy of its claim to religious legitimacy." He adds that during the twelfth century the Church shirked its duty to differentiate between "true" and simulated religion. It seems clear, however, that even the best efforts of canonists to do this in the later Middle Ages were inadequate.

21. Johannes Andreae, *Glos.ord.,* p. 216: *"De erroribus beguinarum et beguardorum Alemaniae."*

22. Ibid., pp. 216–17.

decree, *Cum ex eo* (Clem. 5.10.3)—a decree which becomes a *locus classicus* for canonical commentary on the ecclesiastical status of tertiaries, and that is treated in the next chapter. He reaches much farther back in time, however, for his gloss of the word *insaniam*. Appending a reference to a canon from the Council of Ancyra, 314 A.D. (*Decretum* C.26 q.5 c.12) he suggests that the "insane" behavior of beguines who dare to debate about the nature of sacred doctrine might be compared to the soothsaying and magical arts *(sortilegam et magicam artem)* of the women condemned in this ancient canon: gullible women, who styled themselves minions of the goddess Diana and claimed to fly across the countryside on the backs of beasts.[23]

With its mention of pagan rites, demonic phantoms, and airborne women, this fourth-century canon strikes the modern reader as a decidedly curious proof text. But to the bishops of Ancyra, and so to Johannes Andreae, it was not so much witchcraft *per se* but the occasion that this sort of self-deception provided for leading others into error that was at issue: "For an innumerable multitude, deceived by this false opinion, believe this to be true, and so believing, wander from the right faith. . . ."[24]

By using this decree as his proof text, Johannes lends credibility to the image of the deluded, deceitful beguine that had become a trope among satirical poets, and even canonists like Hostiensis. It is an image that will henceforth appear in more than one guise in the commentaries, and one that Johannes seems to find particularly apposite since he reiterates it almost immediately. At the word *sanctitatis* he adduces Pope Gregory the Great's maxim that the semblance of equity is doubly evil by virtue of the fact that such duplicity creates an evil while entirely consuming the good.[25] Feigned piety, like

23. Friedberg, *Corpus, Decretum* C 26.q 5.c 12, 1:1030. Hefele and Leclerq, 1:1:325 note that this canon was included in the *Decretum*. For an English translation of it, see Koors and Peters, *Witchcraft*, pp. 29–31.

24. Friedberg, *Corpus*, 1:1030. "*Nam et innumera multitudo hac falsa opinone decepta hec vera esse credunt et credendo a recta fide deviant . . .*"

25. Johannes Andreae, *Glos.ord.* p. 217. "*Simulata aequitas duplex est iniquitas; ratio est quia malum facit et abutitur bonus.*"

false teaching, threatens to corrupt, perhaps irreversibly, the simple Christians who encounter it.

Beguine eagerness to engage in theological discussions suggested "a kind of insanity" to Clement V, and the list of proof texts in the ordinary gloss at the words *disputent* and *praedicent* respectively help to explain why. As evidence that such disputation is prohibited to lay*men*, Johannes cites a letter from Pope Innocent III to the bishop of Metz (X 5.7.12).[26] In it, the pope warns of the serious problems that a casual attitude toward theological discussion among the laity can raise, and stresses the need for oversight and guidance by those ordained to explicate doctrine. Johannes also lists a canon of the Second Council of Lyons restating the doctrine of the Holy Trinity, and excoriating those who would ignore the *magisterium* of the hierarchical church in matters of faith.[27]

If the right to participate in debate about matters of doctrine was strictly confined by law to the clergy, the right to preach publicly also belonged to a minority of Christians, none of whom were women.[28] Johannes' citations at the word *praedicent* well illustrates this limitation. He adduces a decree from the Council of Carthage (*Decretum* at D.23 c.29) that begins: "A woman, no matter how

26. Friedberg, *Corpus,* 2:784–87.

27. As found in *VI* 1.1.1, Friedberg, *Corpus,* 2:937.

28. Yet note the important role that itinerant preaching had in the *vita apostolica* as aspired to by believers, both orthodox and heretical, male and female: Grundmann, *Religious Movements,* pp. 219–26. For the distinction between moral and dogmatic preaching see Grundmann as well, p. 36. That women might find the opportunity to preach publicly as Cathars or Waldensians has been noted in recent scholarship, see, for example: Berverly Mayne Kienzle, "The Prostitute-Preacher: Patterns of Polemic Against Medieval Waldensian Women Preachers," pp. 99–113, and Anne Brenon, "The Voice of the Good Woman: An Essay on the Pastoral and Sacerdotal Role of Women in the Cathar Church," pp. 114–33, both in *Women Preachers and Prophets Through Two Millenia of Christianity,* ed. Beverly Mayne Kienzle and Pamela J. Walker (Berkeley: University of California Press, 1998). But heretical preachers, male or female, were not the only concern. Regulation of mendicant preaching, especially as it interfered with parochial privileges, is a major theme in the canon law. The attractiveness of the Franciscans and Dominicans as fiery preachers was one of the reasons for the secular clergy's continued hostility toward friars.

well-educated *(docta)* and holy, must not presume to teach men in a convent," and concludes with the more expansive warning, "In the presence of a cleric, neither should a lay*man*, save for asking questions, dare to teach *(docere)*."[29]

Not only women and laymen, but clerics themselves were denied the right to preach publicly unless they had cure of souls or a special license to do so. And as an example, Johannes cites another decree from the Council of Vienne found in the Clementines at 3.7.2.[30] This legislation restricted Franciscan and Dominican preachers to sermonizing in their own churches and in public places, unless specially invited by a parish priest to speak to his congregation—a restriction necessitated by the wrangling between parochial clergy and the friars about the rights of the latter to preach, hear confessions, and bury the dead in a parish, since these activities undercut the authority and depleted the revenues of parish priests.

Distinctions between the rights of secular and regular clergy merit mention again in the penultimate section of Johannes' gloss, but this time with reference to the penalty of excommunication incurred by *"praedictis religiosis"* (aforesaid religious) who aid or counsel beguines. Johannes interprets these words strictly, saying that the pope wished to exclude secular clergy from this ban and sought to apply the ultimate sanction to regulars alone. As later commentators will prove, Johannes' interpretation takes on special significance for Dominican and Franciscan friars since they were the regulars most often associated with beguines and most often resented by secular clergy.

Given the conservatism of his gloss thus far, Johannes' approach to the final passage of *Cum de quibusdam*, that escape clause exempting "faithful women, whether or not they promise chastity," from condemnation as beguines, is not unexpected. Nevertheless, the deftness with which he succeeds in casting suspicion upon even these orthodox women is worthy of note. Singling out only one word from the saving clause, *humilitatis*, Johannes appends a string

29. Friedberg,*Corpus*, 1:86.
30. Friedberg,*Corpus*, 2:1161–64.

of authoritative references to illustrate not only the essential character of this virtue but also the dangers of false humility.

He begins with two passages from Bernard of Clairvaux's treatise, *On the Steps of Humility and Pride.*[31] The first defines humility as the virtue by which a man, truly knowing himself, recognizes his own vileness. The implication that deception, in this case self-deception, obstructs the attainment of genuine humility, is reinforced and given a social dimension by the second passage. In it Bernard condemns the false humility of those who make a pretense of penitence; those who insincerely confess their sins merely to avoid greater punishments.

Johannes reiterates Bernard's condemnation by following it with a reference to Pope Clement IV's decree (VI 5.2.11) which incorporates the scriptural warning found in Matthew 7:15: "Beware of false prophets which come to you in sheep's clothing but inwardly they are ravening wolves."[32] The pope's decree admonishes inquisitors to be alert to the fact that accused heretics might make false confessions and, although not truly repentant, be allowed to mingle among the faithful as wolves in sheep's clothing *(fallentes sub agni specie lupum gerunt).*

Johannes concludes his gloss with a series of comments drawn from the works of John Cassian, Ambrose, and Gregory the Great, all of which extol the virtue of humility as nothing less than the key to the kingdom of heaven.[33] The fact that some of the greatest names in the history of monasticism are featured in this conclusion was surely not lost on Johannes' readers. Those readers had, after all, just finished a gloss condemning a group which Johannes cast as imitative of, but lacking in the essentials of, that venerable institution.

If true humility was cultivated by the "true" religious and monastic *regulae* supplemented by centuries worth of ascetic counsels helped the monk or nun to achieve it, then the quasi-religious

31. See Bernard of Clairvaux, *Bernard of Clairvaux, Selected Works,* trans. G. R. Evans (New York: Paulist Press, 1987), pp. 103 and 136 respectively.
32. Friedberg, *Corpus,* 2:1073–74.
33. Johannes Andreae, *Glos. ord.* p. 217.

woman, no matter how well intentioned, was at a disadvantage. Absent both a monastic rule and an established *contemptus mundi* literature, she lacked adequate guidance and so might fall prey to self-deception, and much worse. Once again the quasi-religious woman suffered by comparison with the religious woman, strictly speaking.

By starting with the depiction of the deceptive beguine provided by Hostiensis and ending with oblique references to sham humility even among "those faithful women" whom Clement V seemed to place above suspicion, Johannes Andreae achieved a symmetry and an internal consistency in his gloss of *Cum de quibusdam* that the decree itself lacked. Although his was not the earliest commentary (that distinction belongs once again to Guilelmus de Monte Laudano), it became the most influential gloss of Clement V's decree, the ordinary or standard interpretation. In fact, as Jacqueline Tarrant has observed, only one academic commentator raised any challenge to Johannes' interpretation of *Cum de quibusdam* as a blanket condemnation of all beguines.[34]

About 1323, a papal chaplain and auditor of the Rota, Albericus Metensis (also known as Alberic of Metz, d. 1354) produced his *Apparatus* on the *Clementines*. His was one of the earliest commentaries on this collection.[35] Albericus' departure from the standard gloss consists of a short but significant comment that he makes in his gloss to *Cum de quibusdam* at the words *in suis hospitiis:* "By this it appears that the prohibition of this constitution does not extend to the beguines of Metz, Verdun, and many other places in which they live in their own homes *(per hoc apparet quod prohibicio istius constitucionis non extendit se ad beguinas metenses virdui et in pluribus locis que in domibus propriis morantur). "*[36]

Displaying, as his name and early career in Paris and Orléans suggest, an ultramontane perspective, Albericus distinguishes be-

34. Tarrant, "The Clementine Decrees," p. 308 n.25

35. For this and other information about Albericus see Domenico Maffei, "Alberico di Metz e il suo Apparato sulle Clementine," *BMCL* 1 (1971): 43–56.

36. As quoted from Albericus' manuscript by Maffei, Ibid., p. 55 n.47. *"per hoc apparet quod prohibicio istius constitucionis non extendit se ad beguinas metenses virdui et in pluribus locis que in domibus propriis morantur."*

tween the orthodox and the heretical beguine. Unlike Johannes Andreae, he sees Clement V's decree as a condemnation of only one misguided group of these women. Yet, upon close inspection, even Albericus' reading of *Cum de quibusdam* does not unreservedly assert the right of beguines *living in community*, those whose institutional forms might lead people to regard them as "true" religious, to exist unmolested. In *Cum de quibusdam*, the words *in suis hospitiis* are used to refer to the living arrangements of "those faithful women" whom Clement exempts from condemnation. Albericus specifically places certain beguines in this group as well, but he refers to those beguines as living *in domibus propriis.* The shift in language is telling.

Defined as an inn or lodging in classical Latin, the term *hospitium* generally meant "residence" or "dwelling" in the fourteenth century, but it retained some lingering connotations of liberality and hospitality consistent with its earlier definition.[37] Albericus avoids these old associations by using the word for private home, *domus,* instead of *hospitium* in his exoneration of orthodox beguines such as those living in Metz and Verdun. "Good" beguines do exist, he seems to be saying, but they are the ones who avoid the appearance of religion by leading their devout lives in the privacy of their homes.

However cautiously, Albericus Metensis did claim that one could, and should, distinguish among beguines. There were women called beguines, he said, who lived lives above suspicion and were therefore no more liable to condemnation by *Cum de quibusdam* than "those faithful women" referred to in the saving clause. This interpretation of the decree might very well have been closer to reflecting Clement V's original intentions; it was not, however, a reading that later canonists would endorse.

37. See the examples in J. F. Niermeyer, *Mediae Latinitatis Lexicon Minus* (Leiden: Brill, 1976; rpt.1997), p. 503. It is telling that modern translations of, and references to, the segment of the saving clause that contains this word are not at all consistent. Gordon Leff, *Heresy,* p. 315, translates *hospitii* as 'beguinages'; Robert Lerner, *Heresy,* p. 47, uses the words 'communal houses'; McDonnell, *Beguines and Beghards,* p. 527, prefers 'convents' while in Tanner, *Decrees* II, p. 374, we find the word translated as 'hospices.' See Walter Simons, "The Beguine Movement," pp. 67–68 who distinguishes among the *curtis beguinage,* the beguine convent and house as they existed in the southern Low Countries.

Albericus' *apparatus* had only a limited circulation and we do not find his name referenced by other fourteenth- and fifteenth-century commentators on *Cum de quibusdam*. What we do find is a predictable repetition and/or expansion of the sentiments of Johannes Andreae—predictable since, as Richard Helmholz reminds us: "The canonists belonged within a common legal tradition. They did not work in isolation or set out purposefully to create new theories of either law or government. They followed one another. They copied one another."[38] And given the near tyranny exercised over the text of a law by the ordinary gloss on that law, such imitation becomes even more understandable.

All this is not to say that the canonists who came after Johannes Andreae produced colorless, repetitive, glosses on *Cum de quibusdam*. A commentator could easily endorse the interpretation of the ordinary gloss while at the same time demonstrating his own particular strength, such as a penchant for legal research. Citing authoritative texts, both ancient and contemporary, that had not found their way into Johannes Andreae's gloss became a common method by which subsequent canonists distinguished themselves.

Writing his *Commentaria super Clementinas* a year after the publication of the ordinary gloss, Jesselin de Cassagnes (d. 1334–35), adopted this technique.[39] Although the bulk of Jesselin's work on the canon law remains in manuscript form (only his *apparatus* on the *Extravagantes Johannes XXII* has been printed in full), Jesselin was a canonist of international repute in his own lifetime. [40] A teacher of law at Montpellier, papal chaplain in Avignon, and member of the Roman Rota, Jesselin's curial experience added heft to his opinions and established him as a respected authority among his contemporaries.[41] When glossing Clement V's decree, Jesselin used

38. Helmholz, *The Spirit*, p. 397.

39. Jesselin de Cassagnes, *Commentaria super Clementinis*, Paris, BN lat. 14331 fol. 137v.

40. Jacqueline Tarrant, "The life and works of Jesselin de Cassagnes," *BMCL* 9 (1979): 37–64.

41. See above, as well as: Paul Fournier, "Jesselin de Cassagnes, canoniste," *Histoire de la Littérature Française* 35 (Paris 1921): 348–61; R. Naz, "Jesselin de Cassagnes," *DDC* 6 (1957): 130–31; and Schulte, *QL* 2:199–200.

the work of one of those contemporaries to produce an interpretation consonant with, but not purely imitative of, the ordinary gloss.

As we know, the earliest commentary on the *Clementines* appeared three years before that of Johannes Andreae and included a brief gloss of *Cum de quibusdam* written by Jesselin's fellow countryman, Guilelmus de Monte Laudano.[42] Jesselin modeled his own short commentary on that of Guilelmus, thereby highlighting elements missing from or underdeveloped in the *glossa ordinaria.* Jesselin's references to Guilelmus' work are so consistent in fact that we do neither canonist a disservice by treating their two glosses of *Cum de quibusdam* together.

At the word *obedientiam,* Guilelmus had noted that neither a simple promise of obedience nor renunciation of personal property sufficed to confer true religious status since religious profession, either tacit or express, is the *sine qua non* for the regular.[43] Guilelmus' comments accorded well with the ordinary gloss on this matter, and his mention of religious profession—that public action which, coupled with the assumption of a distinctive habit, solemnized the monastic vows of poverty, chastity, and obedience—added a legal dimension absent from Johannes' gloss.[44]

Perhaps it is for these reasons that Jesselin appropriates Guilelmus' observations.[45] He also includes in his own commentary Guilelmus' parody of beguine practice, found at the word *approbatam.*[46] In it, brown-habited beguines wearing "sheep's clothing," ravage the flock and pervert penitential practice: While tertiaries eschew sexual relations with their lawful spouses on certain days, in accordance with their penitential way of life, beguines use these days to consort with their lovers.[47]

42. See Chapter 1 for background on Guilelmus and his gloss.
43. Guilelmus de Monte Laudano, *Apparatus in Clementinas,* Paris, B.N. lat. 14331, fol. 102r. *ad verbum: obedientiam.*
44. See VI 3.15.1 for the Bonifacian legislation to this effect.
45. Jesselin de Cassagnes, *Commentaria, ad verbum obedientiam,* fol. 137.
46. Guilelmus, *Apparatus,* fol. 102r.
47. Ibid. *ad verbum: approbata,* fol.137 v, ". . . *vestes brunas portant male ornatas et frequenter sub specie agni gerunt . . . quasdam que dum mariti earum per tres dies iuxta eorum ritum abstinenbant a thoro maritali ipse illis diebus cum amortoribus begunnatum duplicabant.*"

Finally, at *sane*, the first word of the saving clause, Jesselin, like Guilelmus before him, opines that Clement V's exception applies to those "faithful women" remaining at home *(honeste vivendo in domus suis nequam prohibetur).*[48] As with Albericus Metensis, the shift in language signifies, since once again Clement's exception is being interpreted very narrowly: Any woman endeavoring to lead a quasi-religious life should do so in truly private and restricted circumstances, relinquishing any idea of community, no matter how limited.

Several of Guilelmus de Monte Laudano's references were pithy enough to have been appropriated by Jesselin de Cassagnes, and the words of both men, particularly the parody of beguine spiritual practice, are quoted quite frequently in the writings of later commentators. Neither Guilelmus nor Jesselin, however, had wasted much ink on *Cum de quibusdam* and some of their colleagues and successors bequeathed even less.

Two of the most famous jurists of the Middle Ages, the Perugian law professor Baldus de Ubaldis (1327–1400) and the Sicilian-born Nicolaus de Tudeschis (Panormitanus, 1386–1445) produced only a few derivative lines on the decree.[49] Stephanus Hugonetti (1280–1332) wrote a terse restatement of received opinion, and the Florentine abbot Lapus Tactus (flo. mid fourteenth century) decided to ignore the decree entirely.[50] Perhaps a lack of time or inclination ac-

48. Jesselin, *Commentaria*, fol. 137.

49. Baldus de Ubaldis, *Lectura super Clementinis*, Vat. lat. 5925 *ad verba Sorores minorum*, merely repeats received wisdom about tertiaries and Sisters of St. Clare as well as the stipulation against unauthorized preaching by clergy or laity; Nicolaus de Tudeschis (Panormitanus), *Lectura in Clementinas* (Venice, 1490, no pagination), contains a gloss to *Cum de quibusdam* that is barely a paragraph long and simply restates key points in the ordinary gloss. However, his apparent neglect of the decree in academic commentary by no means implies a lack of knowledge of or interest in it, as my later examination of one of his *consilia* will demonstrate. The lives and work of both of these important canonists will be dealt with in subsequent chapters.

50. See, with cautions similar to those issued for Panormitanus: Stephanus Hugonetti (Stephaus Provincialis), *Apparatus super constitutionibus Concilii Viennensis* (Philadelphia, University of Pennsylvania Library), MS Lat. 95, fol. 43v–44r; and Lapus Tactus, *Lectura super Sexto et Clementi-*

counts for these facts; we can only speculate. But in at least two instances, a lack of first-hand knowledge about the beguines compelled brevity.

Both Johannes Andreae's student Paulus de Liazariis (d. 1356) and the French canonist Petrus Bertrandus (1280–1349) betray humility uncharacteristic of lawyers when they claim ignorance of the facts and unwillingness to draw conclusions based only on rumor.[51] Petrus' comment, echoed by his colleague, reads: "and I have heard that there are many such beyond the mountains [Alps] but not having any on this side I am not able to provide an apt example *(et audivi quod ultra montes sunt multa de talibus sed citra montes non habemus et ideo exemplum bonum proponere non possum)."*[52]

Happily, at least for the historian, the Avignonese cardinal Bonifacius Ammannati (d.1399) was not as scrupulously distrustful of hearsay.[53] To judge from the length of his gloss, he would seem to have welcomed any and every bit of information regarding the subjects of Clement V's decree.[54] Despite (or maybe because of) its length, Bonifacius' extensive commentary was not widely circulated in manuscript and even when it was eventually published it appeared under the wrong name![55]

---

nas (Rome, 1589). Not much is know about the life of Lapus Tactus. See however: F. Rubod, "Lapus Tactus," *DDC,* 6 (1957): 344; and Schulte, *QL* 2:238–39.

51. For biographical details on Paulus see Schulte, *QL* 2:246–47 and R. Chabanne, "Paulus de Liazariis," *DDC* 6 (1957): 1276–77. For Petrus see, M. Déruelle, "Bertrand (Pierre)," *DDC* 2 (1937): 789–92; and Schulte, *QL* 2:235–36.

52. Paulus de Liazariis, *Lectura super Clementinis,* Paris, BN lat. 4136 (part 3) *Cum de quibusdam, ad verbum beguinnarum* and Paris, BN lat. 4102, fol. 50. Petrus Bertrandus, *Apparatus Sexti libri Decretalium cum Clementinis,* Paris, BN lat. 4085, fol. 154.

53. On the life and works of Bonifacius see: D. Maffei, *"Profilo di Bonifacio Ammannati giurista e cardinale," Genèse et débuts du grand schisme d'occident* (Paris, 1980), pp. 239–51.

54. Filling folio pages 85v–88r of his *Lectura Clementinaurm,* Toledo Bibliteca del Cabildo, Codex 23-1, *Pseudo Bonifacio de Vitalinis.*

55. This erroneous attribution continued well into the twentieth century. Even Schulte, *QL* 1:255–56 still credits one Bonifacius de Vitalinis with Ammannati's work.

At times displaying all of the worst traits of the scholar engaged in frenzied bouts of dialectical legerdemain, Bonifacius nevertheless presents us with a truly fresh reading of *Cum de quibusdam*. Like his predecessors, he repeats the words of the ordinary gloss and piles up the usual authorities. But unlike many who came before him, he does not flinch from identifying and then attempting to clarify many of the vagaries of this watershed legislation.

In the first part of Bonifacius' gloss, we find the standard references to the precise nature of beguine status, the rationale for their condemnation, and their relationship to papally approved tertiaries and other "faithful women" exempt from the taint of unorthodox behavior.[56] There are suggestions throughout this section that Bonifacius finds it difficult to reconcile *Cum de quibusdam*'s saving clause with the body of the text:

> Note that the status of female penitents, whether or not they promise chastity, is approved, or at least not condemned . . . note that although they don't promise chastity they ought to preserve chastity as long as they remain in community *(quamdiu ibi manent in communi debent servare castitates)* . . . and thus it [the saving clause] ought to be understood in this sense: That these women are allowed to live in their own dwellings [*in proprio suis hospitio*] and that the status of beguine alone is condemned . . . as to the question of whether these same women are able to live communally in their own dwellings *(an iste mulieres possint in suo hospitio habitare communiter)* it seems that they ought not do so, since it [the decree] reads: 'in their own dwellings' *(hospitiis)* nevertheless in many places beguines are tolerated despite the words of this constitution *(tamen in pluribus paritibus sunt beginae tolleantur contra huius constitutionis).*[57]

The issues are the same as those we have encountered previously, but the difference in approach is apparent. Albericus Metensis, Guilelmus de Monte Laudano and Jesselin de Cassagnes had all al-

56. Bonifacius Ammannati, *Lectura*, fol. 85r deals fully with the status of beguines, and beguines by any other "vulgar" name, as well as supplying the traditional explication of the term "religious"; fol. 87r rehearses the arguments used to exempt the second and third orders of St. Francis from similar condemnation.

57. Bonifacius Ammannati, *Lectura*, fol. 86r.

luded to the right of "faithful" quasi-religious women to live in community, but they had not bluntly denied them that right. They left the reader to speculate, as I have done, that by substituting the word *domus* for *hospitium* they envisioned a strictly private living arrangement for these women. Bonifacius, on the other hand, leaves no room for inference: whatever lingering classical connotations the word *hospitium* possessed (and if the word *hadn't* still possessed those connotations, Bonifacius' clarification would have hardly been needed) it was *not* a term synonymous with beguinage. According to Bonifacius, Clement V had not intended to approve a communal life for quasi-religious women, even if those women were above suspicion.

Having observed that, despite canonical prohibition, communities of beguines continue to exist throughout Europe, Bonifacius goes on to offer an explanation for their resilience. Beguines are a danger because they deceive others by appearing holy, he says, and there is no doubt that their status is not now approved by the holy see; at one time, however, that status had been acceptable; before *Cum de quibusdam* beguines, like canonesses, had been tolerated by the church *(ante istius clem. status eorum sicut canonicarum fuerat tolleratur).*[58]

In addition to likening the status of secular canoness to that of the beguine, Bonifacius thus explains why beguines (like canonesses) are still so much in evidence. With the publication of Clement V's decree, beguines lost their right to exist; their unorthodox behavior and beliefs triggered that loss, but the message had still not been fully accepted in the provinces where beguine communities were established institutions.

Bonifacius relies almost completely on the opinions of Guilelmus de Monte Laudano, Jesselin de Cassagnes, and Paulus de Liazariis when next defining the term "religious." And his assertion that promises of chastity and obedience alone do not suffice to confer religious status, strictly speaking, is scarcely original. What is original is the author's citation of a piece of new papal legislation to support all of his assertions.

58. Ibid., fol. 87v.

This legislation, a decretal issued in 1317 by Clement V's successor John XXII, was known as *Sancta Romana*.[59] *Sancta Romana* condemned the Spiritual Franciscans and those tertiaries in Italy and Southern France who had come under their influence: *fraticelli, fratres de paupere vita;* and *bizochi,* or *beghini;* it will be treated at length in the next chapter. Here it is noted because Bonifacius cites this decretal to emphasize the fact that papal approbation of an order or a way of life suffices to distinguish it from otherwise similar quasi-religious groups. Thus, members of the Third Order of Saint Francis, whom John XXII refers to as members of the Order of Penitence, having such approbation from the pen of Pope Nicholas III [*sic*], escape censure; the beguines, along with the *fraticelli* named in *Sancta Romana,* do not.[60]

To bring this last observation into line with his earlier comments about the nature of the true religious, Bonifacius is once again forced to make a concession to practice. Although women who are not professed in some approved religious order are not technically religious persons (with all the rights and privileges that classification denotes), there are cases in which quasi-religious women continue to retain their way of life without penalty of excommunication. For

59. This decretal was included in the unofficial collection of twenty post-*Sext* decrees known as the *Extravagantes Johannis XXII* at 3.7.1. The Latin text can be found in Friedberg, *Corpus,* 2:1213–14 and in the new critical edition edited by Jacqueline Tarrant: *Extravagantes Johannis XXII, Monumenta Iuris Canonici,* Series B: *Corpus Collectionum,* vol. 6, (Vatican City: *Biblioteca Apostolica Vaticana,* 1983), pp. 198–204.

60. Bonifacius Ammannati, *Lectura,* fol. 87r. Note that it was Pope Nicholas IV who formally approved the Third Order and issued a new rule for tertiaries in 1289. See Gerald J. Reinmann, *The Third Order Secular of St. Francis* (Washington, DC: The Catholic University of America Press, 1928), pp. 37–38. Note also that the *beghini* mentioned in *Sancta Romana* are not even female quasi-religious, and were known as *beguins.* Not surprisingly, as we shall see, there was much confusion surrounding these references—confusion which continues to arise even among modern scholars. See for example Joyce Pennings's remark that, "In 1317 Pope John XXII's bull *Sancta Romana* dealt the semi-religious women a heavy blow, forbidding women to dwell together, unless they should do so in seclusion from the world," p. 116 in "Semi-Religious Women in 15th Century Rome," *Mededelingen van het Nederlands Historisch Instituut te Rome* XLVII/ns 12 (1987): 115–45.

the second time, Bonifacius uses the example of secular canonesses to support his conclusion, in this instance by citing the well-know decretal *Dilecta*.[61]

By the close of his gloss, Bonifacius has raised and resolved some thorny issues. Although he has reiterated the common opinion that *Cum de quibusdam* should be read as a condemnation of all beguines, he has shown a particular skill in pointing up the "apparent" inconsistencies in the decree. He has also demonstrated a more positive, even defensive, attitude toward those quasi-religious women, in the tradition of secular canonesses, who remain untouched by Clement's prohibition.

In his final remarks, Bonifacius reiterates what has come to be a theme of this gloss. Women who are not professed religious, he says, are not religious women strictly speaking and should not be allowed to live as such—here citing Boniface VIII's decree *Periculoso* directing nuns to live in strictly cloistered communities.[62] But women who do not make profession yet live religiously continue to exist because they are not specifically prohibited *(quod non derogatur)*.[63] Once again, the issue seems to be whether the communal organization of quasi-religious women might lead others to presume erroneously that they are true religious.

Bonifacius Ammannati's level of engagement with his subject was not to be duplicated in his lifetime. In the fifteenth century, the canonists appear to have settled on an interpretation of *Cum de quibusdam* that offered little room for innovation; as noted, the eminent Panormitanus produced a mere summary of the decree. Two other important jurists, Petrus de Ancharano (1333–1416) and his distinguished colleague Cardinal Zabarella (1360–1417) did write glosses of some originality, but only because of their enthusiasm for citing conflicting contemporary opinions.[64]

---

61. Bonifacius Ammannati, *Lectura*, fol. 88v.

62. For details about this decree see the preface of this book.

63. Bonifacius Ammannati, *Lectura*, fol. 88r. *"sic non debent manere patientitur huius feminas non religiosas vitam earum regularum servare sine professionam quia earum statui videlicet derogatus, dici [dico?] autem possunt quod non derogatur."*

64. See Chapter 1 for biographical information on Cardinal Zabarella.

Franciscus Zabarella, for instance, begins his gloss by noting some discrepancies among those jurists commenting on the life and practices of the beguines: "Mattheus Romanus . . . says that beguines (of which there are many *ultra montes*) wear gray habits, and this description accords with the Archdeacon's statements in his gloss on the *Liber Sextus*, but Guilelmus de Monte Laudano says that they wear brown dress, badly ornamented *(male ornatas)*."[65]

So, too, the cardinal mentions that with reference to the unauthorized preaching of beguines the ordinary gloss says merely that women are not to preach. Mattheus, however, holds that in the privacy of the cloister, in the chapter house or in the choir, an abbess may teach her nuns or lay sisters and preach to them, but not publicly. Therefore the injunction against women preaching should be understood as implying merely a preference for men.[66]

Finally, the inclusion of *Sancta Romana* as a proof text allowed some of the later glossators to become even more expansive in listing names which, following local custom and "vulgar" usage, might apply to beguine-like groups. Both Petrus de Ancharano and Cardinal Zabarella condemn those called *continentes* and *bizochi*, who, like the *fraticelli*, make no promise of obedience and live outside of any approved rule.[67] So, too, after adducing *Sancta Romana* as a proof text in his discussion of suspect religious groups, Johannes de Imola (d. 1436) holds that *bizochari* and *continentes* can be classed with the *fraticelli*.[68]

Based on this overview of the academic commentary to which *Cum de quibusdam* gave rise, it is safe to conclude that if Clement V

Petrus de Ancharano, born in Tuscany in 1333, had noted students, as well as colleagues; he numbered Panormitanus, Antonius de Butrio and Johannes de Imola among them. For further information on his teaching and public service career see: Charles Lefebvre and R. Chabanne, "Pierre d'Ancarano," *DDC* 6 (1957): 1464–71; Schulte, *QL* 2:278–82.

65. Franciscus Zabarella, *Lectura in constitutiones Clementinas* (Venice, 1499) fol. 138ra. Both Petrus and Zabarella also allude to Guilelmus' story about beguine sexual license as a parody of the ascetic practice of tertiaries and add that some are also said to be apostates and to live by begging.

66. Zabarella, *Lectura*, fol. 139rb.

67. Ibid., fol. 138ra; Petrus de Ancharano, *Lectura*, fol. 77.

68. Johannes de Imola, *in Clementinas*, (Venice, 1492) fol. 137r.

had intended to distinguish between "good" and "bad" beguines, between those meriting condemnation and those whose orthodox beliefs exempted them from censure, then his purpose was thwarted by the glossators. With the exception of Albericus Metensis, the commentators completely upheld the position taken by Johannes Andreae and given currency in his *glossa ordinaria.*

Distinctions made in the decree between beguines and other quasi-religious women were noted and sometimes, as in the work of Bonifacius Ammannati, carefully drawn; but in their academic glosses the canonists overwhelmingly interpreted Clement V's words as a sentence of excommunication directed against all beguines. In later commentaries we even see that condemnation extended (with the support of *Sancta Romana*) to those "beguines by any other name": *continentes, bizzoche, pinzocarae* and the like.

Before concluding, it is important to point out that this consensus among academic canonists might have been easily undermined by their inclusion, as an authoritative proof text, of another of John XXII's decrees. *Ratio recta*, issued only one year after *Sancta Romana*, responded to the undifferentiated persecution of quasi-religious women referred to at the start of this chapter. Its purpose was to clarify *Cum de quibusdam*, and to a great extent it did just that.[69]

Beginning with a recognition that the beguines condemned by Clement V merit censure because of their heretical leanings, it then vigorously restates the saving clause in *Cum de quibusdam*. "In many parts of the world there are those women who are also called beguines but who live in their own homes, in those of their parents, or sometimes in community, but who lead lives beyond reproach. If those beguines do not engage in preaching or disputation about doctrine, and if they attend church regularly, submitting to the authority of local clergy, they must not be molested and should be allowed to retain both their habits (distinctive dress) and their way of life."[70]

69. See the discussion in: Lerner, *Heresy,* pp. 48–49, 95; McDonnell, *Beguines,* p. 536; and Leff, *Heresy,* pp. 333–39.

70. *Ratio recta* is found in another unofficial collection of *extravagantes,* which eventually came to be known as the *Extravagantes communes:* A col-

Although *Ratio recta* stopped short of giving orthodox beguines papal approbation, the decretal did help to restrict persecution, at least for a time. And if academic canonists had given the decree some attention, it might have helped much more, since it quite clearly limited the scope of *Cum de quibusdam*. *Ratio recta* stated that Clement V had not meant to condemn *all* beguines, and it distinctly exempted the orthodox among them, *even if they continued to live in communities and to wear a distinctive habit,* from harassment; *Ratio recta* was duly issued by a pope to help clarify legislation that had proven difficult to enforce because of its apparent ambiguity. Why then was John XXII's decree ignored by academic commentators?

Ratio recta may well be the decree to which Johannes Andreae alluded in the introduction to his gloss on *Cum de quibusdam*. He had heard of a relevant new papal ruling, Johannes admitted, but had been unable to acquire a copy of it, and there was even some doubt about its authenticity: *"dicitur quaedam declaratoria super hac constitutione emanasse, quam de curia habere non potui: eta quibusdam audivi,quod a curia non manavit."*[71]

Unlike *Sancta Romana* which, as part of a small private collection of John XXII's decretals entitled the *Extravagantes Johannis XXII* (1325), found its way into the late medieval law schools, *Ratio recta* circulated independently until much later.[72] Nor is there any indication that it ever entered the medieval law school curricula. It would seem then that the unavailability of the decretal, or the unavailability of an authenticated copy, might logically account for its absence from both Johannes Andreae's and subsequent commentary.

As attractive as this explanation appears, however, it cannot fully

---

lection of 70 decretals from Urban IV (1261–64) to Sixtus IV (1471–84). The Latin text can be found in Friedberg, *Corpus*, 2:1279–80.

71. Jacqueline Tarrant mentions this comment as an example of the fact that although commentators were interested in the *extravagantes* they were often inaccessible: *Prolegomena* to *Extavagantes Johannis*, ed. Tarrant, p. 4.

72. Brundage, *Medieval Canon Law*, pp. 55–56. The compiler of this collection was either Jesselin de Cassanges or Guilelmus de Monte Laudano: *NCE* 5:770. Tarrant, "The life and works of Jesselin de Cassagnes," p. 56, says that it is likely that he compiled as well as glossed the *Extravagantes.*

account for the canonists' failure to cite *Ratio recta* in their commentary on *Cum de quibusdam*. If Johannes Andreae did not have *Ratio recta* at hand when he wrote his gloss on the *Clementines*, he would surely have read it by the time he wrote his *Apostillae* or additions to that work. Dated between 1324–30, the *Apostillae* included John XXII's other decree, *Sancta Romana* at Clem. 5.3.3.[73] And we can say with certainty that other canonists with whom we have dealt in this chapter definitely knew the contents of *Ratio recta*. Guillelumus de Monte Laudano, for example, wrote a brief gloss to *Ratio recta* which was circulated with the decree, and Panormitanus cited *Ratio recta* as a proof text in at least one of his *consilia*.[74]

There is a possibility that *Ratio recta* was not referred to by any of the academic commentators on *Cum de quibusdam* because that decretal was not readily available. It is also possible and indeed probable that the neglect of this important piece of qualifying legislation is simply part of a trend evident in canonical activity in the later Middle Ages. Publication of the *Extravagantes Johannis XXII* in 1325 heralded what might be called the end of an era. Decretal letters which had for so long been the focus of learned interpretation began to assume less importance in the writing of the jurists. Popes certainly did not stop issuing decretals, but canonists stopped relentlessly collecting them. As Tarrant points out in the *prolegomena* to her critical edition of the *Extravagantes*, far fewer papal letters were being collected in the fourteenth and fifteenth centuries than in the twelfth—over 700 decretals were collected for Pope Alexander III for example, while only about 170 were collected during the entire late-medieval period.[75]

Late medieval canon lawyers became more preoccupied with the application of already existing law in the courts, especially the Roman Rota, and the concomitant increase in the collection of the de-

---

73. For the date of these additions see Kuttner, "Apostillae," p. 200.

74. Guilelmus' gloss includes the confusing marginal note: *"Religiose mulieres quod facere debent."* See *Extrav. comm.* 3.9.1 in *Corpus Iuris Canonici* (Venice, 1584), p. 303; For Panormitanus, whose *consilium* will be treated in Part II of this book, see Panormitanus, *Consilia* (Strasbourg, 1474).

75. *Extravagantes Johannis XXII*, ed. Tarrant, *Prolegomena*, pp. 16–17.

cisions of that court attests to this preoccupation.[76] The perspective of late medieval canonists changed, and so did the character of the legal literature that they produced. The long-favored academic gloss and commentary on a huge volume of legislation gave way to the monograph and to the *consilium*, or legal opinion. Often written at the request of a sitting judge in actual litigation, *consilia* always treated the law relevant to some specific situation, and specificity had come to matter a great deal.[77]

Having said this, it becomes easier to explain why some of the most respected canonists of the fourteenth and fifteenth centuries neglected to consider *Ratio recta* in their academic commentary of Clement V's decree. By the second half of the fourteenth century, academic commentary on *Cum de quibusdam* had been shaped definitively by the work of Johannes Andreae. For a distinguished canonist such as Panormitanus to do more than provide a quick summary of that work must have seemed like an empty exercise.

Canonists of the caliber of Panormitanus were interested in writing *consilia* since they were richly paid for their efforts.[78] The genre also allowed them to test their skills in applying existing law to actual, specific situations, and we will analyze quite a few of those legal opinions, as well as Rota *decisiones*, in the second half of this book. Before proceeding to that analysis, however, we need to take one more look at the academic commentary, this time the commentary concerning a third group of quasi-religious women so often confused with, and thus persecuted as, beguines: female tertiaries.

76. Ibid.

77. Less often the *consilium* could be an academic exercise, but even when it was its structure corresponded to that of a brief which might be employed in actual litigation. The later canonists apparently enjoyed the possibilities which this genre gave them to exercise their interpretative skills, focusing on some very specific situation. More information on this genre can be found in the second part of this monograph.

78. On the attractive payments received for writing *consilia* see: Ingrid Baumgärtner, ed., *Consilia im spätenmittelalter: Zum historischen Aussagewert einer Quellengatung, Studi/Schriften des Deutschen Studienzentrums in Venedig,* Bd. 13 (*Sigmaringen:* Thorbecke, 1995); and Mario Ascheri et al. eds., *Legal Consulting in the Civil Law Tradition* (Berkeley: The University of California Press, 1999).

T H R E E

Cum ex eo, Sancta Romana, and Tertiaries

T he indiscriminate persecution of quasi-religious women which sometimes took place in the years following the publication of *Cum de quibusdam* is well documented.[1] Whether as a consequence of local resentments, especially those harbored by secular parish clergy toward the friars who often supported such women, or as the result of the decretal's ambiguous wording, Clement V's legislation proved a useful weapon against any and all "beguine-like" activity.

A moving account of such undifferentiated harassment of quasi-religious women was written by the Franciscan chronicler John of Winterthur between the years 1340–47:

> When it was published, and, although poorly understood, stubbornly and deceitfully promulgated in the chanceries of Germany, innumer-able hearts of the sisters of the third order of St. Francis and of many others were sorely wounded. For, having laid aside their religious habit, they had to don the secular. Many had been serving the Lord in chastity and the other virtues and by good works in their own or their parents' houses for forty years and more in gray, black, and white gar-ments. Now they are obliged by their fellow parishioners to wear reds,

1. John Moorman, *A History of the Franciscan Order* (Oxford: Clarendon Press, 1968), pp. 422–23; McDonnell, *Beguines and Beghards,* pp. 528–34.

yellows, greens, and blues. . . . How much ridicule, contempt, foolhardiness, and rashness these modest and chaste sisters endured God alone knows! They were turned into a spectacle and a proverb by all men. O how often they suffered great humiliation when they were shamefully dragged and mauled in public. The confusion that was brought upon them under pretext of the Clementine decree [*Cum de quibusdam*] was, sad to say, the cause of ruining many. For those who had long practiced celibacy for the Lord returned to the world, now that the vow of chastity had been broken, and either contracted marriage or what is worse committed all kinds of fornication.[2]

From among those "many others sorely wounded" John, a Franciscan, singled out female tertiaries, allowing us to see how easily these women might be confused with their "heretical" sisters: They dress in grays, blacks, and whites, and beguines wear habits of grey and brown; like beguines, they make promises of chastity and, just like the beguines condemned in Clement V's decree, they live in their own or in parental houses rather than in monastic enclosures.

John of Winterthur's German ordinaries, perhaps out of malice or confusion, or a little bit of both, interpreted *Cum de quibusdam* as a condemnation of female tertiaries.[3] Nearly a hundred years later, the Dominican polemicist John of Mulberg would cite the same legislation when endeavoring to show that tertiaries might be as tainted by heresy as beguines.[4] Yet those who had actually been charged with the task of interpreting Clement V's decree for the law schools, whether writing in the fourteenth or the fifteenth century, staunchly resisted such conclusions.

Following the lead of Johannes Andreae, the canonists who

2. The translation of this account is taken from McDonnell, *Beguines and Beghards*, pp. 530–31.

3. The matter was by no means limited to this time or place either. Persecution of female tertiaries follows very much the same cyclical pattern as that of the beguines, with periods of papal defense of the orthodox giving way to renewed efforts at eradication of the heterodox persecution strafing all. These cycles are clearly presented in McDonnell, *Beguines*, especially chapters V and VII; Lerner, *Heresy*, pp. 47–55, 85–105; and Leff, *Heresy*, pp. 333–37.

4. Lerner, *Heresy*, pp. 104, 154–55; Jean-Claude Schmitt, *Mort d'une hérésie*, pp. 152–160, 207–9.

glossed Clement V's decree carefully distinguished between beguines and women who were members of the Third Order of St. Francis. The latter, they insisted, were exempt from condemnation because they possessed the one thing that made their semi-religious way of life permissible, the *sine qua non* which beguines, like secular canonesses before them, lacked: papal approbation.

Although lay affiliation with religious orders had deep roots, papally approved tertiary status of the sort alluded to by the canonists is a thirteenth-century phenomenon.[5] In 1201, Pope Innocent III had provided members of the Lombardy-based lay poverty movement, the Humiliati, with a rule for those whose familial obligations prohibited them from fully renouncing the world.[6] These tertiaries, although married and living in their own houses, were obliged to observe certain ascetic practices, abstain from oath-taking, and to receive spiritual instruction from one among them under the watchful eye of their diocesan bishop.

Innocent III's integration of married laity into the *Ordo Humiliatorum*, which also had a monastic and clerical division, set the example for Pope Honorius III who, in 1221, approved a rule for some lay penitents inspired by the religiosity of the Friars Minor. By 1289, the Third Order of Saint Francis had been solemnly approved. In that year Pope Nicholas IV issued his bull *Supra montem*, which provided the brothers and sisters of the order of penitence—or tertiaries, as they were now explicitly designated—with an approved rule.[7]

For the sake of clarity it is worth noting here that penitents had long been associated with the Dominicans as well, and that it was only in the 1280s that the mendicants distinguished between those affiliated with the Order of Preachers and those who followed the Minorites.[8] Nevertheless, when Pope Nicholas IV, himself a Francis-

5. For examples of older practice see Reinmann, *The Third Order,* chapters I–II; Miramon, *Les "donnés",* chapters I–III.

6. Grundmann, *Religious Movements,* pp. 32–40; Reinmann, *The Third Order,* pp. 17–20; Moorman, *Franciscan Order,* p. 41–42.

7. *Bullarium Romanum,* vol.4. pp. 90–95. Reinmann, *Third Order,* p. 37 and 59; Moorman, *Franciscan Order,* p. 217.

8. Lehmijoki-Gardner, *Worldly Saints,* pp. 34–38.

can, favored the Minorites by granting penitents supervised by Franciscans a *regula bullata*, the canonical commentators were quick to recognize its importance.

The *regula* with which the pope favored Franciscan tertiaries contains precise stipulations about admission to and government of the order, as well as the dress and comportment of its members. Prospective tertiaries were to be examined for evidence of good character and sound beliefs. Once admitted to the fraternity, members were bound to remain in it, save to enter an approved religious order. They were obliged to dress in simple clothes, to fast and abstain with something more than ordinary rigor, and to avoid disreputable feasts and entertainments. They were to observe the canonical hours, to attend mass as a group once a month, and to confess and receive communion three times a year. The bearing of arms and oath-taking were permitted only in specified circumstances.

For the academic lawyers glossing *Cum de quibusdam* this recent history made all the difference. In contrast to beguines, who "neither promise obedience to anyone . . . nor profess any approved rule," female members of the Third Order of St. Francis had received approval for their penitential *modus vivendi* from the pope himself. A legal distinction had been thereby created which, if sometimes lost on local ordinaries and polemicists, was crucial to jurists, allowing them to support the activities of tertiaries while condemning those of the beguines whom they so closely resembled.

But would this technical distinction be enough to preserve tertiaries from suspicion when the jurists encountered them in other, specifically negative, legislative contexts? That is the question which this chapter raises, and that canonical commentary generated by two decrees, issuing from the chanceries of popes Clement V and John XXII respectively, allows us to answer.

The two decrees, *Cum ex eo* and *Sancta Romana*, both cast tertiaries in the role of potentially problematic, if not overtly heretical. Both decrees entered into the *Corpus iuris canonici*, and both became *loci* for academic commentary dealing with, among other things, distinctions between beguines and female tertiaries and the classification of third-order members as ecclesiastical persons. They provide us, therefore, with the means to gauge canonical commitment to a position protective of female tertiaries in an ecclesiastical climate which fostered suspicion of quasi-religious women generally.

Cum ex eo, issued as canon thirty-seven of the Council of Vienne (1311–12), was incorporated into book five of the *Clementines* (5.10.3).[9] It is a sternly worded warning to the Friars Minor "not to receive brothers or sisters of the Third Order of Saint Francis, who are also known as *continentes* or penitents, into their churches to hear the divine offices in time of interdict."[10] This practice, the decree continues, is a source of scandal to those who are excluded at these times and it debases the force of ecclesiastical censure. Consequently, the friars who persist in such practices are to be automatically excommunicated, not withstanding any privileges which they or the tertiaries might have relative to this practice—privileges which, the pope adds, "we certainly do not favor" *(quae ipsis [privilegiis] in nullo prorsus quoad hoc volumus suffragari).*

That the "privileges" to which Clement V refers were routinely given to members of religious orders, and that the right of access to churches, even in times of interdict, had been expressly given to tertiaries in the past is undeniable—in 1224, for example, Honorius III permitted tertiaries to say their offices and to receive the sacraments during such times.[11] Equally obvious is the fact that the privilege of immunity to interdict was frequently abused, leading, as a canon from the Fourth Lateran Council put it, to a loosening of ecclesiasti-

9. Friedberg, *Corpus*, 2:1192; For an English translation of the canon see Tanner, *Decrees*, vol. 1, p. 391.

10. Interdict is defined as an ecclesiastical punishment imposed upon a person, group, or whole territory, that stops some or all church functions in a particular place, or prohibits those affected by interdict from participation in divine services. Reception of sacraments other than baptism and the Eucharist (for the sick or dying) would be prohibited, masses would be celebrated privately, and burial in consecrated ground would be banned as a matter of course. Mitigations of the interdict, usually treated as *ad hoc* privileges, abounded, however. See *DMA*, 6:493–97 for a good overview of the subject.

11. Moorman, *Franciscan Order*, p. 44; Reinmann, *Third Order*, p. 62; McDonnell, *Beguines*, p. 259.

cal discipline that threatened to make the sentence of interdict con-
temptible.[12]

Commonplace or not, however, the abuse of papal privilege was
serious business and members of the Third Order of St. Francis had
been implicated by *Cum ex eo*. Would this canon further obscure the
distinction between female tertiaries and their erring sisters, the beguines? Johannes Andreae, author of the ordinary gloss on the
Clementines, certainly thought it might.

At the very beginning of his gloss proper, Johannes alerts the
reader to the difference between these two groups of quasi-religious
women, appending a reference to papal legislation *(Cum de quibusdam)* that highlights that distinction by condemning the beguines.
Citing the words *sorores tertii ordinis*, Johannes states: "These women,
however, are not the beguines who are spoken of in this same collection under the title *de religiosis domibus, capitulum primum*."[13]

Cardinal Zabarella's *prolegomena* to this gloss, which appears in
some printed versions, explains why Johannes Andreae had felt the
need for such clarification: "Note that women of the third order of
the blessed Francis are called 'sisters.' On account of this, the [ordi-
nary] gloss mentions that they are not Beguines and it says this because tertiaries owe obedience following the traditions of the third
order; Beguines, on the other hand, are certainly not bound by obedience."[14]

The cardinal's explanation of Johannes Andreae's reasoning
points up a patent source of confusion for jurists dealing with tertiaries and beguines. In direct address, beguines were generally

12. Tanner, *Decrees*, vol. 1, p. 261. Moorman, *Franciscan Order.*
13. Johannes Andreae, *Glos. ord.* to Clem. 5.10.3 in *Corpus Iuris Canonici* (Venice: 1584), p. 312.
14. Ibid., p. 311. This same explanation occurs as a marginal note over
the *sigla* of Franciscus Zabarella in some printed editions of the *Clementines*, for example: *Clementis Quinti Constitutiones* (Basilee: Joannes Amer-
bach, 1511), fol. 68; it is also found at the very beginning of Cardinal
Zabarella's own gloss to *Cum ex eo:* "*Nota quod mulieres de tertio ordine beati
Francisci dicuntur sorores ex hoc insertur glos. quod non sunt begine et insert hoc
ex eo quia sunt sub obiedientia secundum traditiones tertii ordinis predicte; beguine
vero non sunt sub obedientia.*" Franciscus Zabarella, *Lectura super Clementinis*
(Venice, 1492), fol. CXCVI.

called "sister" and we find the terms *sorores conversae, paupercule sorores,* and *sorores castitati dedicate* used to refer to them in the documents.[15] Use of the title "sister" to refer to both beguines and tertiaries added just one more element to the already confusing situation.

Elsewhere in his gloss on *Cum ex eo,* Johannes Andreae defines tertiaries as married people who have renounced neither the world nor their possessions. Although practicing sexual abstinence at certain times (following ancient penitential practice), they were assuredly not "continent" in the strict sense of the term, since they take no vow of continence, nor, properly speaking, were they regulars.[16] He is quick to add, however, that their way of life has nevertheless received undisputed papal approval.

As in so many other cases, subsequent commentary on *Cum ex eo* followed the model set down by Johannes Andreae. Many important glossators repeated his distinction between female tertiaries and beguines, stressing that the two groups ought not be conflated; the latter, at best, lacked an approved rule and at worst tended toward heresy. As Bonifacius Ammannati put it: "Note that the third order instituted by the blessed Francis is composed of men and women and these people are not beguines *(beginni nec beginnae)* since the beguines are not an order and are rather heretics than religious despite the fact that they wear habits and have their own visitors *(visitatores)* as it says in *cum de quibusdam. . . .*"[17]

Brothers and sisters of the Third Order "*non sunt beghine sed appellantur fratres et sorores de penitentia,*" wrote Johannes de Imola, adding

15. See references to these and other titles in: Norman Tanner, *The Church in Late Medieval Norwich* (Toronto: Pontifical Institute, 1984), p. 65; Dayton Phillips, *Beguines in Medieval Strassburg* (Stanford: Stanford University Press, 1941), p. 3.

16. Johannes Andreae, *Glos. ord.* to *Clem. 5.10.3 ad verba tertio et continentes,* p. 312. For a discussion of sexual abstinence by tertiaries see: Vauchez, *The Laity in the Middle Ages,* p. 121 and Dyan Eliott, *Spiritual Marriage,* pp. 197–99.

17. Bonifacius Ammannati, *Lectura Clementinarum, Toledo, Biblioteca del Cabildo, Codex 23-1,* p. 281 vb: "*Nota quod ordo tertia ab sancti Francisci institus est virorum ac mulierium et non sunt beginni nec beginnae nam iste nullus ordo erat ad heretics . . . etsi religiosis isti habebat habitum et eorum visitatiores.*"

that the Third Order was founded for married men and women who did not renounce their property and who might be properly said to have a *modus vivendi* rather than a rule.[18] "The third order was devised for married men and women," echoed Panormitanus, "and those professing this rule possess property, even private property, and the third order is more precisely called a way of life than a rule, being nevertheless approved by Pope Nicholas. . . ."[19]

So too, Johannes Andreae's reservations about using the term "continents" to describe tertiaries were repeated again and again, with virtually no alteration. "It appears that the brothers of the third order shouldn't be referred to as *continentes* since they have wives . . . ," reasoned Johannes de Imola, "but my response is that they are not called continent because they take a vow of continence, but rather because of the fact that following their [penitential] way of life they refrain from sexual relations on certain days of the week, just as the priests of the old testament used to abstain weekly from their conjugal duties."[20]

What is more interesting, and less common, is the way in which subsequent writers reflecting on *Cum ex eo* departed from the model established for them by the *glossa ordinaria*. Johannes Andreae had accorded tertiaries legitimacy by virtue of papal approval, but some later canonists wondered if he should have stopped there. Were members of the Third Order not sufficiently "religious" to warrant something more than mere legitimacy? Might not the sanctity of their founder and the penitential nature of their lives allow them to be recognized as ecclesiastical persons? Since *Cum ex eo* had ecclesiastical privilege as its fulcrum, the commentators saw in it an appropriate opportunity to argue this point.

18. Johannes de Imola, *In Clementinis* (Venice, 1492), fol. 181vb.

19. Panormitanus, *Lectura in Clementinas* (Venice, 1490), gloss to *Cum ex eo*, n.p.; Stephanus Hugonetti, *Apparatus super constitutionibus Councilii Viennensis* (Philadelphia, University of Pennsylvania Library), MS Lat 95, fol. 68r; and Petrus de Ancharano, *Lectura super Clementinas* (Venice, 1493) p. 104.

20. Johannes de Imola, p. 181 ra. We find the same sentiments in Bonifacius Ammannati, *Lectura*, p. 281v; Panormitanus, *Lectura*, gloss to *Cum ex eo*, n.p.; Petrus de Ancharano, *Lectura*, p. 104, and Cardinal Zabarella, *Lectura*, fol. CXCVI, to name just a few.

Although, as the name suggests, the package of special rights referred to as clerical privileges attached first of all to ordained clergy—those men who exercised the offices of worship—but by the later Middle Ages some of these privileges had been extended to a variety of other persons broadly classed as ecclesiastical. Chief among these privileges were the *privilegium fori,* which reserved to ecclesiastical courts all cases dealing with clergy; *privilegium canonis,* which protected the person of the cleric from physical abuse; *privilegium immunitatis,* which exempted clerks from requirements to pay taxes set by secular authorities and relieved them of the obligation to hold public office; and *privilegium competentiae,* which forbade the reduction of a clerk to penury in redeeming his indebtedness.[21]

Writing in 1338, Lapus Tactus argued cogently that ecclesiastical privilege be granted to tertiaries: "Should the brothers and sisters called the brothers and sisters of penitence who are treated here [in *Cum ex eo*] enjoy ecclesiastical privilege or immunity? It ought to be said that they do . . . for it is undeniable that these people are ecclesiastics in the broad sense of the term and even religious, so they certainly should enjoy ecclesiastical privilege at least with respect to their goods, if not their persons."[22]

Lapus here refers to two separate privileges, namely the one that encompassed exemption from taxes *(privilegium immunitatis)* and that which guarded the person of the cleric from physical attack by prescribing excommunication as punishment for such acts of violence *(privilegium canonis).* Lapus supports his concession of these privileges by noting that tertiaries live by a rule that forbids them to reenter secular society after their profession *(in regula ipsorum prohibentur professi eiusdem regulae post professionem ad saeculum redire).*

21. On this topic see: *DMA,* "Clergy," 3:445; John E. Downs, *The Concept of Clerical Immunity* (Washington, DC: The Catholic University of America Press, 1941); Gerard Campbell, S.J. "Clerical Immunities in France During the Reign of Philip III," *Speculum* 39 (1964): 404–24. Chapter 5 examines some of the practical ramifications of this idea of extension of clerical privileges to quasi-religious.

22. Lapus Tactus, *Lectura super Sexto et Clementinas* (Rome, 1589), p. 243: *"non enim potest negari, quin ipsi sint ecclesiasticae personae largo sumpto vocabulo, et etiam religiosae: quae tamen ecclesiastico privilegio gaudent etiam in bonis suis, nedum in personis . . ."*

This prohibition obligates them to observance that is even stricter than that required of the Friars Minor themselves, since those wishing to become Friars Minor are allowed to return to the world, provided that they leave the order before the end of their probationary year. If tertiaries live under obligations similar to or even stricter than those of the friars, and if "he who is subject to the burden ought also to enjoy the advantage," then tertiaries should be accorded ecclesiastical privilege.[23]

Lapus' reasoning might have effectively supported his argument, but it did little to convince other canonists that his was the correct opinion. A lively battle of words began among the canonists glossing *Cum ex eo*. Bonifacius Ammannati, whose thorough treatment of the vagaries of *Cum de quibusdam* we observed in the previous chapter, highlights this fact in his (equally involuted) gloss of *Cum ex eo*.[24]

Bonifacius says that according to Guilelmus de Monte Laudano, tertiaries do not enjoy clerical privilege with respect to their persons or their goods *(nec in personis nec in rebus gaudent privilegio clericali)* and are, in fact, about as worthy of clerical status as newborn babes *(et ideo iudicat eos ut nudos omnio privilegio clericali quasi de novo egresso de utero matris)*. Other jurists, he admits, grudgingly grant members of the third order religious status "broadly speaking" while being careful to distinguish between monastic profession and the mere promise of obedience, such as is made by tertiaries. And Bonifacius himself cautions that as married people who continue to live in their own homes *(manentes in domo proprio)*, tertiaries may claim immunity from secular jurisdiction only by special privilege *(ut laici coram judice seculari, nisi aliud habent)*.[25]

By the fifteenth century, legal opinion on this issue had become, if anything, even more various. For instance, Johannes de Imola, whose commentary on the *Clementines* appeared early in the century, writes:

23. Lapus cites the rule of law: *regula LV "Qui sentit onus, sentire debet commodum, et e contra."* Friedberg, *Corpus*, 2:1123. According the their 1289 rule, tertiaries were allowed to enter an approved religious order after their profession, but forbidden to "return to the world."
24. Bonifacius de Ammannati, *Lectura*, pp. 283r–284v.
25. Ibid., p. 284v.

Guilelmus [de Monte Laudano] says that members of the third order of blessed Francis are neither true clerics nor true religious since they don't have power over their own bodies (their wives do); and he goes on to say that they consequently do not enjoy benefit or privilege of clergy, neither with respect to their persons nor goods and he judges them to be devoid *(nudos)* of all clerical privilege just as if they were newborn babes; Zenellius [Jesselin de Cassagnes] maintains the contrary, saying that they enjoy privilege of clergy and Johannes de Lignano also takes this position, as does Bartolus [de Saxoferrato] who deals extensively with it in a *consilium* . . .[26]

Johannes goes on to discuss the particular argument of Bartolus, who draws a parallel between tertiaries and members of some military orders who are classed as ecclesiastical persons despite the fact that they do not renounce marriage or property.[27] Johannes finds Bartolus' parallel a bit troubling, however, noting that the military orders have an express privilege exempting them from secular jurisdiction, not to mention taxation and civil service—the mention of which brings him to cite the *consilium* of yet another civilian, Dynus.[28]

Dynus makes it clear that at least in some quarters tertiaries were treated no differently than laity—the magistrates in Perugia, for example, requiring tertiaries to both appear before lay judges and to pay taxes. Johannes suggests that he finds this approach acceptable in the absence of express papal immunity to secular imposts, but finally avers that "perhaps the opinion of Bartolus is more just *(forte verior est opinione Bartolo)."*[29]

26. Johannes de Imola, *In Clementinis*, pp. 181ra–rv.
27. According to Johannes, Bartolus (d. 1357) also accords freedom from secular jurisdiction to *deo devoti*, which, as we have seen, is a name still used for secular canonesses. For Bartolus' life and works see Manlio Bellomo, *The Common Legal Past of Europe 1000–1800,* trans. Lydia Cochrane (Washington, DC: The Catholic University of America Press, 1995), pp. 190–95; and J. A. Clarence Smith, *Medieval Law Teachers and Writers* (Ottawa: University of Ottawa Press, 1975), pp. 81–82.
28. The citation, simply *Dynus*, might refer to Dino Mugellanus (d. 1303), a civilian and canonist who taught in Pistoia and Bologna. See Smith, *Medieval Law Teachers and Writers*, pp. 55–57; Schulte *QL*, 2:176–77; L. Falletti, "Dinus Mugellanus," *DDC*, 4:1250–57.
29. Johannes de Imola, *In Clementinis*, p. 181ra.

Johannes de Imola wrote a gloss that made it clear that there was a dispute among canonists regarding the issue of ecclesiastical status of tertiaries. He also showed how civilians like Bartolus and Dynus had naturally become a part of that dispute, since it was one with very practical ramifications for municipal governments. When Johannes cited these civil law experts, moreover, he cited not their commentaries or treatises but their *consilia*.

Cardinal Zabarella's commentary on *Cum ex eo* demonstrates all of these same features.[30] In addition, it adds one Johannes Calderinus (d. 1365) to the list of bickering luminaries. The cardinal cites Calderinus' opinion as expressed in one of his *consilia:* granted that tertiaries are an approved order, "I think that they enjoy no ecclesiastical privileges because they strictly and properly speaking are not ecclesiastical persons, neither clerics nor regulars."[31]

Apparently convinced by this argument, Cardinal Zabarella concludes that tertiaries should be numbered among the laity and should not enjoy ecclesiastical privileges without special dispensation. Petrus de Ancharano also joins the opposition with the caveat that an express papal privilege of immunity would alter the *status quo.*[32] One prominent late-medieval canonist, however, chose to remain above the fray, at least at this juncture.

As he had done when glossing *Cum de quibusdam*, Panormitanus wrote a gloss of *Cum ex eo* that was little more than a summary of the words of Johannes Andreae; in consequence, he never even broached the issue of ecclesiastical status for tertiaries.[33] Yet, as in that earlier instance, it would be wrong to construe this omission as proof that the famous canonist lacked either knowledge of, or interest in, a crucial issue of his day. A few years after writing his com-

---

30. Zabarella, *Lectura*, fol. CXVI.

31. Johannes Calderinus, *Consilia* (Venice: Bernardinus Benalius, 1497), *Consilium IIII*, fol. LVI . See chapter 5 of this book for more discussion of the work of Johannes and his son.

32. Petrus de Ancharano, *Lectura*, p. 104: "*concludit quod non debet dici persone ecclesiastice nec privilegiis ipsarum gaudeant fatetur tamen quod si a papa habent de hoc privilegium est eis servandum.*"

33. See the previous chapter for Panormitanus' uninspired gloss of *Cum de quibusdam.*

mentary on the *Clementines,* Panormitanus produced a *Lectura* on the decretals of Gregory IX, and his comments on one of those decretals more than made up for his earlier silence.[34]

In his gloss of the decretal *Nullus,* which became the *locus classicus* for academic discussion of the extent to which a vast array of quasi-, semi-, and loosely affiliated *familiares* were entitled to clerical privilege, Panormitanus found his voice as an opponent of the extension of such privilege to tertiaries.[35] Furthermore, his exposition of the arguments of Federicus de Sensis *(contra),* Paulus de Romanus *(pro),* and Antonio de Butrio *(pro),* which precedes that conclusion, allows us to add the names of these jurists to our already long list of debaters.

The thoroughgoing and lively disagreement among academic commentators on *Cum ex eo* regarding the status of tertiaries as ecclesiastical persons confirms an observation made some years ago by Génestal. In the absence of any explicit legislation on the topic, canonists were free to draw their own conclusions concerning the exact nature and extent of ecclesiastical privilege enjoyed by tertiaries (not to mention any number of other quasi-religious persons in late-medieval society).[36] These conclusions would be drawn, and not only in the pages of academic commentary.

Differences of learned opinion on the matter gave sitting judges and their legal consultants considerable latitude when it came to decision-making in the courts. And the ramifications of this flexibility in matters ranging from the payment of tithes and testamentary succession to right of patronage will be more fully explored in a subsequent chapter. For the present, however, it is not the variety of academic opinion but the consensus that matters.

The jurists who commented on *Cum ex eo* did not retreat from the

---

34. Panormitanus, *Lectura super primo-quarto et quinto Decretalium....* (Lyon: 1521–22), X 2.2.2 *ad verbum Nullus,* p. 49.

35. Panormitanus' argument in this gloss and its relevance to one of his *consilia* will be treated in the next chapter.

36. R. Génestal, *Le Privilegium Fori* (Paris, 1921), vol. 1, pp. 32–33. Note, however, the transcription error in footnote 4, p. 33, line two should read: *"hic dominus Antonius (de Butrio)et etiam Paulus (de Romanus) in Clementina."* Laurentius de Pinu is mentioned only on line four.

position established in their glosses of *Cum de quibusdam*. They were unanimous in their defense of tertiaries as an orthodox manifestation of lay piety and they carefully distinguished female tertiaries from beguines. As we have just seen, many canonists had even been prepared to use *Cum ex eo* to justify extending ecclesiastical privileges to tertiaries. Would that same unanimity in defense of tertiaries be seen in the literature generated by *Sancta Romana*? *Cum ex eo* had censured disobedient tertiaries, and then only indirectly; *Sancta Romana*, however, referred to those among them who were overtly heretical. The shift in content would, at the very least, require the canonists to take a different approach in their defense of the Third Order.

Issued by Pope John XXII as part of his campaign against the Spirituals, *Sancta Romana* condemned a congeries of men *(prophane multitudinis viri)* living in a variety of places but especially in parts of Italy, Sicily, and the south of France.[37] The bull stated that men known commonly as *Fraticelli, fratres de paupere vita, bizochi sive beghini* defied the dictates of canon law (specifically here, the oft-cited decree of Lateran IV prohibiting the formation of new orders) by acting as if they were members of a religious order approved by the holy see; specifically, by organizing themselves into congregations, electing their own superiors, constructing buildings in which they lived in common, and publicly begging.

Some of these men claimed to be members of the order of Friars Minor by virtue of privileges granted to them by Pope Celestine V (notwithstanding the fact that these privileges had been revoked by Boniface VIII). Others claimed to be members of the Third Order of Blessed Francis, called penitents, in spite of the fact that their *status et ritum* was merely cloaked by that name, since the rule of the Third Order conceded none of the rites practiced by them. Therefore, the

---

37. For the text of this decree see *Extravagantes Johnnis XXII*, ed. Tarrant, #10, pp. 198–204. It is also found in Friedberg, *Corpus*, 2:1213–14. David Burr, *The Spiritual Franciscans* (University Park, PA: Pennsylvania State University Press, 2001), chapters 8–11 recount details of John XXII's campaign.

status sive sectam et ritum of *Fraticelli* and tertiaries alike was condemed.

The difficulties in distinguishing between orthodox and heretical tertiaries, especially given the variety of their organizational forms, and the numbers of people who claimed tertiary status merely to escape secular imposts and military service, led local ordinaries to read *Sancta Romana* as a condemnation of the Third Order.[38] Bishops read it as a prohibition against the formation of tertiary communities, a development that had proven to have its own momentum in the fourteenth and fifteenth centuries. Like *Cum de quibusdam* before it, *Sancta Romana* fostered confusion and indiscriminate persecution. Once again, local authorities seemed content to work with, or even to exploit, the ambiguity of papal law; once again, the canonists sought to erase such ambiguity.

Although it was never part of an officially promulgated canonical collection, *Sancta Romana* was well known to and widely cited by late medieval canonists. The appropriate context for such citation was suggested to them by Jesselin de Cassagnes, compiler of the *Extravagantes Johannis XXII* and author of the *glossa ordinaria* to *Sancta Romana*.[39]

Jesselin's intent is clear from the outset. At the words *habitum novae religionis assumere* he writes: "the habit, that is, of the new religious *Fratricellorum vel beguinorum*."[40] At the words *statum huiusmodi* he not only reminds his readers of the importance of papal approba-

38. Moormann, *Franciscan Order,* pp. 216–19 recounts conflicts with civic authorities and Phillips, *Beguines,* pp. 219–21, as well as Moormann, *Franciscan Order,* p. 421, note that the adoption of the Third Order rule by existing beguine and beghard communities increased local or inquisitorial suspicion that such communities harbored heretics. See Moormann, *Franciscan Order,* pp. 562–66 regarding persecutions undertaken as the result of the publication of *Sancta Romana.*

39. Jesselin de Cassagnes, *Glos. ord.* to *Extrav. Jo.* XXII 3.7.1 in *Corpus iuris canonici* (Venice, 1584), pp. 70–75.

40. The Dominican inquisitor Bernard Gui used the same terminology when writing of the errors of the beguines in Provence. He entitled this section in his inquisitor's manual *de secta beguinorum.* See Malcolm Lambert, *Franciscan Poverty* (London: S.P.C.K., 1961), p. 217.

tion for any truly religious community to exist, but cites as his supporting text Clement V's anti-beguine legislation *Cum de quibusdam*. This same decree condemning beguines is cited in two more places in the gloss, at the words *subiicimus* and *abolemus* respectively.

After linking the *bizochi* and *beghini* of *Sancta Romana* to the beguines, Jesselin carefully distinguishes these self-proclaimed tertiaries from members of the Third Order of Saint Francis. He never uses the word tertiary to refer to the *bizochi /beghini* condemned by the decree—they are imposters. Should the reader need clarification of the words *de tertio ordine*, he is referred to *Cum ex eo*.

The ordinary gloss deflected suspicion of heresy from tertiaries by simply refusing to acknowledge that the *bizochi/beghini* were tertiaries. But it did more than that. By interpreting *Sancta Romana* as a condemnation of unapproved sects which, *ipso iure*, excluded members of the Franciscan Third order, it lumped the anathematized *bizochi* and *beghini* together with beguines. Consequently, later canonists were encouraged to cite *Sancta Romana* when they needed to buttress their arguments against beguines.

Bonifacius Ammannati, as we have seen, was among the first to do so. In his commentary on *Cum de quibusdam*, he noted that tertiaries were distinct from beguines and that beguines, like the *Fraticelli* of *Sancta Romana*, merited censure because they lacked papal recognition. Petrus de Ancharano, Cardinal Zabarella, and the fifteenth-century glossator Johannes de Imola also adduced *Sancta Romana* in support of this line of reasoning.

It goes without saying that these commentators were fully aware of the fact that they were citing a law aimed at a group of men in southern Europe to support their judgments about a group of women popular in the north. For the academic canonists, however, differences in gender and geography were less significant than juridical similarities. Or, to put it in more starkly medieval terms, despite their different names and faces, all heretics are joined by their tails, since they are all alike in their pride.[41]

The absence of papal approval, like the sin of pride, bound *Frati-*

---

41. I paraphrase the famous canon 3 of the Fourth Lateran Council.

celli and beguines, *bizochi* and *beghini;* papal approbation distinguished and redeemed tertiaries. Whether this legal technicality—
this academic distinction—survived in, or even reached, the ecclesiastical courts where practicing lawyers faced vested interests,
jurisdictional conflict, inconsistent terminology, and paying clients,
remains to be seen.

Part II

Consilia and *Decisiones:* Practical Application
of Legal Theory

F O U R

Panormitanus and the *Inhumati, A Consilium*

Founded by the mystic and reformer St. Bridget of Sweden (1303–73),the Bridgettines embodied the saint's unique vision of earthly renewal.[1] Although governed by an abbess, Bridgettine monasteries admitted a fixed number of priests and brothers to serve the daily liturgical needs of the sisters. In 1370, the monastery at Vadstena, established by St. Bridget herself, was given official recognition by Pope Urban V, and in 1379 Urban VI approved the Bridgettine rule. But on February 13, 1422, Pope Martin V issued a bull denying the right of the Bridgettines to establish any more double monasteries. The bull declared that bishops were to oversee the separation of the nuns and monks living in such monasteries, allowing the nuns to remain and compelling the monks to find or construct new buildings for themselves.[2]

1. Bridget Morris, *St. Brigitta of Sweden* (Woodbridge, Suffolk, UK: Boydell Press, 1999), is one of the most recent studies of the Saint and her contributions. For insights about the significance of the order's structure see: Joan Bechtold, "St. Birgitta: The Disjunction Between Women and Ecclesiastical Male Power," In *Equally in God's Image,* ed. Julia Bolton Holloway, et al. (New York: Peter Lang, 1990).
2. A full account of this incident can be found in Hans Cnattingius, *Studies in the Order of St. Bridget of Sweden, I: The Crisis in the 1420s, Acta uni-*

Faced with effective dissolution, the Bridgettines and their royal supporters, Henry V of England among them, sent letters and even embassies to Rome, but failed to alter papal policy. Then, in 1423, the English confessor general of the order, Thomas Fishbourne, engaged the services of one of the most eminent canonists of the day, a professor at the University of Bologna named Nicholas de Tudeschis (1386–1445), better known as Panormitanus, since he later held the office of archbishop of Palermo.[3]

For a fee of ten silver ducats, the learned doctor produced a *consilium*, or certified legal opinion, upholding the canonical legitimacy of the Bridgettine Order.[4] Panormitanus argued that the Bridgettine monastery was not in fact a double monastery at all. It was rather a convent for nuns whose spiritual care was entrusted to individual clerics residing nearby, and as such it violated no canonical regulations. As for the binding nature of Martin V's "bull of separation," as

---

versitatis Stockholmiensis, Stockholm Studies in History 7 (Stockholm: Almquist & Wiksell, 1963).

3. For biographical details, see the recent overview by Kenneth Pennington, "Nicolaus de Tudeschis (Panormitanus)," in *Niccolo Tedeschi (Abbas Panormitanus) e i suoi Commentaria in Decretales,* (Roma: Libri di Erice 25, 2000), pp. 9–36. For information about Panormitanus' conciliarist stance at the Council of Basel (1433), to which he had been sent as a delegate by Pope Eugenius IV, see for example, Knut Wolfgang Nörr, *Kirch und Konzil bei Nicholas de Tudeschis,* Forschungen zur Kirchlichen Rechtsgeschichte und zum Kirchenrecht 4: Böhlau, 1964; the relevant essay in Morimichi Watanabe, *Concord and Reform: Nicholas of Cusa and medieval political and legal thought in the fifteeth century,* ed. Thomas Izbicki and Gerald Christianson (Burlington, VT: Ashgate, 2001); Brian Tierney, *Foundations of the Conciliar Theory* (Cambridge: Cambridge University Press, 1955); Charles Lefebvre, "Panormitain," *DDC* 6 (1957): 1195–1216; and Schulte *QL* 2:312–14.

4. This *Consilium, # VIII,* appears in many printed collections of the work of Panormitanus. I have consulted Panormitanus, *Consilia* (Lyon: Siber, 1500) Hain #7187; See also Cnattingius, *Studies,* pp. 138–41. Walter Ullmann, "The Recognition of St. Bridget's Rule by Martin V," *Revue Bénédictine,* 3–4 (1957): 190–201 contains an analysis of this opinion but because the author misdated it, confuses the issue of Bridgettine privileges and gives the impression that all struggles for recognition were over long before 1435. That struggle was clearly still raging at the Council of Basel (1431), where the validity of St. Bridget's revelations was also challenged.

it was called, Panormitanus pointed out that even the pope can be the victim of false information. If a pontiff makes a ruling based on misinformation, that erroneous judgment might be rescinded. Clearly, in this case, Martin V had been wrongly informed when told that the Rule of St. Bridget called for the establishment of double monasteries.

Panormitanus' *consilium* was put in the hands of the pope sometime in September or early October, and by November Martin V had issued a decree revoking the bull of separation insofar as it concerned the English Bridgettines. This was only the first in a series of decrees by which the bull was eventually nullified in its entirety.[5]

Apart from illustrating the vulnerability of the late medieval papacy to political pressures, especially in the wake of the Great Schism, this story about the Bridgettines helps to explain why the legal genre known as the *consilium* achieved such prominence among fourteenth- and fifteenth-century jurists. Reacting to external pressures exerted by those hostile to the Bridgettines, and armed with canonical prohibitions against double monasteries, Martin V had used all the authority of a newly invigorated papacy to rule against the continued existence of the order in the form envisioned by its founder. Pro-Bridgettine forces needed more than entreaties or even bribery to reverse such a decision. Where costly "gifts" and royal petitions had failed, one well-crafted *consilium* that allowed the pope to save face while withdrawing from his original position succeeded.

And although he was astute in his choice of expert counsel, Thomas Fishbourne was far from unique in recognizing his need for outside legal advice. The heads of religious orders, their lay patrons and benefactors, and late medieval litigants generally, encountered a bewildering mass of law when they sought legal redress, and they

---

5. It should be noted that by "explaining away" the double monastic character of their monasteries and reducing the role of the abbess from that envisioned by St. Bridget, the spirituality of the Bridgettines was fundamentally altered. See Auke Jelsma, "The Appreciation of Bridget of Sweden (1303–73) in the 15th Century," in *Women Without Vows,* pp. 163–75.

had become accustomed to viewing legal consultation as the *sine qua non* of victory.

Distinguished advocates claimed popes and kings as clients. Often plagued by legal problems, officials and administrators of church and state frequently needed the advice of lawyers to justify their actions or to weigh the strength of their positions before taking action. Pope John XXII, for instance, sought the opinions of seventeen canonists regarding the kind of aid he should offer to the king of France for a crusading venture.[6]

Notwithstanding the popularity of the *consilium* prepared for an individual (usually one of the parties in a case), the opinion given in response to a question put to a jurist by the court itself was even more common.[7] Such a response, called the *consilium sapientis iudiciale*, was delivered directly to the sitting judge under the seal of the jurist who wrote it, and judges in both ecclesiastical and civil courts availed themselves of such learned consultation. In some cases a jurist asked his colleagues for advice, and collaborative opinions—at times involving an entire law faculty—survive from the thirteenth century on.[8]

Judges, like litigants, faced an ever more specialized and academically formed body of Romano-Canonical law and an increasingly sophisticated court procedure. Requesting expert legal advice allowed a judge to achieve greater impartiality, expedite justice, and decrease the number of appeals from his court. For an itinerant judge employed by an Italian commune or a French king, the need to deal with local customary law and to work within overlapping ju-

6. Zacour, *Jews and Sacracens*, p. 5.

7. A good survey of the types and uses of *consilia* can be found in the introduction to Pazzaglini, *Consilia,* and in the introduction to Zacour, *Jews and Saracens*. For detailed reference see Guido Rossi, *Consilium sapientis iudiciale* (Milan: A. Giuffrè, 1958). See also Norbert Horn, "Die legistische Literatur der Kommentatorem und der Ausbreitung des gelehrten Rechts," in *Handbuch der Quellen und Literatur der neueren europäischen Privatrechtsgeschichte,* I, *Mittlelalter (1100–1500),* ed. Helmut Coing (Munich: C. H. Beck, 1973), pp. 336–40.

8. The defense of the Sisters of the Common Life (1398) by the law faculty of the University of Cologne is an excellent example of this type of collective opinion—see chapter six.

risdictions made the consultation of local experts less an option than a necessity.[9]

Consilia started to be collected as their popularity increased. One of the earliest collections was made by an advocate at the papal court in Avignon, Oldradus de Ponte (d. 1337), who began to edit his more than three hundred *consilia* for publication in the early fourteenth century. Renowned jurists such as Bartolus de Saxoferrato, Baldus de Ubaldis, Johannes de Imola, Petrus de Ancharano, Antonius de Butrio, and Panormitanus, would continue that practice into the fifteenth century, their collections serving as manuals which were regularly consulted by practicing and academic lawyers well into the early modern period.

Now we return to Panormitanus—although not to the Bridgettines—in order to examine a *consilium* that he chose for inclusion in his 1433 collection.[10] *Consilium LV* directly addressed the issue of the status of quasi-religious men and women since it involved a dispute between the Friars Minor and a quasi-religious group designated as "those paupers commonly known as the *inhumati*" *(illos pauperes qui vulgariter appellantur inhumati)*. This rigorously penitential group, sometimes referred to as the *Jesuati*, was founded in Siena by Giovanni Colombini in about 1360, and a female branch of the society was added at the time of Colombini's death.[11] To support his argu-

9. It was even customary in Italian towns to audit the decisions of the *podestà* and his chief judges at the end of their terms in office. This practice of assessing judicial liability made for even greater caution and reliance on the *consilium*. Pazzaglini, *Consilia*, p. xv.

10. See: "Panormitain," *DDC* 6:1203 for information about the collection. *Consilium* LV in Niccolo de Tudeschi, *Consilia*, (Lyon: Siber, 1500), extends from fol. xxx (va) to xxx (rb) and I have used that edition for what follows. I have also consulted an earlier edition, Niccolo de Tudeschi, *Consilia cum tabula Ludovici Bolognini* (Strassburg: Heinrich Eggestein, 1474) and where readings differ, I note discrepancies.

11. The identification of the *inhumati* with the *Jesuati* is further confirmed by the 1423 bull issued by Martin V in favor of the *Iesuati*—a bull alluded to as an indulgence in *Consilium LV*. See *Bullarium diplomatum et privilegium sanctorum Romanorum pontificium*, vol. 4, p. 730. For more information on the *Iesuati* consult: *DIP*, vol. 4, *Gesuati*, pp. 1116–30; *NCE*, 7:893; and for the founder, Giovanni Colombini (d. 1367) see *DCB*, p. 269. Panormitanus uses only the masculine gender when referring to this

ments in this *consilium,* Panormitanus adduced all the significant papal legislation relevant to quasi-religious women that had been incorporated into the corpus of the canon law. Because this is the same legislation that generated the hostile academic commentary that we have examined in previous chapters, *Consilium LV* provides us with a fine opportunity to assess the ways in which legal opinion differed from that commentary and the practical implications of these differences for quasi-religious men and women.

Consilium LV is a tightly wound skein of technical argument and proof texts, and what follows is less a translation than an attempt to unravel that skein for the benefit of the modern reader. While preserving characteristic structure and aiming for integrity of content, I have truncated some strings of supporting authorities or "proof texts" in the interests of clarity. I have also abbreviated two segments which pertain to the law of property so as not to deflect attention from what is for us the main focus: the legal status of the quasi-religious.

> A single tract of land, intended as the site of an oratory, was donated first to the *inhumati* and subsequently to the Friars Minor. Each claimant contests the proprietary right of the other, and the *inhumati* appear to have the weaker case.
>
> The *inhumati* seem to have no right to this donation, although they were the original beneficiaries, since their society appears to be condemned by canon law. Should this be the case in fact, the brethren would be barred from legal acquisition of any property, as a look at the relevant section in the *Codex Justinianus* demonstrates.[12] See as well Jo-

---

group in his *consilium* but we must remember that the canonists do the same when referring to the Brethren of the Common Life, a majority of whom were women.

12. Reference here is to one of the four parts of the *Corpus iuris civilis,* a compilation of Roman law made in the reign of the Byzantine Emperor Justinian (482–565). Of the four parts, *Institutes, Digest, Codex,* and *Novels,* Panormitanus makes most use of the *Digest,* as will be evident. The text cited at this juncture, *Codex. de here. insti., lex collegium,* can most conveniently be found in the modern edition of the *Corpus iuris civilis,* ed. Paul Krueger, Theodor Mommsen, et al., 3 vols. (Berlin: Weidmann, 1872–95), at Cod. 6.2.4.8.

hannes Andreae's gloss of "Religionum diversitatem," VI 3.17.1 [a decree of the Council of Lyon (1274) forbidding the founding of new orders without papal permission] in which he states that unapproved societies are not able to legally acquire property.[13]

And the Minorites contend that there is much evidence to support
the fact that the college or society of the *inhumati* is not approved—evidence such as the aforementioned decree which bans the founding of
new religious orders without papal approval. Since it cannot be denied
that religious orders each have their own distinctive habits which reflect contempt of the world, and that these habits are of a particular
color and form as dictated by a rule or constitution, and since the *inhumati* have such distinctive habits it follows that they must be a new religious order, which, having come into existence in opposition to the
papal ban, is consequently unapproved.

We do have to note here, however, that at the word *habitum*, the
standard gloss to "Religionum diversitatem" says that individuals who
live together in a college do not violate the provisions of the decree,
provided that they do not all don the same dress, thus avoiding the appearance of a religious community.

So too, we might adduce Clement V's decree "Cum de quibusdam"
(Clem. 3.11.1) as evidence against the *inhumati*, since in it the pope
condemns "certain women who live together under the guise of religion." But we can cite this decree only if we note that in it the pope
also states that he does not intend thereby to prohibit "faithful women,
whether or not they promise chastity, from living a penitential life in
their dwellings *(in suis hospitiis)* serving the Lord in virtue and humility." Whence, because of those words *in suis hospitiis*, I wonder on what
account living religiously *(sub quandam umbra religionis)* in a hospital or
college *(in hospitio seu collegio)*, for penitential purposes, is illicit.

Then we must also take into consideration the decretal "Indemnitatibus" (VI 1.6.43), in which the pope [Boniface VIII] expressly says
that he does "not intend to extend official papal approval to the status,
order, or rule of certain women [secular canonesses] who neither re-

---

13. This decree is a repetition and expansion of the ban on new religious orders, *Ne nimia religionum*, promulgated by the Fourth Lateran
Council in 1215, which found its way into the *Corpus iuris canonici* via the
decretals of Pope Gregory IX: *X 3.36.9*, and from here into the works of
important commentators on the canon law, like Johannes Andreae.

nounce property nor make regular profession," as is the case with secular canons. And of course when we introduce this text into the discussion, we pose a real dilemma, since it now appears that it is illicit for some to gather together for the sake of religion [as per *Cum de quibusdam*] and yet licit, if not strictly speaking approved, for others to do so even if they do not renounce their property or profess a rule [as per *Indemnitatibus*].

We can see from Bartolus' [de Saxoferrato] gloss of the Digest (D.47.22.1), however, that people may gather together for the sake of religion and still retain their lay status provided that they do not live continually *(assidue)* under one roof, nor wear the same habits, thus enabling people to distinguish them from ecclesiastics.[14] Hence we can surmise that the above canons many times limit the ways in which people might assemble for religious reasons simply because of the confusion and scandal to which this practice might give rise in the church of God.

We must also note that the papal ban on new religious orders not only expressly prohibits the founding of new orders but also the building of new religious houses, save with papal permission, and that the *inhumati* ordinarily erect such houses for themselves; indeed, they wish to build one on the disputed land, which would not be licit, thus nullifying the donation to them.

Similarly, it seems as if Pope John XXII in his decree *Sancta Romana*, [*Extravagantes Jo.* 7.1] expressly if not censoriously condemns the status of the *inhumati*, particularly in that part of the decree that prohibits collegial public mendicancy. And since both canonical and civilian opinion forbids public begging without evident necessity, it appears that the status of these paupers is condemned by both civil and canon law.

Now, from all of the above, it might be concluded that the *inhumati* are incapable of legally asserting their right to this donation and that they should cede that right to the second claimants, the Friars Minor,

---

14. This is the same Bartolus whom the commentators on *Cum ex eo* referenced in the previous chapter. Here Panormitanus cites Bartolus' comments on the *Digest* 47.22.1–4, which refers to the right to assemble for religious purposes so long as no public law is contravened. For this and subsequent references to the *Digest* see *The Digest of Justinian*, ed. Mommsen, Krueger, and Watson, 4 vols. (Philadelphia, PA: University of Pennsylvania Press, 1985) which features the Latin text and an English translation.

whose order *is* approved by the church. And it might also be surmised that those friars in turn ought to apply to Pope Martin V for a special license to gain possession of the land in question, since there could be objections raised to such a transfer of title on several grounds [all having to do with technicalities involving property law].

For instance, it might be objected that Antonius Johannis, the brother who accepted the donation in the name of the *inhumati,* cannot now surrender that donation since he never had full mandate from his society to accept it in the first place; consequently, because he never acquired dominion over it, the original donor would be fully within his rights to bequeath it to another.[15] And in support of this argument see the Digest (D.41.1.20 and D.41.2.1).

Notwithstanding all that has been alleged above, however, I think that the *inhumati* have the stronger case in this matter, not least because they were the ones to whom the bequest was first made. The Roman law says that a perfect donation can neither be revoked after the fact nor have conditions applied to it after receipt, as is clear from a reading of the Codex, so the donor in this case could not subsequently give the aforesaid land to the Friars Minor, since the *inhumati* already possessed it and you cannot give what you do not have. For supporting texts, see the Digest (D.41.1.20.)

Nevertheless, it is obvious that I shall need to refute all the charges against the *inhumati* that I adduced previously in order to safeguard their rights in this matter, hence:

In the first place, the *inhumati* themselves say that they do not have distinctive habits, that is, of a particular color and form; they say they are free to dress in different ways and that they might put on one kind of clothing one day and another kind the next and that there is nothing stated in their constitution which compels them to do otherwise. Thus we are not able to say that these men have a particular or distinctive kind of habit.

The *inhumati* also contend that they are unconditionally laity *(dicunt se esse puros laicos),* that they have no religious superior, and that they merely come together for the sake of devotion as did the apostles and

---

15. This allegation as well as two more that follow all involve problems related to property law and especially to the idea that illegal possession could not be the source of legitimate title. For an interesting survey of this idea as it emerges in the law of prescription see Helmholz, *The Spirit,* chapter 7.

other holy Christians in the primitive church who were of one heart and one spirit and held everything in common, as the psalmist says: "Behold how good and how pleasing it is for the brothers to live as one" (Psalm 133).

And they deny that their houses are religious, saying rather that they are profane, as I think they are, since they are dedicated without episcopal authority and they do not contain churches but only oratories of the sort that one might find in a private home for devotional purposes.[16] And on this issue note the words of Pope Innocent III (X 3.24.8) and what Bartolus says in his gloss of the Digest (47.22.1–4), namely that benevolent colleges characterized by ascetic discipline are approved by law.

Indeed, when we look at what Antonio de Butrio says, we see that he actually approves of the *inhumati* by name.[17] In his commentary on the decretal "Nullus" (X .2.2.2), Antonio states that while not required to make profession, the *inhumati* live regularly and are ecclesiastical persons who enjoy ecclesiastical privilege. And Antonio supports this statement by citing the decrees *Indemnitatibus* and *Dilecto* [sic].

He also says that those under penitential discipline who go around discalced are always under ecclesiastical jurisdiction and belong to a status approved by the church; nor are these penitents required to adopt an approved rule, since, although they are not called regulars (having taken no perpetual vow), their way of life is approved by the church. In support of this argument, see the decree of John XXII which begins *"Ratio recta"* [*Extravagantes commu.* 3.9.1] and states that those women known as beguines who live honestly and who do not get involved in preaching are to be tolerated.

All these authorities then ought to suffice to respond to the previous allegations against the *inhumati*. As for what has been contended about begging, it can be said that some of the *inhumati* work, while others beg, and that mendicancy is not condemned *de iure*, as we see in

16. This legal distinction hinges on episcopal authorization. Mario Sensi, "Anchoresses and Penitents," pp. 56–83, notes that the construction of an oratory or chapel, with the authorization of the bishop, conferred *titlus,* which was the juridical basis for a foundation.

17. This important gloss, to which we shall refer again later, appears in Antonius de Butrio, *Super prima primi . . . Decretalium commentarii* (Venetiis: Apud Iuntas, 1578), fol. 30vb–ra. It will be cited subsequently by its more common title, *Super Decretales.*

the *Decretum* (D. 92.c.1). But I do not intend to pursue the legal sub-
tleties that remain, since I am mindful of the fact that Pope Martin V
himself has issued an indulgence to the *inhumati* and we can assume
by this action that he intended to tolerate them, since an indulgence is
not extended to those in a state of sin but only conceded to the truly
penitent and shriven, as can be inferred from arguments found in the
Digest.[18]

To conclude, although the status of the *inhumati* is undoubtedly a
dubious one *(Non enim negari potest quin istorum inhumatorum status sit
dubius)*, the granting of a papal indulgence appears to be a declaration
that their status is not illegal. Thus we may defend the right of the
aforesaid *inhumati* to come together in three ways: on the basis of law
alone *(mero iure)*, as a consequence of the tacit declaration of their legitimacy by Pope Martin V, or on the basis of his dispensation/indul-
gence awarded to them. And so the many allegations made against
their society are refuted.

After a brief rebuttal to the objections made by the Friars Minor
with reference to the possessory rights of the *inhumati*—a refutation
crafted almost exclusively from the civil law related to mandates
and procuration—Panormitanus brings *Consilium LV* to an end: "I
conclude that those brothers or poor men who are called *inhumati*
have the better title to those lands which are at present contested.
And let this suffice."

We do not know if this legal opinion did suffice to settle the
property dispute, but it more than suffices as an example of the
working jurist's goals and methods, as well as of the gulf that could
exist between academic commentary and *consilia*. That gulf is not
immediately apparent, however, if we confine ourselves strictly to
questions of method.

Like the law professor, the *iurisperitus*, or legal expert, sought to
clarify difficult points of law and used conventional scholastic forms
to do so. Panormitanus made his case for the *inhumati* by stitching
together arguments *contra et pro* with authoritative citations from

18. See *The Digest*, 1.4 , in which the inviolate character of praetorian
decree is under discussion. The parallel between papal indulgence and
such a decree appears to be obvious.

canon and Roman law. And the frequency with which he cited the latter—passages from the Codex and Digest of Justinian and the comments of renowned civilians like Bartolus de Saxaferrato—is not in itself a distinguishing characteristic of *consilia* either.

Given the fact that *consilia* were often written at the behest of secular magistrates and that they involved disputes which crossed the permeable boundary between secular and ecclesiastical jurisdiction, we might expect them to be richer in references to Roman law than academic commentary. But commentary too might be larded with such citations, depending upon the subject being glossed: for instance, a canonical decree which posed questions about representation or consent within corporate bodies.[19]

The consultor, like the commentator, made regular use of the Roman law, since Roman statutes and rules of law supplied solutions to many practical problems. Civilian legal theory proved relevant too in canonical discussion of a variety of large issues, including the sources and limits of papal power itself. By the later Middle Ages, the interdependence of civil and canon law had become so pronounced that an aspiring canonist's university curriculum included formal training in the Roman law.[20]

Of course all canonists also agreed that the Roman law could never obviate the need for church law. Representing as it did a venerable and most sophisticated legal tradition, Roman law could be mined for useful arguments and principles, but ecclesiastical inde-

19. A classic study of this and related issues is Gaines Post, *Studies in medieval legal thought: public law and the state, 1100–1322* (Princeton, NJ: Princeton University Press, 1964).

20. Brundage, *Medieval Canon Law*, pp. 110–12. The intellectual interaction between practitioners of the two laws, the regular borrowing, when needed, to settle a dispute in the absence of apposite custom or statute, led in fact to the acceptance of Romano-canonical law as a *lex omnium generalis*, or *ius commune* in courts throughout Christendom. See Manlio Bellomo, *The Common Legal Past of Europe 1000–1800*, trans. Lydia G. Cochrane, Studies in Medieval and Early Modern Canon Law, vol. 4 (Washington, DC: The Catholic University of America Press, 1995) for a detailed account of the relationship between local, customary, and regionally distinctive law and the *ius commune* in medieval and early modern Europe.

pendence demanded that the canonists never be in thrall to that or any other secular law.

Panormitanus acknowledged this need for jurisdictional independence and for preserving a sphere of action for the church that was entirely separate from that of the temporal courts when he adduced an argument in favor of the *inhumati's* right to *privilegium fori*. Not incidentally, it is at this juncture that Panormitanus' *consilium* takes a shape that fully distinguishes it from academic commentary—his own as well as that of others.

As evidence of the *inhumati's* fully orthodox, and indeed privileged, status, Panormitanus paraphrased Antonio de Butrio's gloss on the decretal *Nullus* [X 2.2.2]. The gloss itself reads as follows:

> In general, all who live regularly are ecclesiastical persons and even if they do not make religious profession, as is the case with the *Iesuati*, they enjoy privilege of clergy, as noted in the gloss to and text of *Indemnitatibus* and *Dilecta*. This is true of the *Iesuati*, both men and women *(pro istis Iesuatis et maribus et mulieribus)*, since they are subject to the bishop to whom they promise voluntary obedience, chastity, and poverty for as long as they remain with the group *(quamdiu ibi sunt)*, and although they do not bind themselves by perpetual vows, they forbid anyone to stay among them who subsequently wishes to possess private property or who does not wish to remain chaste any longer.[21]

Panormitanus used this gloss as a supporting text because in it Antonio de Butrio specifically awarded the *inhumati/Jesuati* the status of ecclesiastical persons. Panormitanus presented Antonio's positive assessment *as if it were representative*. There is no hint that other canonists, many other canonists, held contrary opinions. Yet we know that Panormitanus was not only well aware of the arguments offered in opposition to the extension of clerical privilege to quasi-religious persons, but that, not long after he finished *Consilium LV*, he himself wrote such an opposing argument when glossing the decretal *Nullus:*

21. Antonio de Butrio, *Super Decretales*, fol. 30v. The decretal *Nullus* had become the *locus classicus* for canonists discussing the extension of clerical privilege to those not in orders.

I say that those called *Iesuati*, who go around discalced and in white hoods and who all wear the same kind of clothes are not entitled to privilege of the forum, and are not clerics since they are not in orders, and are not true religious since they lack the substance of religious life. . . . Antonio holds the opposite, that such as they are penitents and so are under ecclesiastical jurisdiction, . . . but I respond to him: first, that penitents do not enjoy privilege of the forum, and furthermore that these [the *Iesuati*] are not simply penitents, but that they rather live as if religious and so are called brothers and have dormitories and refectories and in other things comport themselves as if religious. And this order, since it is not approved by the holy see, is prohibited by it [citing the Lateran decree and *Sancta Romana*] . . . and see what I have to say at length about this group in my *Consilium LVI* [*sic*]. It is only because of a concession granted them quite recently by Pope Martin V that these *Iesuati* are permitted to exist.[22]

Panormitanus, then, clearly disagreed with Antonio de Butrio's assertion that the *inhumati* were ecclesiastical persons, but in *Consilium LV* he refrained from mentioning his reservations, or those of a considerable number of his fellow commentators, although he was just as clearly aware of the lack of consensus on the issue. In an academic gloss, the goal of which was to resolve any "apparent" contradictions posed by the issue at hand, such an omission of opposing opinion might signal a lack of training or expertise on the part of the commentator—either he was not fully conversant with the opposition, or insufficiently confident of his ability to reconcile conflicting authorities. In a *consilium*, however, the ability to judiciously select from a number of differing authorities those that most cogently supported the case at hand was the earmark of the successful and sought-after consultant.

When we turn to Panormitanus' exposition of the canon law related specifically to quasi-religious women, we find the practicing jurist willing not only to select from, but to bypass entirely, academic commentary, thus freeing himself to persuasively interpret the law in ways that might be at odds with received opinion.

22. Panormitanus, *Lectura super primo-quarto . . . Decretalium* (Lyon: 1521–22), *ad verbum Nullus*, p. 49. See also Miramon, *Les <<donnés>>*, pp. 223–26 for a treatment of Panormitanus' rebuttal.

From the very outset of *Consilium LV*, Panormitanus adduced legislation such as *Cum de quibusdam, Dilecta,* and *Indemnitatibus*—decrees that had entered the *Corpus iuris canonici* and that had consequently become *loci* for academic discussions about the legal status of quasi-religious women. As we have seen, those discussions were overwhelmingly negative in character, since most glossators echoed the sentiments expressed by Johannes Andreae in the *glossa ordinaria*. In fact, Panormitanus' own contribution to the academic commentary on *Cum de quibusdam* aptly illustrates the conservatism that was the norm. His brief, entirely derivative gloss on the decree, paraphrases portions of the ordinary gloss.[23] It contains no suggestion that Clement V's decree should be read as anything other than a blanket condemnation of all women called beguines. *Ratio recta* is not cited, nor is there any attempt to distinguish between "good" and "bad" beguines. There is no hint that "those faithful women" untainted by heresy might validly live in community. In *Consilium LV*, however, Panormitanus approached *Cum de quibusdam* in a very different manner. Warning that Clement V's decree, specifically directed against beguines, should not be read as a blanket condemnation of all women without vows, Panormitanus quoted the saving clause that exempted "faithful women living a penitential life in their own dwellings" from condemnation. He then wondered about the wording of that saving clause too. Might not use of the word *hospitium*, with its classical denotation as a hostel or inn, suggest that the pope continues to permit "faithful" quasi-religious women to live in community and not just as penitents isolated in their private homes?

Next, he used the example of the venerable institution of secular canonesses to illustrate the fact that such communities had been traditionally tolerated, if not officially approved, by the papacy. Adducing the decrees *Indemnitatibus* and *Dilecta* for support, he demonstrated that the status of secular canonesses paralleled that of other orthodox quasi-religious women whose *modus vivendi* fell short of being awarded formal approval.

23. Panormitanus, *Lectura in Clementinas* (Venice, 1490), contains this derivative gloss, as noted in chapter two.

As a final defense of the right of such women to live "as if religious," Panormitanus cited the decree of John XXII, *Ratio recta*. Promulgated in an attempt to clarify *Cum de quibusdam,* and to eliminate the indiscriminate persecution of tertiaries and other "faithful women" to which that decree had given rise, *Ratio recta* distinguished between orthodox and heretical beguines—it was, as Panormitanus pointed out, fully exculpatory of the former.

In *Consilium LV* then, Panormitanus proved that he was completely conversant with the canon law regarding quasi-religious women. Defense of the *inhumati/Jesuati,* a quasi-religious group with a substantial female component, required that he scrupulously deploy that legislation and that he tease out the ambiguities inherent in it. But that defense required that he just as scrupulously avoid citing any of the standard, consistently negative, academic commentary to which this legislation had given rise—even if that commentary was his own.

As is so often the case, we do not know the exact circumstances which occasioned *Consilium LV.*[24] To judge from the conclusion of this opinion, however, it is certainly possible that the *inhumati/Jesuati,* and not the court, had solicited it—an arrangement parallel to that arrived at with the Bridgettines. Under these circumstances, Panormitanus would have had special incentive to exploit the ambiguities inherent in the law concerning quasi-religious since the vigorous defense of one's client was prescribed by late-medieval ethical codes. From the early thirteenth century on, the canons of church councils, legatine decrees, and municipal statutes set standards of behavior for canon lawyers that emphasized the faithful and skillful representation of clients.[25] And repetitive legislation condemning the suborning of perjury, coaching of witnesses, and introduction of spurious evidence suggests that unbridled zeal on behalf of a client was also not unheard of.[26]

---

24. Norman Zacour, *Oldraldus,* p. 12, comments similarly about many of Oldradus de Ponte's legal opinions.

25. James Brundage, "The Medieval Advocate's Profession," *Law and History Review* 6 (1988): 439–64, notes this steady trend.

26. James Brundage, "The Calumny Oath and Ethical Ideals of Canon-

But, even if *Consilium LV* had been requested by the court rather than by one of the litigants (making it a *consilium iudiciale* technically speaking), Panormitanus would have been more concerned about the legality and crisp persuasiveness of his arguments than about whether those arguments reflected his personal opinions or those of his academic colleagues. It was a preoccupation that had not gone unnoticed by contemporaries. At the Council of Basel, for example, the cardinal of Arles is said to have been baffled by Panormitanus' keen defense of Pope Eugenius "since no one had on other occasions shown up papal errors more than Panormitanus, through whose activity and persuasion the warning decree had been passed against Eugenius, and his suspension had been carried. He [the bishop] was quite unaware of the reason for the change, seeing that Eugenius had not changed his life . . . [and] he asked Panormitanus to consider carefully whether he was speaking in accordance with his conscience."[27]

It was the law, after all, and not legal opinion, however hallowed, that was binding, and medieval jurists, like their modern counterparts, drew a clear distinction between the sort of legal advice that the *consilium* represented and justice *per se*. The consultant was under ethical obligation to provide an opinion regarding one or more disputed points in a case, and that opinion was in no way to contravene the law; it was up to the judge to issue an official verdict. And while it is true that a judge was sometimes bound by a *consilium*, when he was ignorant of the law for instance, procedural law never obliged him to request such an opinion in the first place.[28]

---

ical Advocates," *Proceedings of the Ninth International Congress of Medieval Canon Law*, Munich, 13–18 July, 1992, *Monumenta Iuris Canonici*, Series C: *Subsidia*, Vol. 10.

27. Aeneas Sylvius Piccolomini's report on the actions of Panormitanus at the Council of Basel in *De gestis concilii basilensis*, trans. Denys Hay and W. K. Smith (Oxford: Clarendon Press, 1967), p. 177. An additional note on Panormitanus' ability to argue contrary to his personal beliefs is found in his alleged lament that he failed to make his case at Basel because his instructions from the King of Naples did not allow him to follow his personal opinion, p. 173.

28. Pazzaglini, *Consilia*, pp. xvi–xvii; Helmholz, *The Spirit*, p. 30.

In sum, the *iurisperitus* had to resolve an issue and not merely explore it. He argued his way to a conclusion exclusive of all others or suffered the consequences of breach of promise. And although, in the long run, it was not Panormitanus' arguments in favor of the legitimacy of quasi-religious communities which established the claims of the *inhumati* (evidence of papal approbation as expressed in Martin V's indulgence did that), these arguments nevertheless represent a milestone in the history of the relationship between canon lawyers and quasi-religious women.

The inherent ambiguities in so much of the law relating to quasi-religious women, coupled with the failure of academic commentators to arrive at a consensus about the ecclesiastical status of tertiaries and others, had given Panormitanus a great deal of flexibility when mounting a defense of the quasi-religious *inhumati*. He had been able to point out (in good conscience and quite legally) that even decrees like *Cum de quibusdam* and *Indemnitatibus* could be used to exculpate some varieties of female quasi-religious activity, that canonical regulation of quasi-religious organizations in the interests of minimizing scandal did not necessarily imply the prohibition of such organizations, and that a valid analogy could be drawn between contemporary quasi-religious associations and those common among primitive Christians.

Consilium LV demonstrates the practical use to which canon law and commentary could be put, and although it is the work of a master of the genre, it is not unique. Other fourteenth- and fifteenth-century canonists would use the same methods, if not always as adeptly, in defense of their own quasi-religious clients.

FIVE

Tertiaries, Canonesses, Beguines, and Case Law

Academic commentators on the canon law related to quasi-religious women insisted on a distinction between quasi- and "true" religious based on the *substantialia* of monastic life. No matter how closely quasi-religious women resembled regulars they were not, strictly speaking, religious because they lacked the essentials, the *substantialia*, of monastic life: three vows of poverty, chastity, and obedience as pronounced upon formal profession into an approved religious order.

Since the canonists often reiterated these distinctions between formal and informal pious practice, adding comments about deceitful beguines or unedifying canonesses, it is easy to regard their comments as just another assertion of the inferiority of lay religiosity. In and of itself, however, the distinction between "true" and quasi-religious as established by the possession of the *substantialia* was a morally neutral one.

In practice, this dichotomy, based on juridical technicalities, allowed lawyers to distinguish between the two groups, not in order to determine their relative merits, but rather to decide their specific legal rights. And although meeting the qualifications for true religious status might enhance a pious woman's position in the next world, it did not always increase her legal rights in this one.

The regular, or true religious, was *ipso iure* an ecclesiastical person and, as we have seen in Chapter 3, this meant that she enjoyed by extension certain legal privileges traditionally reserved for the clergy. These privileges usually included *privilegium fori* (forbidding the trial of a cleric in secular courts) and some form of the *privilegium canonis* (protection of the person of the ecclesiastic, via threat of excommunication, from violence at the hands of a layman). But by the same token, a woman whose status as ecclesiastical person rested on religious profession faced clear restrictions on her actions in the secular sphere.

As a consequence of her solemn vows, the professed religious could never put aside her monastic habit. As an apostate religious, she would incur *ipso facto* excommunication and could be forcibly returned to her monastery where, should she remain unrepentant, penalties such as imprisonment might be imposed.[1] Individually, the professed woman's vows carried specific obligations.

The vow of chastity created what the canonists called a diriment impediment to marriage. This meant that a marriage entered into subsequent to religious profession was not only unlawful but also invalid.[2] A woman who had taken solemn vows of poverty and obedience could not claim an inheritance nor assume a worldly office or title which would have required her to wield power outside of the cloister—we even find canons denying nuns the right to fill the

1. Helmholz, *The Spirit*, pp. 233–37 encapsulates the issue of irrevocable monastic vows. He notes that even though papal power to dispense from solemn vows of religion was being rather widely discussed by the thirteenth century, the indult of exclaustration was uncommon before the Early Modern periods. See also James A. Brundage, *Medieval Canon Law and the Crusader* (Madison: University of Wisconsin Press, 1969), pp. 39–65, for the evolution of canonical thought on vows of chastity to the thirteenth century; *NCE*, 14:756–56 for an introduction to the origins and consequences of simple and solemn vows; F. Donald Logan, *Runaway Religious* (Cambridge: Cambridge University Press, 1996), for a full discussion of apostate religious in England.

2. Helmholz, *The Spirit*, pp. 243–47, on monastic vows and subsequent marriage. See McDonnell, *Beguines and Beghards*, pp. 129–31, discussing the distinctive consequences of simple and solemn vows with reference to beguines.

role of godmother, which entailed both social and legal obligations of some consequence.[3]

Given the serious implications of profession, we would expect there to be instances when a religious woman litigant would find it an asset rather than a liability to be classed as quasi- as opposed to fully-religious. The collected *consilia* of prominent fourteenth and fifteenth-century jurists yield some examples of just such cases.

Ludovicus Pontanus (1409–39), also called Ludovicus de Roma, studied in Perugia and later became the student of Johannes de Imola at Bologna.[4] He took his doctorate at Bologna in 1429 and taught for a time in Siena, but then became a practicing lawyer, first in Florence and then in Rome. Although he left behind a treatise on relics and a guide to some points of law, it was the practice of the law that most intrigued him. He wrote more than five hundred legal opinions during his short life and one of these, which concerns the contested right of a female tertiary to succeed to a fief, is of particular interest.[5]

Consilium CCCLXVII is a foray into the complexities of feudal law touching on questions of inheritance, gender, and marital as well as religious status, and Ludovicus does not begin to discuss the last issue until he has established that the woman in question cannot be deprived of her rights solely on the grounds of her sex.[6] To those who would oppose her enfeoffment because she is a tertiary, he offers the following challenge:

---

3. See, for instance, the examples given in Eileen Power's classic study *Medieval English Nunneries* (Cambridge: Cambridge University Press, 1922), pp. 34–37, regarding inheritance. Refer also to Joseph Lynch, *Godparents and Kinship in Early Medieval Europe* (New Jersey: Princeton University Press, 1986) and Bernhard Jussen, *Spiritual Kinship as Social Practice* (Newark, DE: University of Delaware Press, 2000) for information on the legal ramifications of becoming a godparent.

4. See Schulte *QL*, 2:395; *DDC* 6:684.

5. Ludovicus Pontanus, *Consilia et allegationes* (Venice: Bonetus Locatellus, 1500). *Consilium CCCLXVII fol.* 121v–122v.

6. *Consilium CCCLXVII fol.* 122r. Mention of the status is made a page earlier but it is only at this juncture that Ludovicus squarely faces the issue: *"Nec validitati dicte donationis refragabitur quam dicta mulier sit de sororibus tertii ordinis et consequeriter tamquam religiosa in feudo non succeceret."*

It has been contended that, since this woman is a sister in the third order, she cannot assume control of her feudal holdings, since religious are legally prohibited from succeeding to fiefs. But, although it is a papally approved way of life, the third order of the Blessed Francis is much more aptly called a *modus vivendi* than a religious state strictly speaking, as noted in the gloss to *Cum ex eo* and *Cum de quibusdam*.[7]

The life of the tertiary lacks the *substantialia* of religious life: vows of chastity, obedience, and poverty. For how can members of the third order preserve continence when they have spouses, or poverty when they have personal property? How can they render unquestioning obedience to a superior when they remain married folk who have no power over their own bodies having given that power over to their spouses?[8] And it is for this reason that Federicus de Sensis at the end of his *Consilium CXLV* [sic], rightly opines that tertiaries are not to be counted as religious persons.[9]

Like Guilelmus de Monte Laudano, who in his commentary on *Cum ex eo* quipped that tertiaries had about as much right to clerical privilege as newborn babes, Ludovicus de Pontanus rejects arguments in favor of classifying tertiaries as ecclesiastical persons. He elaborates on Johannes Andreae's gloss to *Cum ex eo*, both by stressing the fact that married folk who still possessed property could hardly be called true religious and by citing *Cum de quibusdam* to distinguish the papally approved tertiary from the "renegade" beguine.

7. Ibid. *"Quoniam respondeo quod ille tertius ordo beati Francisci potius inducit quemdam modum vivendi approbatum a Papa quam veram religionem."*

8. Ibid. *"Quia tria sunt substantialia cuiuslibet religionis, scilicet castitas, obedientia et paupertas. Ad isti tertio ordine nec continentiam servant cum habeant coniuges, nec paupertatem cum habeant proprium, nec omnino possunt servare obeientiam quia cum maneant in coniugio non habent omnino potestatem sui corporis."* Ludovicus is obviously quoting lines we have often seen in previous commentaries on the clerical status of tertiaries. On the right here referred to, see Elizabeth Makowski, "The Conjugal Debt and Medieval Canon Law," *Journal of Medieval History* 3 (1977): 99–114.

9. Fredericus de Sensis, cited by Panormitanus in his gloss of the decretal *Nullus*, was a noted canonist who numbered Baldus de Ubaldis among his students. See Schulte, *QL*, 2:237–38. The *consilium* mentioned here can be found in Federico Petrucci, *Consilia sive mavis Responsa . . .* , (*Venetiis: Apud Joannem Antonium Bertanum*, 1576), p. 74, in which it is numbered *CL*, not, as Ludovicus notes, *CXLV*.

He then uses an argument from another *consilium*, that of Sienese canonist Federicus Petrucius (de Sensis), to justify his own conclusion.[10]

Provided that the litigant is otherwise capable of succession, Ludovicus finds that her tertiary status could not impede her enfeoffment.[11] To be sure, municipal governments would be likely to benefit from such an opinion. If they were legally regarded as laymen and women, the ever-growing numbers of tertiaries in the cities could be subject to urban taxes and tolls and made to respond to secular rather than ecclesiastical judgments, if they failed to meet their obligations.[12] Yet, in the case at hand, Ludovicus' insistence on the quasi-religious status of a female tertiary had only positive, and we may assume profitable, results: it enabled her to benefit from an inheritance that her religious (strictly speaking) sister would have had to forego.

Ludovicus had declared that the enfeoffment of a female tertiary was valid because she was not, strictly speaking, a religious woman. She could therefore accept landed wealth from the hands of a secular power and/or fulfill feudal obligations—actions inimical to the

10. Federicus' *Consilium CL* concerns the right of a bishop to claim a portion of a testamentary bequest made to a group of tertiaries. Federicus argues against that claim by stating that tertiaries are subject to secular and not episcopal jurisdiction, and that they are religious persons only in the general sense that *"totus populus Christianus dicitur Christiana religio."*

11. The rubric found in a printed edition of Ludovicus' *consilia, Consilia vie responsa . . . , (Venetiis: Horatii Mandosii,* 1568), *Consilium XXXLXVII #14,* p. 260, puts it succinctly: *"Ordo tertius sancti Francisci est potius quidam modus vivendi quam religio, ideo foemina alias capax feudi per ordinem illius susceptum feudo non privatur."*

12. In practice, different cities seem to have applied different standards and municipal statutes evince both diversity of opinion and change over time. In 1320, for instance, the city fathers of Florence agreed to exempt tertiaries from all taxes, regarding them as religious persons (Moorman, *Franciscan Order,* p. 428), while canonists commenting on *Cum ex eo* remark how insistently the civil authorities in Perugia demand dues and taxes from members of the third order and compel them to appear before lay judges (see especially Johannes de Imola's gloss p. 181ra). In the city of Toulouse, on the other hand, tertiaries appear to have been considered ecclesiastical persons throughout the late Middle Ages and to have been judged only in the episcopal court (Génestal, p. 33).

goals of "true" religious life—actions which, if taken by one solemnly vowed to that life, would be *ipso iure* invalid. Following this reasoning, a marriage contracted subsequent to entry into a religious
community would be not only morally wrong, but also legally invalid. In an opinion significant for both male and female litigants,
Gaspar Calderinus (1345–99) deals with the validity of a marriage
contracted subsequent to entry into a quasi-religious community.[13]

Son of the more famous Johannes Calderinus (d. 1365), Gaspar
Calderinus studied in Bologna, taught there, and, just like his father
before him, took an active part in urban politics. Interests and ideas
of father and son must have often overlapped, since we find Gaspar's *consilia* collected along with those written by the elder Calderinus.[14] The latter, it might be recalled, had resisted the extension of
ecclesiastical status to those who lacked the *substantialia* of religion
and in the *consilium* that concerns us here, *Consilium VI*, Johannes'
influence is clear.[15]

Gaspar tells us that a certain layman became a *conversus* in a Minorite convent, promising true obedience to the Guardian of the
Friars Minor.[16] But after a while, he married and at the end of his
life he wrote a last will and testament: *"Lapsu temporis ipse contraxit*

13. Johannes Calderinus, like his teacher and stepfather the renowned
jurist Johannes Andreae, was one of very few married laymen to become
a canon lawyer. See: *NCE*, 7:996; and Schulte, *QL*, 2:247–52. For
Gaspar/Caspar, see Schulte, *QL*, 2:264–65.
14. Johannes Calderinus,*Consilia* (*Venezia: Bernardinus Benalius*, 1497).
Gaspar's contributions bear his name. Note that in other collections, both
father and son are named as authors: *Consilia Johannis Calderini et Gasparis
Calderini* (Rome: Adam Rot, 1472).
15. Johannes Calderinus, *Consilia* (*Venezia: Bernardinus Benalius*, 1497),
Consilium VI fol. LVII. We have encountered Johannes' views in Chapter 3
and they are conveniently recapitulated in this collection in *Consilium IIII
fol. LVI*, where Johannes denies Franciscan tertiaries any ecclesiastical
privileges, saying that they are simply not religious persons: *"Sed contrarius
puto quod nullo privilegio ecclesiastico gaudeant quia stricte et proprie loquendo
non sunt persone ecclesiastice nam non sunt clerici et hoc planum nec religiosi idest
religiosi per sedem apostolicam approbate religati scilicet professi . . ."*
16. *Consilium VI, fol. LVII,* *"Laicus promisit Guardiano fratrum minorum re-
cipienti nomine conventus veram obedientiam et ominia facere, quae erunt ei im-
posita dicto nomine et de iure debita: qui Guardianus recepit ipsum in conversum
et familiarem dicti conversus."* As noted in the Introduction, *conversus* is one

matrimonium et in fine vitae condiddit testamentum." In order to determine whether the man's marriage and his testamentary provisions should be regarded as legitimate (with obvious consequences for his putative spouse and heirs), Gaspar is required to resolve several legal points.

First, he attempts to define terms. There are many kinds of conversion, says Gaspar: the conversion of the sinner to godliness; conversion from lay to ecclesiastical status; and, within that broad category, conversion to the secular or regular state *("ad ecclesiam secularem/ad religionem")*. The case at hand concerns conversion to religion, but Gaspar uses the term religion in its broadest sense, noting that if one entered an unapproved order, for instance, subsequent marriage and the right to draw up a will would certainly not be illicit *("Et si regula non est approbata plane quod potest contrahere matrimonium et facere testiamentum").*[17]

The same could be said regarding someone who entered a community which *was* papally approved but which had a rule of life that did not forbid marriage or the making of a will. The rules of the Third Order of St. Francis, the Humiliati, and similar groups *(et similium)* allow these things, and this enables an entrant into any one of them to possess both a spouse and personal property. In support of this statement, Gaspar cites *Cum ex eo* as well as a canon from the *Extravagantes Joannis* (6.1) which privileges marriage vows over vows of religion taken subsequent to marriage.

Gaspar next distinguishes between professed religious who take three vows and so can be regarded as possessing the *substantialia* of the regular, and *conversi* who, like the man in question, make only a

---

of those "complicated and illusive" terms connected with medieval religious practice, and its use tends to vary with changing times and altered contexts. Called *famuli, conversi,* or *conversi barbati* (to distinguish them from the clean-shaven monks) they were either lay brothers or "various types of lay people who associated themselves in one way or another with a religious house" (Constable, *Reformation,* p. 10). The single most important characteristic for Gaspar, however, is the fact that the *conversus* did not take vows. See also Miramon, *Les <<donnés>>,* pp. 74–75.

17. The supporting text is the decree from the *Liber Sextus* in which Boniface VIII sets down the guidelines for full religious profession with solemn vows: VI 3.15.1.

promise of obedience. This single promise by no means creates the presumption of a three-fold obligation, as some would "absurdly" contend *("Esset enim absurdum quod quis intelligeretur obligatus ad id quod non promisit. . . . Item quod promissio obedientie non inferat professionem")*. The perpetual obligation to observe the solemn vows that bind the regular—the obligation that is created by formal profession into an approved religious order—is simply not created by anything short of it. Therefore, Gaspar concludes that both the man's marriage and his last will and testament are valid.

Although the litigant in this case was male, Gaspar Calderinus' arguments supporting his right to marry and to dispose of private property would apply to his female counterparts as well. A woman might attach herself to a monastery by a promise of obedience. As the female equivalent of *conversi, conversae* or *familiares* performed any number of mundane tasks for the religious to whom they were bound, although they generally lived apart from the professed nuns.[18] So too, the Humiliati, tertiaries, "and similar groups" which Gaspar lists as relevant illustrations of the limits of quasi-religious obligation had a large, sometimes disproportionately large, female membership.

It is also instructive that Gaspar makes only legal, not moral distinctions in his *consilium*. Entrance into a sect or community which has not received papal approval is for him merely another way by which one acquires quasi-religious status. There is no censorious reference to the morality of such a choice, as might be found in the work of the commentators, since for Gaspar, becoming a member of an unapproved religious group has exactly the same legal ramifications as the decision to become a tertiary—neither decision binds the entrant to life-long observance of vows, since neither one requires formal profession of those vows.

18. The term *conversae* is also imprecise, and it was used to refer to women with a variety of relationships to monastic communities; see McNamara, *Sisters*, pp. 242–43, 262–63; Lehmijoki-Gardner, *Worldly Saints*, p. 29; and Berman, *The Cistercian Evolution* (Philadelphia, PA: University of Pennsylvania Press, 2000), pp. 131–32, 213–14. Again, absence of solemn vows is the only crucial element of that relationship for Gaspar.

As *iurisperitus*, Gaspar Calderinus noted common practice, irrespective of its moral valence, since he was interested only in the legal ramifications of such practice. In so doing, he illustrates the way in which the *consilium* linked legal theory and practice. He also demonstrates how it was possible for other jurists to find that even "suspect women" like beguines and secular canonesses could make creditable legal claims.

Both Ludovicus de Pontanus and Gaspar Calderinus rendered legal opinions that favored quasi-religious claimants by arguing that these people were not ecclesiastical persons, since they were not regulars. In both cases the litigants gained rights in the secular sphere, but they did so only by being divested of all special privileges that the church accorded the "true" religious. A *consilium* written by the illustrious doctor of both laws Baldus de Ubaldis (1327–1400) proves that this trade-off was not always necessary.[19]

Regarded by historians as one of the most exceptional jurists of the late Middle Ages, Baldus de Ubaldis, or "de Perusio" as his contemporaries called him, studied both canon and civil law in Perugia, where he received his doctorate around 1347. While he held many public offices in his native city, Baldus remained a teacher all his life, numbering men like Petrus Ancharanus, Franciscus Zabarella, and Johannes de Imola among his students.

During his long career as teacher, consultant, and public official, Baldus de Ubaldis was particularly drawn to the resolution of practical problems, a tendency that is graphically illustrated by his commentary on feudal law and by the vast number of *consilia* that he wrote—approximately 2500 in the printed editions of his work.[20] In

---

19. Baldus de Ubaldis of Perugia had famous teachers in both Roman and canon law: Bartolus de Saxoferrato and Fredericus de Sensis, respectively. For biographical background on Baldus, see Kenneth Pennington, "Baldus de Ubaldis," *Rivista internazionale di diritto commune* 8 (1997): 35–61, which contains much new information on the man and his works; Brundage, *Medieval Canon Law*, p. 207; Schulte, *QL*, 2:275–77; *DDC* 2:9–52. The *consilium* under discussion can be found in Baldi Ubaldi Perusini, *Consiliorum,sive responsorum* (*Venetiis*, 1575; rpt. Torino, 1970),*Consilium LX*, pp. 36–37.

20. Pennington, "Baldus," p. 35.

Consilium LX, Baldus treats one such ordinary problem as it relates to the classification of a quasi-religious woman.

The facts of the case were these: a certain female tertiary made a donation of some possessions to a Minorite community in the town of Assisi. This donation was made formally *in comitatu Fulginei* and in the presence of the *custos* of the order, another female tertiary. But the donation was being contested on the grounds that in Assisi a woman who wished to draw up a contract of any sort was required by municipal statute to get the consent of a certain kindred *(consanguineorum)*—a regulation with which the non-resident tertiary had obviously not complied.[21]

As usual, there were several legal questions that required answers before the case could be resolved. Baldus asks whether the contract, which is not recognized in Assisi because of the aforesaid ordinance, might be valid elsewhere, and whether the ordinance in question is person- or place-specific. In determining the answers to both of these questions he draws heavily on the Roman law, especially that which concerned actions begun in one venue and concluded in another.[22] Finally, and most important for our purposes, Baldus raises the issue of whether the city statute binds sisters of the Third Order or if, as ecclesiastical persons, they are exempt from such secular regulation *(an istud statum liget istas sorores tertii ordinis, sive personae ecclesiasticae, vel exceptae seculari iurisdictione sint)*.[23]

Baldus admits that on the question of tertiary status the jury is, so to speak, still out. He cites Johannes de Lignano, as saying that tertiaries, like members of the military orders, are ecclesiastical per-

---

21. *Consilium LX*, p. 36: *"verum in civitate Assisii est quoddam ordinamen quod contractus mulierem non valeat ipso iure, nisi interveniente praesentia et consensu certorum consanguineorum quorum consensus et praesentia hic non intervenit."*

22. For example, Baldus twice cites D 13.4.1 *"De eo quod certo loco dari oportet,"* which abrogated older legislation, decreeing that one could sue a delinquent party *only* in the place where under the terms of the stipulation the payment was to be made. A remedy was clearly needed in this case, since a debtor might simply avoid returning to the place where the obligation had been incurred.

23. Ibid.

sons and therefore immune from secular jurisdiction, while at the same time he observes that the ordinary gloss, which refers to tertiaries by their common name of *continentes*, states that theirs is only a way of life and not an order properly speaking.[24]

Unwilling to simplify the situation but determined to resolve it, Baldus falls back on a categorization popular with the commentators—tertiaries are not completely ecclesiastical persons, but neither are they completely lay people *(Ego dico quod non sunt omnino personae ecclesiasticae, nec sunt omnino personae seculares)*. Accordingly, there will be certain instances in which they are regarded as ecclesiastical persons and certain instances in which they are not.

Tertiaries are free to distribute the alms they collect from their members, for example, and they are not compelled to swear oaths, save for that broad affirmation of good faith, the oath *de calumnia*.[25] Tertiaries are allowed to have religious superiors whose task it is to govern and to protect them, and they are permitted to make a last will and testament (this was to be done within three months of admission to the order according to their rule approved by Pope Nicholas IV). In these particulars, all of them stemming from papal privilege, tertiaries are treated as ecclesiastical persons, and Baldus acknowledges that he has observed this treatment in practice *(ut ego similiter vidi in publica forma)*.

On the other hand, there are certain instances in which tertiaries are not treated as ecclesiastical persons. Clerics, for instance, enjoy the *beneficium competentiae* (the courts never permitted a creditor to reduce to utter penury a cleric who had contracted too many debts), but tertiaries have to fully satisfy their creditors.[26] What then of the

24. Ibid: *Sed gl.vulgatis dicit quod ordo dictorum continentium Non est proprie ordo, sed quidam modus vivendi*. See chapter three for Johannes Andreae's full statement to this effect.

25. Reinmann, *The Third Order*, notes the difficulties that sometimes surrounded the administration of goods/alms collected from the members for distribution to the poor; see especially p. 38 and p. 61. Helmholz, *The Spirit*, pp. 153–54, discusses the oath *de calumnia*.

26. *Consilium LX*, p. 37: *"non tamen sunt personae ecclesiastice si delinquerent, nec contraherent, qui possint pro delictis et suis contractibus conveniri. . . ."* See Chapter Three for discussion of the different types of clerical privilege.

case at issue? Should this female tertiary be subject to a civil statute or should she be exempt from its restrictions on the basis of her "quasi-clerical" status?

Baldus opts to exempt the litigant from secular jurisdiction and concludes that her donation is legal and binding *(dictam donationem valuisse)*, and he does so for several reasons. First, the woman in question made her donation under the aegis of her religious superior, who acts for her with an authority backed by papal privilege.[27] Second, it has been established that that same papal privilege extends to female tertiaries the right to execute a last will and testament and, according to Roman law, anyone who is deemed legally competent to draw up a will is regarded as competent to draw up a contract.[28] Third and finally, a general statute like that existing in Assisi cannot apply to those possessing a specific, and superior, privilege *(Item quia generale statutum non intelligitur de personis nominatim a superiore privilegiatis)*.

Harkening back to academic commentary, and actually employing the arguments of Johannes Andreae, Bonifacius Ammannanti, and others, Baldus classed tertiaries not as laity but as religious *largo modo*. Unlike his more theoretically inclined colleagues, however, he did not stop at classification; he dealt with a possible consequence of such labeling, all the time aware that his opinion might be perceived as threatening to undermine civil jurisdiction.

Knowing that the exemption that he granted to a female tertiary would, if multiplied, heighten tensions between ecclesiastical and secular authorities, Baldus twice mentioned the fact that he had personally observed secular magistrates according tertiaries similar exemptions. By doing so, he implied that his conclusions in the case at issue flowed from, rather than challenged, common legal practice. He was also careful to limit the number of prerogatives that he

---

27. Ibid. *dico quod in contrahendo sufficit dictae donatrici authoritas sui superioris nam quantum ad ista statuta quae tangunt de directo personas istae sorores de poenitentia non includuntur in statuta; sufficiens esset eis proprii superioris permissio.*

28. Ibid. *Item cum dictae personae* [aforementioned tertiaries, *continentes* and widows] *sint habiles ad testandum ergo ad contrahendum : quia licitum est arguere de ultimis voluntatibus ad contractus.*

claimed for members of the Third Order and to anchor those rights firmly to the doctrine of papal privilege.

According to Baldus, the exempt status of the tertiary in *Consilium LX* resulted from a confluence of special rights, all of them imbedded in the rule of the Third Order of St. Francis promulgated by Nicholas IV. In instances where no such privileges could be invoked, the litigant would be as bound by secular law as any other laywoman. What is more, the language of a privilege needed to be strictly interpreted. In another, related *consilium* Baldus demonstrates just how strictly.[29]

In his rule for tertiaries, Pope Nicholas IV had stated that if tertiaries were ever harassed by local authorities or if they found their privileges infringed upon by local lords, they were to direct their case for redress to the bishop.[30] In *Consilium CCLXXII* Baldus analyzes this statement. Did it entitle members of the Third Order of St. Francis to bring their cases before the bishop, rather than a secular magistrate; that is, to claim *privilegium fori (Nunc videamus de foro, an huiusmodi persone sint de foro episcopi, ita quod sub iudice laico non astringantur)*?[31]

Baldus decides that it does, but only conditionally. He says that the court of the bishop should be merely a court of appeals, and that tertiaries should normally consider secular courts the courts of first instance. Tertiaries may have recourse to the ecclesiastical forum only if there is a defect of justice in the secular *(Non ergo videntur subesse foro episcopi, nisi propter defectum iustitiae iudicis saecularis: quia iurisdictio conditionaliter non principaliter ad tributa episcopo)*.[32]

Now, since according to canon law *all* Christians were entitled to

29. Baldus, *Consiliorum sive . . . ,Consilium CCLXXII*, pp. 163–64. *Consilium CCLXXII* deals with the general categorization of members of the Third Order of St. Francis, and it is worth noting that in it Baldus arrives at roughly the same definition of the tertiary as in *Consilium LX*, although he expresses it in more memorable terms. Tertiaries, he says, *"ergo mere non sunt personae seculares, sed aut ecclesiasticae aut est genus per se. . . . sed quid ergo denominari potest alter utro modo, sed non simpliciter."*

30. Ibid. p. 164; See *Bullarium Romanum*, 4:93 for the *regula*.

31. *Consilium CCLXXII* p. 164.

32. See Helmholz, *The Spirit*, pp. 132–34 on ecclesiastical jurisdiction *ex defectu justiciae.*

invoke ecclesiastical jurisdiction *ex defectu iustitiae*—that is, in cases when secular justice had been grossly inadequate—we may wonder whether in this instance Baldus accorded tertiaries any special privilege at all. It appears that he did, but that the privilege was a subtle one.

At one end of the legal spectrum there were those such as ordained clerics, whose status as ecclesiastical persons was undoubted. They had the privilege of being cited exclusively in an ecclesiastical court. Laymen and women were at the other end, recognizing the ordinary jurisdiction of secular courts, with two exceptions: matters reserved by canon law (and custom of region) to the church courts, and matters in which defective justice had been meted out by the secular courts. In order to take advantage of the latter exception, however, the average layperson would first have had to exhaust all the remedies provided him by the secular law.[33]

Baldus does, therefore, give tertiaries some advantage over their lay (or shall we say "fully lay") counterparts, since by referring to the bishop's court as their appellate court, he allows tertiaries to short-circuit the ordinary judicial process—a not inconsiderable benefit, considering the costly and time-consuming character of late-medieval litigation. Tertiaries would be able to proceed to the court of the bishop immediately, whereas the layperson "strictly speaking" would first have had to exhaust all the remedies afforded him by the secular courts.

Despite his cautious approach when dealing with the practical consequences of papal privilege, the conclusions arrived at by Baldus de Ubaldis were in line with those articulated by the academic commentators that we encountered in Chapter 3. Baldus stated that tertiaries were in some sense, at least, ecclesiastical persons, and that as religious "broadly speaking" they were entitled to enjoy certain legal advantages over the ordinary layman. All of the academic commentators had agreed with him. They upheld the right of the brothers and sisters to their quasi-religious *modus vivendi*, orthodox in content and approved by the pope, and about half of them had

33. *Consilium CCLXXII*, p. 164.

gone so far as to heap upon them far more clerical privileges than Baldus was willing to allow.

In conclusion, Baldus, like other practicing jurists, found plenty of support for his arguments in academic commentary. But what if his cases had involved canonesses or beguines? As we have observed, academic commentators grudgingly tolerated secular canonesses whose way of life, however hallowed, disrupted the "right order" of institutional religious life for women. They argued that the religious status of canoness was not a good or virtuous one, but merely a lesser evil; a dangerous option which some women continued to exercise, but without papal approbation.

Beguines fared even worse. With the exception of Albericus de Metensis, academic commentators interpreted Clement V's decree *Cum de quibusdam* as a condemnation of all beguines. They drew no distinctions between heretical women and those whose religious practice presented no threat to orthodoxy, preferring instead to construct collages of authoritative texts that established the duplicitous character of beguines as a group.

It is quite clear then that any practicing jurist who attempted to accord legitimacy (much less ecclesiastical status) to canonesses and beguines would, unlike Baldus, find little support for his argument among those charged with interpreting the law. Considering how slavishly most canon lawyers relied on such supporting authorities, this would seem to be a position into which few jurists would willingly put themselves. Yet it is precisely the one assumed by the distinguished judges of the Roman Rota when they questioned, or simply ignored, academic opinion regarding canonesses and beguines.[34]

As their formal title of "Papal Chaplains Auditors of the Sacred

34. G. Dolezalek, "Reports of the 'Rota' (14th–19th centuries)," in *Judicial Records, Law Reports, and the Growth of Case Law*, ed. John H. Baker (Berlin: Duncker & Humbolt, 1989), pp. 69–99, mentions the way in which the authority of the Rota judges enabled them to give an occasional "turn to the wheel" of justice, overriding precedent and lending credibility to the quip: *Rota quandoque rotat*, p. 81. This article also offers an excellent introduction to court proceedings as a whole.

Apostolic Palace" suggests, the first Rotal judges received their commissions in order to deal with the flood of litigation inundating the papal curia in the thirteenth century.[35] Every case that was appealed to the highest power in Christendom could no longer be heard personally by the pope and so began to be referred to chaplains in the papal household who were also called auditors.

Initially, the auditors made their legal opinions known to the pope, who acted as ultimate judge, but by the time of Pope Innocent III they were empowered, in some cases, to give judgments. When the curia moved to Avignon, the term "Rota" was in use to refer to the papal court staffed by the auditors (presumably because of the marble ornamentation in the shape of a wheel on the floor of the audience hall).

The *decisio* of a Rota auditor, much like a *consilium sapientis iudicale*, applied the law to a specific case, and both forms of legal opinion allow us to observe how the law was applied in actual fact. But unlike a *consilium*, a *decisio* was written by a jurist who had himself taken part in the litigation and was binding. This jurist, normally the auditor, gave a short account of the facts of the case, listed arguments and the legal questions involved, and finally stated the verdict reached by the court.[36]

Auditors consulted each other and took notes during deliberations, and each judge had from one to four notaries working for him who kept a chronological record of actions and a separate dossier for each case.[37] Reports of debates and opinions about legal issues (but usually not about a case as a whole) known as *decisiones Rotae* began

35. *DDC*, 7:744–70; *NCE*, 12:683–85 presents a summary history of the development of the court. See also E. Cerchiari, *Capellani Papae et apostolicae sedis auditores causarum sacri palatii apostolici*, vols. 1–4 (Rome, 1919–21) and Dolezalek, "Reports."

36. Helmholz, *The Spirit*, pp. 30–31, notes that despite the name, *decisiones* are not the actual court sentences, since the latter contained no authorities or reasons for the judge's verdict. This is because, as Dolezalek points out, it was considered unwise, since a judgement might be nullified solely on the basis of erroneous legal reasoning.

37. Dolezalek, "Reports," p. 74.

to be privately collected in the fourteenth century, and by the fifteenth some of the more popular collections made their way into print.[38] But because there was no systematic mechanism for their publication before the Rota's reorganization in 1870, many more *decisiones* remained, and still remain, in manuscript.

Two *decisiones Rotae* which found their way into fourteenth-century compilations exemplify the distinctive course taken by the auditors as they tried cases dealing with the rights and obligations of canonesses and beguines. They are recorded in a collection of Rota reports called the *Decisiones antiquae*—a congeries of earlier collections including the one made by Bernard du Bosquet, auditor between 1355 and 1365, and that of Guillaume Gautier, auditor who collected reports between 1372 and 1374 and whose work forms the first section of the *Decisiones antiquae*.[39]

Decisio CLXVII from this compilation involves secular canonesses.[40] The legal issue at stake is the right of secular canonesses to enjoy the clerical privilege known as the *privilegium canonis:* the privilege which prescribed automatic excommunication for anyone who dared to lay violent hands upon a cleric.[41]

38. On these early collections see Schute, *QL*, 2:69–70; G. Dolezalek and K. W. Nörr, "Die Rechtsprechungssammlungen der mittelalterlichen Rota," in *Handbuch,* 1:851–56.

39. Dolezalek, "Reports," pp. 78–79; Bernard Guillemain, "Les tribunaux de la cour pontificale d'Avignon," in *Cahiers de Fanjeaux, Collection d'Histoire religieuse du Languedoc aux XIIe et XIVe siècles* 29 (Editions Privat: Toulouse, 1994) p. 348. The *Decisiones antiquae* also includes decisions or excerpts of decisions collected between 1374–75 and 77–78 by the well-known auditor Gilles Bellemère (Aegidius Bellemera) and those of other Rota judges as well. Given the amount of material gathered together, it is difficult to date specific decisions even if the identity of the collecting auditor is given.

40. *Decisiones rote nove et antique cum additionibus casibus dubiis et regulis cancellarie apostolice, diligentissime emendate* (Lyon, 1507) *decisio II,* fol. CCXLIIII. Note that this case, in abbreviated form, is also found at fol. CXXIX as decision CLXVII. See also *Decisiones antiquae et novae rotae romanae, a variis auctoribus collectae et editae* (Rome, 1483) Hain #6049, *decisiones* II and CLXVII.

41. Helmholz, *The Spirit,* pp. 384–89, treats the development of canonical thought regarding the penalty attached to this privilege.

The auditors begin by reporting their debate. Some are of the opinion that as long as secular canonesses remain in their state of life, they remain ecclesiastical persons and that, although they are not regulars, they should still enjoy *privilegium canonis*.[42] Support for this position is culled from the *Decretum* and the *Liber Sextus*, with special mention of a decree of Celestine III (X 1.6 13). In that decree Celestine confirmed the election of a hermit as abbot of a monastery, thereby (in the words of the *decisio*), "according ecclesiastical status to hermits despite the fact that [like canonesses] they neither make formal profession nor renounce property."[43]

Contrary opinion, the auditors continue, follows Johannes Andreae in maintaining that the status of secular canonesses is condemned rather than approved *(immo reprobatus)* and that therefore these women do not merit the *privilegium canonis*. Support for this opinion comes in the form of the oft-cited decree *Indemnitatibus*, and from Johannes Andreae's gloss of *Dilecta*. And it is this contrary opinion that stands, the *decisio* adds, since "it is said that the chancery does not ordinarily issue letters [of excommunication] for that [which is done] contrary to this immunity."[44]

Decisio CLXVII does not, however, end with this judgment. It concludes instead with the admission that "others continue to draw distinctions, saying that as long as canonesses are wearing their habits and are in the service of God they should be considered ecclesiastical persons enjoying ecclesiastical privilege and that they lose this status only when they leave the service of God and live in their own

42. *Quidam dicuntur quod sic quamdiu remanent in tali statu etiam si non sint religose sunt tamen persone ecclesiastice vel deo devote igitur gaudeant*

43. *Decretum*, C 17 q 4 c. 22, a decree of Pope John VII which includes *"Deo devotis"* in the list of ecclesiastical persons, violence against whom is construed as sacrilege; and C 11 q 1 c. 7, St. Jerome's mention of *"clerici et Deo devoti"* as members of that segment of humanity specially dedicated to God (the other segment being the laity, whose rewards would be concomitantly smaller in the next world). *VI* 5.11.21, a decree promulgated by Pope Boniface VIII dealing with the excommunication of those who did violence to anyone tacitly or expressly professed.

44. *Et hanc opinionem conservat ut dicitur chancellaria que non daret eis litteras contra tales immunitates.*

homes."[45] Nor is this admission a mere aside, since it is followed by a full array of supporting authorities.

The dissenting opinion draws its support from a decree of Pope Boniface VIII (VI 5.11.11) in which wearing clerical garb is deemed to create a presumption of clerical status and to afford a malefactor privilege of the forum, at least until that presumption can be undermined. The Roman law dealing with the right of immunity (D 50.6) is also adduced, and, somewhat ironically, the final citation is to Johannes Andreae's gloss to X 3.3 *de clericis coniugatis*.[46]

Although ultimately reiterating negative academic opinion in the form of Johannes Andreae's gloss of *Dilecta*, the judgment recorded in *Decisio CLVII* was far from unanimous. *Obiter dicta*, complete with appendices of supporting texts, were recorded, and not only *before* the majority pronouncement (arguments *contra* were commonly presented at that juncture) but *subsequent* to it. Given the lack of unanimity among the auditors, which was highlighted by the very placement of dissenting opinion, it would be unwise to regard this decision as anything like a rejection of the broader right of secular canonesses to come under ecclesiastical rather than secular jurisdiction. Indeed, the very "distinctions" which some of the auditors drew at the end of the decision were commonly drawn in practice. As Génestal observed, privilege of the forum was often extended to canonesses in France well into the early modern era, as long as those *deo devote* remained unmarried.[47]

45. *Alii distinguunt dicentes quod tempore quo portant habitum canonicatus pura suppellicium et in divinis serviunt deo tunc reputentur persone ecclesiastice et gaudeant privilegio: sed quando exierunt et extra servicium dei sunt in domibus propriis, secus.*

46. These citations do not include an indication of the precise law or chapter that the jurists considered relevant. In the case of the Digest, D 50.6.2 would be germane, since it required keeping faith with those who bound themselves conditionally to assume an office or *munera*—conditions remaining as they were at the time at which those individuals agreed to their obligations. In the case of Johannes Andreae's gloss, there are several possibly relevant comments having to do with retaining a clerical benefice only as long as one retains one's chastity.

47. Génestal, *Le Privilegium*, pp. 31–32. With respect to French practice the version of this decision found as CLVII is instructive. The final passage

It is also significant that the pronouncement against extending the *privilegium canonis* to secular canonesses *("Et hanc opinionem conservat ut dicitur chancellaria que non daret eis litteras contra tales immunitates")* gives standard chancery policy decisive clout. Like Baldus de Ubaldis, the auditors factored common legal practice into their decision-making. It was a sober regard for practice more than reverence for academic interpretation that finally effected a ruling in this contested case.

A second Rota decision, found in the *Decisiones Rote nove antique*, involves beguines.[48] In this case *(Decisio CCCXXII)*, the issue is the classification of a right of patronage, that is, the right of a person or community to appoint to a benefice.[49] When the patrons are beguines, does this privilege pertain to the secular or to the ecclesiastical law of patronage? The decision consists of the following assertions:

> A certain cleric, having been collated to a reserved benefice despite the fact that the right of presentation to that benefice belongs to the beguines, claims that he should be able to retain it.[50] He alleges that at the time of his appointment, no mention was made of the fact that the right of patronage belonged to the secular beguines. But, although beguines are seculars, they nevertheless live as religious and wear habits and thus do not seem to be entirely lay *(ideo non videtur mere laice)*.

---

points out that there are those who say that canonesses ought to be treated as ecclesiastical persons, since although they may contract marriage *de futuro*, they nevertheless live as religious in the present and may be compared therefore to clerks in lower orders who, while not bound by vows, are still viewed as ecclesiastics.

48. *Decisiones*, (1507), *fol.* cxl, #CCCXXXII; *Decisones*, (1483), *fol.* 88 #CCCXXXII. This decision can also be found as #365, in an unpublished collection made by the Rota auditor Juan Alfonso de Mella (1397–1467):*Decisiones reverendi patris domini Johannis de Mella*, MS Vat.lat. 2665, fol. 236.

49. The classic study of medieval law of patronage is: Peter Landau, *Ius patronatus: Studien zur Entwicklung des Patronats im Dekretalenrecht und der Kanonistik des 12.und 13. Jahrhunderts, Forschungen zur Kirchlichen Rechtsgeschichte und zum Kirchenrecht Bd.*, 12 (Köln: Böhlau, 1975).

50. *Nota quod clericus cui est collatum beneficium etiam reservatus, posito quod illud beneficium pertineat ad collationem seu presentationem beguinarum: tale beneficium potest licite.*

Also, for religious reasons, they have the right to form an association *(collegium)* just as it is allowed to those laymen who are Friars Minor and Cistercians.[51] Also, because beguines, like widows and other disadvantaged persons *(miserabiles personae)*, may bring their causes before ecclesiastical judges, they must not be classed as mere laity. This especially since beguines wear habits, and since anyone harming them is liable to canonical sentence, as Johannes Andreae notes in his gloss of Dilecta.[52]

Here the decision ends, having established that the beguine right of presentation to a benefice pertains to the ecclesiastical and not the secular law of patronage—the rubric for this decision reads: *Ius patronatus beguinarum censetur ius patronatus ecclesiasticum.* Given the relentless way in which academic commentators had cast suspicion on the beguines, we cannot help but be surprised that orthodoxy is never at issue in this decision. The auditors do not debate the legitimacy of the beguine way of life, they assume it. They never question the legal right of these women to present to a benefice. What is more, the judges support their classification of the beguine right of patronage as an ecclesiastical right by noting that, as *miserabiles personae*, beguines are customarily extended a privilege reserved for clerics, the *privilegium fori.*[53]

51. . . . *propter religionem quam habent videatur facere colleguim . . . ut dicimus in simili quod fratres minores et cistercienses sunt laici.*

52. Ibid.: *..et talibus iniuriando quis incideret in sententia canonis sic intelligitur nota per Jo. an. in c.dilecta. De maio.et obe.* The auditors refer here to Johannes' distinction between secular canonesses *(conversa ecclesiae secularis)* who do not enjoy the *privilegium canonicis* and women who are "converts to religion" who do—they then equate beguines with the latter, privileged, group. Johannes Andreae, *Novella*, gloss to X 1.33.12, p. 267. See chapter one for a full discussion of this gloss.

53. As McDonnell, *Beguines and Beghards,* p. 131, points out, urban magistrates could and did exempt beguinages from civic jurisdiction. The complicated question of beguine status as "disadvantaged" will be taken up in the final chapter of this book. Note that the term *miserabiles personae* covered a very broad sector of humanity according to some commentators, and might include widows and orphans, those suffering from debilitating disease, scholars, captives, pilgrims, serfs who worked on church lands, and many more. See Helmholz, *The Spirit,* chapter 5, for an introduction to the claims and actual practice of church courts with respect to this vaguely defined group. Also see Brian Tierney, *Medieval Poor Law,* and

As in example one, the auditors make scant reference to academic commentary on the law, and rather rely directly on citing the enactments, themselves both canon and Roman. They use supporting texts in unexpected ways as well. For instance, *Cum ex eo* is used not to condemn beguines (because they were an unapproved sect, like the *fraticelli*), but to establish their legal right to form societies (since that right had been given to the Friars Minor, a predominately lay group at the time). Johannes Andreae's gloss of *Dilecta* is used to support the privileged status of a beguine as long as she remains in the habit of a beguine—a condition that, as we saw earlier, was placed on secular canonesses as well.

How can we account for the independence of the Rota auditors, particularly when they render a judgment so at odds both in tone and intent with the legal theory generated by legislation such as *Cum de quibusdam*? And how typical were such decisions? While the answers to these questions remain elusive, a few observations about the men who filled the office of papal auditor, and about the workings of late medieval ecclesiastical courts generally, may be useful.

Canonists employed by bishops or municipal governments might have found the prospect of writing *consilia* or *decisiones* that went against the grain of academic comment intimidating; canonists who served as judges in the highest Christian court were less inhibited. Rota auditors were among the most eminent and well-regarded jurists of their day. A short list of auditors in the fourteenth century, for example, includes the names Oldradus de Ponte, Gilles de Bellemere, Cardinal Zabarella, Ludovicus Pontanus, and Panormitanus.[54] The international reputation of these men, coupled with the authority that was theirs to wield, made them willing to depart from common opinion. *"Rota quandoque rotat,"* it was said, and on more

---

James A.Brundage, "Legal Aid for the Poor and the Professionalization of Law in the Middle Ages," *The Journal of Legal History* 9 (1988): 169–79.

54. *DDC* 7:743. See also M. Henri Gilles, *"Les Auditeurs de Rote au Temps de Clement VII et Benoit XIII (1378–1417): Notes Biographiques,"* *Mélanges d'archéologie et d'histoire publiés par l'École française de Rome* 67 (1955): 321–37.

than one occasion the decisions of the Rota did in fact give new shape to the *Ius Commune*.[55]

But even absent Rotal robes, practicing canonists appear to have been more progressive, more willing to adapt to local custom or circumstance, than their academic counterparts. As we have noted when comparing the work of Panormitanus the commentator with that of Panormitanus the *iurisperitus*, this generalization holds even when practitioner and academic are one and the same person. It also seems to apply in areas of the law that have nothing to do with quasi-religious women, or with the religious life in any form.

James Brundage, for example, points out the disparity between theorists and practitioners with reference to marriage law. He comments that in the fourteenth and fifteenth centuries, "canonical courts at every level were in practice less rigorous than legal theory required and on occasion granted divorces that ruptured the bond of marriage, even though theorists claimed that they could not do so."[56] While observing that, in general, the gap between what ecclesiastical judges did and what academic jurists said they should do was fairly narrow, the consistently conservative trend in legal scholarship was not reflected in the actions of the courts. "Striking and important divergences" existed between the law as taught in the schools and as practiced in the courts.[57]

In practice then, ecclesiastical judges and consultants often had more in common with local ordinaries and city magistrates than with their academic colleagues. In large part this is because the goal of the commentator was diametrically opposed to that of the practitioner.

Academic commentators waged a noble, if losing, battle against legal ambiguity. With respect to the law regarding quasi-religious women, that struggle sometimes reduced them to pure sophistry,

55. Dolezalek, "Reports," p. 81, reproduces the contemporary maxim *"Opinio Rotae facit communem opinionem"* in making this point.

56. James A. Brundage, *Law, Sex and Christian Society in Medieval Europe* (Chicago: University of Chicago Press, 1987), p. 510.

57. Ibid., p. 547.

occasionally produced viable consensus, and was sometimes effectively, although not happily, abandoned—as when the canonists failed to reach a consensus about tertiaries and ecclesiastical privilege. When academics became judges and consultants, however, the rules changed. Legislative ambiguity became an asset, something to be exploited rather than wrestled out of existence.

Faced with difficulties similar to those consistently encountered by urban magistrates required to make mundane decisions about the women who lived in the towns and cities under their jurisdiction, practicing canonists employed similar methods. We have seen that local authorities sometimes used the less than forthright canons issued regarding beguines to persecute tertiaries and other beguine "look-alikes." But they sometimes found in those same decrees, especially in the saving clause appended to *Cum de quibusdam*, a means to protect the integrity of popularly patronized beguine houses and the women who lived in them—women who thought of themselves, and were regarded by their fellow citizens, as true *mulieres religiosae*.[58]

Similarly, what had been the bane of the theorist gave the legal consultant or the auditor needed flexibility in decision making, and a lack of consensus among interpreters made it possible to select among representative authorities, as the needs of case or client dictated. The absence of uniform guidelines encouraged practitioners to return to the law itself rather than to comment on it, not incidentally producing what amounted to a new interpretation of that law.

The legal minds behind the decisions and opinions discussed in this chapter capitalized on the fact that legislation dealing with the religious status of quasi-religious women was often murky and sometimes contradictory. As practicing jurists they were not averse to giving established court practice, even that of the secular courts, a valence equal to, if not surpassing, that which they attached to academic theory.

These *consilia* and *decisiones* testify to the continued participation of all manner of quasi-religious women in the everyday life of late-

---

58. McDonnell, *Beguines and Beghards,* pp. 547–53, features many such examples, especially for France and the Netherlands.

medieval cities. Those opinions that depart from the negativism of academic commentary may even support inferences about the triumph of popular ideas about *mulieres religiosae* over technical, juridical ones, and about the attractiveness of those ideas to jurists who sometimes preferred them to the strict interpretation of the law.

Yet in none of the opinions covered in this chapter were canon lawyers engaged in anything more exalted than sorting out the facts of a specific case and making legal arguments pertinent to those facts. In each instance they confined themselves to dealing with the legality or illegality of specific actions and not with the morality of those actions—Gaspar Calderinus was interested only in the legal ramifications of entrance into an unapproved order, and the Rota auditors decided a case involving patronage rights of beguines without once referring to the ubiquitous expression of papal suspicion about these women.

When we turn to a landmark consultation of the late fourteenth century, however, the moral and the legal become less separable, the issues broaden, and the weight of both theology and law are required to resolve them. In their collective defense of a group of quasi-religious women known as Sisters of the Common Life, the canonists of the University of Cologne argued not about rights, but about *a* right: the right of an entire group of women to continued existence.

S I X

The Cologne Defense of the Sisters
of the Common Life

---

*"Man is corrupted by the honors, favors, and especially the greed that
drives everyone. Through the lucrative arts he becomes so tainted and
enflamed that his natural uprightness is forgotten and his appetites in-
fected; he no longer looks to the things of God, of virtue, or of bodily
good. Whence it is the rarest thing for someone given over to one of the
lucrative disciplines—medicine, civil law or canon law—to be found
upright or balanced in reason, or just or tranquil, or of genuine in-
sight."*[1]

These are the words of Geert Grote (1340–84), impassioned
preacher, visionary reformer, and erstwhile student of the
canon law. Since he had spent a good part of his youth
among law professors at the University of Paris, Grote might have
drawn this unflattering portrait of canonists and civilians from life.
He might just have easily, however, found his models in medieval

1. Geert Grote, "Resolutions and Intentions, But Not Vows," in *Devotio
Moderna, Basic Writings*, ed. John Van Engen (New York: Paulist Press,
1988), p. 67.

literature, which abounded in invective against both types of lawyers.[2] But whatever Grote's diatribe may have lacked in originality, it made up for in irony. Although he had ceased to practice law after his conversion, Grote continued to cling steadfastly to its forms. He filled his sermons and treatises with proof texts and even wrote legal opinions until shortly before his death.[3] More pointedly, it would be a group of men given over to that "lucrative discipline" of canon law who would save Grote's followers from condemnation as heretics.

Born into a wealthy merchant family in the city of Deventer and educated at the Latin grammar school in his hometown, Geert Grote received his Master of Arts degree from the University of Paris by the age of eighteen.[4] He took no advanced degrees, yet spent sixteen more years enjoying the privileges which inherited wealth, education, and the system of ecclesiastical patronage provided. Al-

2. On polemic against medieval lawyers see: John A. Yunck, "The Venal Tongue: Lawyers and the Medieval Satirists," *American Bar Association Journal* 46 (1960): 267–70; John W. Baldwin, "Critics of the Legal Profession: Peter Chanter and His Circle," in Proceedings of the Second International Congress of Medieval Canon Law, ed. Stephan Kuttner and J. Joseph Ryan, *MIC, Subsidia*, vol. 1 (Vatican City: Biblioteca Apostolica Vaticana, 1965), pp. 249–59; James A. Brundage, "The Ethics of the Legal Profession: Medieval Canonists and Their Clients," *The Jurist* 33(1973): 237–248, and "The Medieval Advocate's Profession," *Law and History Review*, 6:2 (1988): p. 454 n.1, where Brundage points out that if criticism of lawyers in medieval literature is in fact a measure of their importance in society, "lawyers were arguably the most prominent single group in the high middle ages, for no other group was so constantly and consistently attacked . . ."
3. Van Engen, *Devotio Moderna*, pp. 38, 42.
4. For biographical details see: Theodore van Zijl, *Gerard Groote, Ascetic and Reformer 1340–1384* (Washington, DC: The Catholic University of America Press, 1963); C. de Bruin, E. Persoons, and A. G. Weiler, *Geert Grote en de moderne devotie* (Zutphen: Walburg Press, 1984); Georgette Epiney-Burgard, *Gérard Grote (1340–84) et les débuts de la dévotion moderne* (Wiesbaden: F. Steiner 1970; rpt. Turnhout: Brepols, 1998). Albert Hyma, *The Christian Renaissance* (Hamden, CT: Archon Books, 1965), pp. 9–40; R. R. Post, *The Modern Devotion* (Leiden: E. J.Brill, 1968), pp. 51–176; Van Engen, *Devotio Moderna*, Introduction.

though these years are not well documented, we know that during this time he pursued further study in canon law, and dabbled in medicine, astrology, and philosophy, received income from two benefices although residing in neither one, and kept up his association with the councilmen of Deventer, with an eye to future employment.

Then, in 1374, at the age of thirty-four, he renounced both his benefices, turned his family home into a hospice for poor women, and imposed a strict penitential life upon himself. And while the phenomenon of conversion is anything but unique in the annals of late medieval history, Grote's determination to avoid the well-trodden path is apparent even at this stage of his devout life.

Although he rejected ordination, which would have meant a subsequent rise into the higher orders of the secular clergy, he did not, as had so many other penitents before him, reject the world entirely. Instead of withdrawing to a monastery, he retained his clerical status of deacon and obtained a license to preach in the diocese of Utrecht. And from 1380 until shortly before his death, he did so with a fervor and forthrightness that gained him both enmity—he was banned from preaching in 1383 after a too-fiery harangue delivered in the court of the bishop of Utrecht—and his reputation as the founder of a movement of religious renewal known as the New Devotion *(Devotio Moderna)*.

We can say with confidence that the individualized vision and the determination of Geert Grote influenced the development of the *Devotio Moderna*. Only Grote's earliest followers—those sisters who lived in his own house in Deventer and the brothers (clerics like himself) who established the first houses for men in Deventer, Zwolle, and Amsterdam—had actually known him personally, but the written and oral accounts of his life and ideals guided generations of the devout.[5]

Those who spontaneously began to form communities designed to foster the spirit of renewal embodied in Grote's life and work are generally referred to today as the Brothers and Sisters of the Com-

---

5. Van Engen, *Devotio Moderna*, p. 7.

mon Life.[6] But as R. W. Southern has pointed out, "even this is too precise a label. The 'Common Life' was simply the irreducible residue that was left when they had cut away all other distinguishing features."[7]

Geert Grote's first followers were unwilling to accept a designation which would set them apart from other pious laymen. They dressed simply but did not wear a distinctive habit. They sustained their physical needs by manual labor and their pious intentions by firm resolutions, not irrevocable vows. They lived communally but remained lay people subject to the secular courts.

Nor should the establishment of the Windesheim Congregation north of Deventer and other communities of regular canons and canonesses be seen as a departure from the ideals of the founder. Geert Grote himself recognized that such approved religious communities could provide support to the far more vulnerable and informally constituted "gatherings" of the lay brothers and sisters.[8] And such informal groups, which are the focus of this chapter, were continuously founded, renewed, or shored up when ranks became depleted throughout the fifteenth century.

The Brothers and Sisters of the Common Life continued to embody the ideal of pious laity attempting to transform the mundane rather than retreat from it. The institutional structures which supported their spiritual life were not prescribed by any monastic rule. And yet there were elements of that life that closely—too closely, some would say—resembled conventional monastic forms. Like the beguines and beghards of an earlier time, the brothers and sisters

6. For overviews of this movement, see: *DMA,* "Brethren of the Common Life," 2:366–69; *DHGE,* "Frères de la Vie Commune," 18:1438–54; *LMA,* "Brüder und Schwestern vom gemeinsamen Leben" 12:734–35; *DIP,* "Sorelle della Vita Comune," 8:1926–28; and "Devozione Moderna," 3:456–63. See also Kaspar Elm, "Die Brüderschaft vom gemeinsamen Leben: eine geistliche Lebensform zwischen Kloster und Welt, Mittelalter und Neuzeit" *Ons geestelijk erf* 59 (1985): 470–74, regarding the quasi-religious status, identified as a "third" or "middle" position between lay and clerical status, of the Brothers and Sisters.

7. Southern, *Western Society and the Church,* p. 345.

8. Ibid., p. 338; Van Engen, *Devotio Moderna,* pp. 21–21.

implicitly challenged the sincerity of those who opted for a formal, life-long, monastic commitment. Like the beguines, the Sisters of the Common Life began to attract the special attention of inquisitors suspicious of yet another self-governing group of quasi-religious women.[9]

Despite the fact that some scholars use the designation *"Brethren* of the "Common Life" when dealing with the New Devout, the sisters not only predated the brothers but also consistently outnumbered them. Their first community was founded by Grote himself shortly before his death, and the majority of subsequent foundations of the New Devout were made for women.[10] By conservative estimate, there were thirty-two houses of sisters in the Netherlands by 1460, compared to eighteen occupied by the brethren.[11]

The most impressive growth in the numbers of women's houses founded in and around the Issel River Valley occurred within a decade and a half of Geert Grote's death. As R. R. Post observed, by the end of the fourteenth century such houses, congregations of

9. The only full-length study devoted entirely to the the sisters is Gerhard Rehm, *Die Schwestern*. Although centering on the German experience, it does treat of the similarities between beguines and sisters, gives a fine introduction to the phenomenon as a whole, and deals with the complex issues of terminology. See also Florence Koorn, "Women without Vows," who notes the differences and similarities between the spirituality of beguines and sisters.

10. There has been some controversy, specifically between R. R. Post and Albert Hyma, about precisely when the women to whom Grote had handed over his family home actually took up the communal life. Hyma claimed that the statutes drawn up to effect this transition are properly dated to 1379, while Post argued that they were written well after Grote's death—in 1395 in fact—and that they were only attributed to Grote in a time of crisis for the sisters. Rehm, *Die Schwestern*, pp. 35–36, appears to have no problem with Post's dating; Koorn, "Women Without Vows," p. 145 n.10, however, writes that Post's arguments "are not quite convincing." For our purposes, John Van Engen's remarks are guide enough: "In the early stages of his conversion, in 1375, he [Grote] seems to have intended little more than a kind of hospice, but by the end of his life in 1384, and then clearly by the 1390s, this had become a distinct religious community." Van Engen, *Devotio Moderna*, p. 18.

11. Post, *Modern Devotion*, pp. 494–95; Bruin, *Geert Groote*, pp. 66–67.

women who ultimately became Sisters of the Common Life, "sprang up from the ground like mushrooms."[12] And if reports of two hundred or more sisters living in a large community may not always be trusted, such numbers were also not unheard of.[13]

This rapid expansion of the sisters made them highly visible in cities and towns, and for many who saw them on a regular basis they appeared to be just another group of beguines. Like beguines, the Sisters of the Common Life were normally addressed in conversation as "sister," and pious bequests, chronicles, and even civic statutes frequently used the terms *beguine* and *sister* interchangeably.[14] Since their houses only gradually achieved a fully communal character, even the living arrangements of the original sisters resembled those of beguines.[15]

Almost from the first then, the Sisters of the Common Life struggled to distinguish themselves from the beguines with whom they were identified. According to one version of the statutes written for the sisters living in Geert Grote's house in Deventer, for example, any sister found to espouse religious views shared by beguines faced immediate dismissal from the community. Nor were sisters allowed to dress like beguines, lest they be thought of as members of that status "prohibited by the pope and the general church under jurisdiction of the ecclesiastical law."[16]

That the sisters and their protectors needed to draw such distinctions is clear. The suspicions about quasi-religious women generated by *Cum de quibusdam* continued to manifest themselves in cyclical and largely indiscriminate persecutions of beguines. Papal mandates

12. Post, *Modern Devotion*, p. 268.
13. Van Engen, *Devotio Moderna*, p. 18.
14. Rehm, *Die Schwestern*, pp. 31–44 addresses the issue of terminology, as well as organization of the sister houses as it relates to the distinction between beguines and sisters.
15. Ibid.
16. Post, *Modern Devotion*, p. 265. Note that it was this defensiveness about their orthodox status that confirmed R. R. Post in his editorial decision that the long version had been drawn up, not during Geert Grote's life, but shortly "before the great attacks on the Sisters of the Master Geert's house and of many other houses, especially in 1396, '97, and '98."

issued after *Cum de quibusdam* (decrees like *Ratio recta,* for instance) had attempted to distinguish "good" from "bad" beguines, but other directives, whether issued by popes or their secular counterparts in the campaign against heresy, actually added to the confusion. In 1369, for example, the Holy Roman Emperor Charles IV, called by Pope Gregory XI *"pugil fidei praefatae magnificus ac promptus haereticorum persecutor,"* expressed suspicion of quasi-religious generally and recommended that the papal inquisition proceed against "beghards, beguines, and *Swestriones* [Sisters of the Common Life] everywhere in Germany."[17]

Inevitably, Charles IV's zeal and Pope Gregory XI's cooperation resulted in the persecution of fully orthodox, as well as heretical, quasi-religious.[18] And, just as inevitably, given the clear pendulum swings in papal policy on this issue, Gregory XI relented. In answer to an anonymous plea for protection, he issued the bull *Ex iniuncto* in 1374, and three years later published an even more conciliatory restatement known as *Ad audientiam.*[19]

Ex iniuncto was addressed to all prelates in Germany, Brabant, and Flanders, and spoke of "the poor people of both sexes" *(personae pauperes utriusque sexus)* who lived humbly, honestly, in poverty and chastity, and attended church regularly. Gregory XI noted that appeals had reached him concerning the harassment of such people and that he wished such appeals to be investigated.[20] *Ad audientim* again referred to "poor people of both sexes" who had been repeatedly molested by inquisitors. As long as orthodox belief could be ascertained, the bull stated, this abuse was to stop. Moreover, those who had been wrongly excommunicated were to be restored to the church.

17. McDonnell, *Beguines and Beghards,* pp. 563–69, on the cooperation between Gregory XI and Charles IV.
18. Lerner, *Heresy,* p. 54 mentions that Gregory had attacked beguines and beghards "in no uncertain terms," in his bulls of 1372–73.
19. Fredericq, *Corpus,* 1:220, pp. 228–31 and 1:225, pp. 23–38 respectively.
20. McDonnell, *Beguines and Beghards,* pp. 569–70, on this decree as well as and *Ad audientiam,* and episcopal reaction to it; see also Lerner, *Heresy,* pp. 53–54 and p. 141.

The promulgation of *Ad audientiam*, coupled with the death of Charles IV in 1378 and the beginning of the Great Schism, led to "a comparative lull in inquisitorial activity."[21] Inquisitorial activity in the 1380s tended to be sporadic and highly localized, and it did not at first seem that the ascension of Boniface IX (1389–1404) to the papal throne would alter the situation.[22] By 1396, however, Boniface IX had issued a decree which not only revoked all the concessions that had ever been granted to *"sectae utriusque sexus homium, vulgo Beghardi seu Lullardi et Zwestriones,"* but also ordered cooperation with papal inquisitors charged with rooting out those who had been spreading heresy "for the past century."[23]

A new cycle of persecution, targeting the *Swestriones* among others, was underway. The pattern of correction and counter-correction was again evident, and Boniface IX had newly empowered inquisitors, one of whom had almost certainly been responsible for effecting the change in papal policy.[24]

About 1393, an inquisitor assigned to the imperial territories of western Germany and the Netherlands, Jacob von Soest, had begun an investigation of the congregation of *Swestriones* who lived in Utrecht and Rhenen. His observations and conclusions, drawn from "the sworn testimony of several reliable persons," were contained in a complaint which he had forwarded to Rome.[25] Because von

21. Lerner, *Heresy*, p. 141, and note 40 in which Lerner shows that the inquisition was by no means inactive even during this period.
22. Lerner, *Heresy*, p. 148; McDonnell, *Beguines and Beghards*, p. 571.
23. Fredericq, *Corpus*, 1:241, pp. 256–57.
24. As Lerner, *Heresy*, p. 149, n.55 notes there is no firm evidence that Jacob von Soest's fellow inquisitor assigned to western Germany and the Netherlands, Eylard Schoenveld, proceeded against the sisters at this time, as a later chronicler had claimed. Post, *The Modern Devotion*, pp. 279–80, says "it is probable that one or both of the inquisitors in question" investigated the houses, sent a report to Rome, and consequently inspired Boniface XI's 1396 legislation. See also Rehm, *Die Schwestern*, p. 149–50.
25. Fredericq, *Corpus*, 2:106, pp. 153–56. See also the version of this report in Walter Ribbeck, "Beiträge zur Geschichte der römischen Inquisition in Deutschland während des 14. Und 15. Jahrhunderts," *Zietschrift für vaterländische Geschichte und Alterthumskunde* XLVI (1888): 129–56. This version, in Appendix 1, pp. 138–44, has supporting citations at its conclusion, to which I shall refer.

Soest's report was the catalyst for the first legal defense of the sisters, as well as for Boniface IX's persecution of them, its contents bear scrutiny.

Von Soest's report contains three distinct parts. The first, the complaint proper, makes oblique references to unorthodox practice among the sisters: the need for "pre-confession" to the community's superior, whom the sisters refer to as Martha; the hearsay testimony of a Carthusian prior that the statutes of the house in Rhenen "*cum statutis ecclesie nullatenus posse stare*"; and the air of secrecy which the informants say surrounds those rules.[26] Yet, above all else, the sisters are indicted for their quasi-monastic lifestyle, and a variety of specific examples are used to support that indictment.

For instance, the superior leads the sisters in saying the blessing and thanksgiving at meals which are taken in a refectory while books are read aloud—all clearly monastic customs. The superior convenes a chapter of faults during which the sisters confess their sins. Sisters are not allowed to hear mass or sermons, to go to confession or communion without license of the superior, and she even assigns particular confessors who are well acquainted with the house ordinances. Those ordinances, in turn, are obeyed by all sisters under pain of expulsion from the community; and although the sisters make no profession, those who leave a house are referred to as "apostates" just as if they had been regulars.[27]

The second part of von Soest's report contains the formulae to be followed in future interrogations of the sisters. It begins with an obligatory oath *(Si nollet iurare vel difficultaret, hereticus est)* and ends with a list of questions to determine whether a respondent has a firm grasp of, and willingness to confess to, the tenets of the faith.[28] Yet even here, amid questions aimed at determining right thinking with respect to Christian doctrine, the issue that had all but monop-

---

26. Fredericq, *Corpus,* 2:106, pp. 153–54; Ribbeck, "Beiträge," pp. 138–14.

27. Post, *Modern Devotion,* pp. 284–85, gives a summary of this first segment of the complaint. See Ribbeck, "Beiträge," pp. 138–41, and Fredericq, *Corpus,* 2, pp. 153–55.

28. Fredericq, *Corpus,* 2, pp. 155–56; Ribbeck, "Beiträge," p. 142.

olized the body of the complaint looms large. That issue is, once again, quasi-monastic practice and organization.

Respondents are to be asked whether they know of the church's ban on the formation of new religious orders and of the condemnation of the sect of beghards, beguines, and sisters which represent such an unauthorized order *(An umquam audierit preceptum ecclesie novam religionem non assumendam et non confirmatam deserendam esse. An audierint sectam, que dicitur begardorum et beghinarum seu swestrionum, dampnatam esse).*[29] With these questions, the issue of canonical prohibitions against the founding of new religious orders is reasserted, and beguines are unmistakably equated with sisters.

The final part of von Soest's report is an appendix consisting of anti-beguine/sister statements followed by citations of the law that support them.[30] In addition to the familiar prohibitions and condemnations from the thirteenth and early fourteenth centuries *(Ne nimia, Cum de quibusdam,* and *Ad nostram),* von Soest cites the most recent fourteenth-century decrees of Pope Gregory XI and the edicts of the emperor Charles IV against beguines and beghards. Although he also mentions Pope John XXII's decree *Ratio recta,* he reads it *a contrario sensu.* This law exculpatory of orthodox beguines proved that heretical beguines, deserving of previously prescribed condemnation, existed as well.

One reference to academic commentary finds its way into von Soest's list: Johannes Andreae's gloss to *Cum de quibusdam,* specifically the tart quotation from Hostiensis with which it opens *(quod perniciosum est genus feminarum a quibus modis omnibus est cavendum).*[31]

Given von Soest's unwillingness to distinguish Sisters of the Common life from beguines, it is significant that he concludes by noting that tertiaries, because of their papally approved *modus vivendi,* are exempt from condemnation by *Cum de quibusdam.* He also mentions church law requiring ecclesiastical approval (episcopal or

---

29. Ibid.
30. As noted above, the document as it appears in Fredericq lacks this appendix. Ribbeck, "Beiträge," pp. 143–44.
31. Ibid. p. 144. See chapter two for the complete quotation, in which Hostiensis makes a slight distinction between beguines and whores.

papal, depending on the venture) for the construction of buildings normally associated with religious orders: hospitals, churches, oratories, and monasteries.

"The intention behind of all this is clear," writes R. R. Post of von Soest's report. "The inquisitor had to have the means of condemning the Sisters and Brethren on the grounds that they had set up a new order."[32] A specific defensive strategy designed to prove the contrary would have to be undertaken. In 1397–98, after von Soest's complaint had reached Rome and resulted in Boniface IX's sweeping condemnation of "those who had been spreading heresy for the past century," the Brethren of the Common Life solicited legal opinions from jurists in the diocese of Cologne testifying to the lawful status of their communities.

The Cologne defense of the Brothers and Sisters of the Common Life has long been recognized by historians as a crucial event in the history of the New Devotion.[33] Some historians, like Post, have summarized the major arguments of the lawyers and some, like Gerard Rehm, have provided a brief history of the earlier legislative assault on the beguines, which helps to make the *consilia* intelligible.[34] Yet no one has examined the Cologne opinions in detail with regard for both mode of argumentation and choice of supporting texts. Nor has anyone studied them within a genre-specific context, such as that provided by the earlier chapters of this book.[35]

The Cologne *consilia* vary in length and quality. There is much overlap of material among them, since they were all written in response to a formulaic question. Some are preserved without attribu-

32. Post, *The Modern Devotion*, p. 285.

33. See, for example, L. Korth, "Die ältesten Gutachten über die Brüderschaft des gemeinsamen Lebens," in *Mittheilungen aus dem Stadtarchiv Köln* 5 (1887): 1–27. More recently: McDonnell, *Beguines*, p. 573; Lerner, *Heresy*, pp. 148–49; 198–99; Southern, *Western Society*, p. 339, to name a very few.

34. Post, *The Modern Devotion*, pp. 280–85; Rehm, *Die Schwestern*, pp. 152–58.

35. A dissertation in progress, "The *Devotio moderna* and Freedom of Association: A Case Study in Medieval Theory of Rights," by J. Michael Raley, promises to fill this gap, since it includes a chapter on the Cologne *consilia* based on extensive archival research.

tion, and some are supplemented by replies which are more expository than juridical in content. Most are the work of individuals, but there exists a corporate response as well, produced in 1398 by the law faculty of the University of Cologne. I have chosen one of these opinions for close examination. It was written a year before the corporate *consilium* by a "doctor of decrees," Arnold, Abbot of Dikningen.[36] Not only would the collective opinion of the Cologne faculty rely heavily on this, a decision of one of its own, but given the formal resemblance of the abbot's opinion to *consilia* already surveyed in previous chapters, it bears comparison with them.

Arnold of Dikningen's opinion consists of seven questions concerning the lawful existence of the Brothers of the Common Life and his reply to each of them. The first question concerns the broad issue, made so much of by von Soest, of quasi-monastic organization. Do these men who live together collegially and conventually violate the papal ban on the establishment of new religious orders or colleges; that is, do they elect their own superiors, make formal profession, or live under a new rule? Papal decrees with which we are already quite familiar, namely *Ne nimia* (promulgated by the Fourth Lateran Council, 1215) and *Sancta Romana* (promulgated by John XXII), as well as the Digest (47.22), are cited to underscore the fact that new, unapproved orders/colleges are in fact forbidden.

The abbot replies that the Brethren do not violate the ban on new orders since they form simple societies and live united in fraternal charity, but without forming a new religious order or constituting a new college. To live in this manner is not only licit but also meritorious, as can be demonstrated with reference to Pope Gregory XI's *Ex iniuncto* (summarized above), as well as John XXII's *Ratio recta*.

Canon law and commentary on it, Roman law, and Scripture provide further justification for the existence of simple, extra-monastic associations. Authorities include Distinction VIII in the *Decretum*, affirming that a communal form of life accords with natural law; Pope Innocent IV's gloss to X 5.31.14 validating the formation

36. Fredericq, *Corpus*, 2:112, pp. 173–76. The abbot was also a consultant in the corporate opinion produced by the Cologne law faculty.

of private societies as long as those societies avoid the use of collegial insignia; and the citation from the Digest (47.22) referenced above, but this time at the qualifying words: "There is, however, no ban on assembly for religious purposes, so long as there is no contravention of the *senatus consultum* which prohibits unlawful *collegia.*"[37]

Scriptural support comes from the ever-quotable Psalm 133: "Behold, how good and how pleasant it is for brethren to dwell together in unity!"; from the (rather weak) suggestion that Christ and the apostles lived a communal life found in John 13:29; and from the forthright statement about the apostles found in Acts 4:32: "And the multitude of them that believed were of one heart and of one soul: neither said any of them that any of the things which he possessed was his own; but they had all things in common."

The abbot concludes this question with a scattering of additional references to the *Decretum* and the statement that the communal life outside religion is not only consonant with Scripture and Church custom, but that it is even habitually used within the Church, as in the case of secular canons.[38] He then immediately takes up the second question, which concerns the specific practice of designating a superior to whom all the brethren owe obedience.

Two references are made to the *Decretals* (X 1.6.20 and X 1.33.6). The first illustrates the hoary canonical principle *par in parem potestatem non habeat* thus establishing the fact that there is no juridical basis for constrained obedience of the Brethren to their superiors, since theirs is a simple society. But the second demonstrates that coercion is not really at issue, since all Christians (even emperors, according to Innocent III, author of this decretal) owe voluntary obedience to godly authority. The abbot then relies on Scripture and moral theology to support his proposition.

He cites the epistles of Peter twice. The first time at the apostle's injunction to those who have purified their souls through obedience to "love one another with a pure heart fervently" (Peter I.1.22) and the second time at the words "submit yourselves to every ordi-

---

37. *The Digest,* 47.22.1–4. The Distinction cited from the Decretum reads in part: "By natural law all things are common to all people . . ."
38. Citations are to *Decretum,* C 12. q 1. c 2; C 15. q 7. c. 1; D 32 .c 6.

nance of man for the Lord's sake." The *Quodlibet* questions of Thomas Aquinas (VI.XI) establish submission of the lower to higher as the order of nature, and Saint Bernard's words *ad fratres de Monte Dei et Augustinus* stress the importance of obedience for the maintenance of domestic harmony.[39]

It seems that unconstrained obedience rendered to one person in the spirit of charity and for mutual benefit is not only permitted but enjoined upon the faithful in general, not just upon monks. But what of another quasi-monastic ritual favored by the Brethren—the confession of faults to another member of the community, who is not a priest? Relying on canonical commentary of Innocent IV, Guilelmus de Monte Laudano, Johannes Andreae, and the Frenchman Henri Bohic (d. 1350), the abbot shows that this practice too is acceptable.[40]

As in the foregoing matter of obedience, the informality and the non-binding character of a practice neither enjoined by law nor having juridical consequences makes it tolerable. Brotherly correction is not sacramental confession. Absolution for sin and imposition of penance are powers reserved to a priest who administers the sacrament of confession. And for guidance on the latter, the reader is referred to the Fourth Lateran decree *Omnis utriusque sexus* (found at *X 5.38.12*), mandating that all faithful Christians confess annually to a priest.

To the fourth question regarding the possession, study of, and translation into the vernacular of books of Sacred Scripture, Arnold of Dikningen replies that study of Scripture is indeed recommended to the laity. He handles his proof texts dexterously here, since they could just as easily be used to support the usual cautions against the

---

39. Lacking any more specific reference, it must be assumed that the abbot finds justification in Aquinas' ideas about the structured cosmos obedient to the will of the creator.

40. Innocent IV, *Apparatus* to the *Liber Extra* at X 5.38.12; Guilelmus de Monte Laudano, *Summa* (this may be a reference to his theological manual, the *Sacramentale*, at the title *de penitencia*; Johannes Andreae's gloss to the *Liber Sextus* at VI 5.10.2, and Henri Bohic's gloss to the *Liber Extra, Distinctiones in Libros V Decretalium*, at X 5.38.12).

128   *Consilia* and *Decisiones*

involvement of lay folk in matters better left to their priestly guides. For instance, when citing a decretal of Pope Innocent III enjoining the bishop of Metz not to permit lay preaching or secret theological discussion (X 5.7.12), the abbot focuses only on the qualifying words in that decree about furthering one's understanding of Scripture through study *("Licet autem desiderium intelligendi divinas scripturas, et secundum eas studium adhortandi, reprehendendum not sit . . .")*.[41]

So, too, while noting that canon law requires the destruction of heretical books or heretical sections of books, he insists that it by no means suggests a ban on edifying books, even if in the vernacular *("boni libri in vulgari editi vel de latino transfusi . . . a contrario sensu liquido permittuntur et approbatur")*.[42] To reinforce this argument, he alludes to the words of Sts. Augustine, Boniface, and John Chrysostom, advising various groups among the laity to engage in the reading of Scripture.

Naturally enough, the abbot is compelled to add the standard warning against exposing laymen to any difficult doctrinal works which, because of their intellectual simplicity *(secundum intellectum parvulis)*, would not be nourishing food for thought. And this cautionary tone is echoed in the proof texts: Hebrews IV, "For unto us was the gospel preached as well as unto them: but the word preached did not profit them, not being mixed with faith in them that heard it"; and the opening words of *Cum de quibusdam*, excoriating "those women who presume to discuss/dispute about articles of faith and the sacraments and so fall into various errors".

Rather than end this reply on a negative note, however, the abbot resumes his praise of *lectio divina* via the Old Testament admonition (Deuteronomy VI) to regard the study of the divine commandments not as something limited to the Sabbath but as a part of one's daily routine: "And thou shalt teach them diligently unto thy children and shalt talk of them when thou sittest in thine house, and when thou walkest by the way, and when thou liest down, and

41. Friedberg, *Corpus*, 2:784–87. Also cited is Innocent IV's gloss to X 1.1.1, which is the confession of faith promulgated by Lateran IV, Friedberg, *Corpus*, 2:1
42. Fredericq, *Corpus*, 2:112, p. 174.

when thou risest up." And he concludes by stressing the particular value of the New Testament in this daily devotion, citing Thomas Aquinas once again as an authority.[43]

The fifth question, regarding the acceptability of the Brethren's practice of *correctio fraterna*, is answered in much the same fashion as question three. Arguing from the "innumerable sayings of the saints and the testimony of Scripture" and inserting references once again to Henri Bohic and Thomas Aquinas, the abbot sees problems if, and only if, the rights of public correction for and punishment of sin that are the preserve of prelates are compromised.[44] Private, brotherly correction done in charitable spirit is clearly allowed to those without, as well as those within, religious orders.

As Jacob von Soest's report had pointed out, the Brethren of the Common Life simulated monastic practice in other ways as well. They regulated their days, setting aside particular times for prayer, manual labor, and meals, and prescribing sacred reading during those meals, in the manner of monks. The abbot considers this organizational issue as question six.[45] He uses the legal commentary of Hostiensis and Johannes Andreae, as well as the theological observations of the ubiquitous Aquinas, to illustrate the distinction between private customs or routines and those undertaken in conformity with an official, legally binding statute or constitution. Monks regulate their daily life according to the latter; the Brethren do so as private individuals, without legal compulsion, as might be done by members of a family in their own home.

43. He cites the *Summa Theologica, secunda secundae q.xvii, a.1.* This reference to the argument about whether hope is a virtue—with Aquinas' comment that according to St. Augustine it is not, because hope, like other passions, is subject to means and extremes—apparently speaks to the distinction between expectation of the savior and his manifestation, Old and New Testament respectively.

44. Henri Bohic, *Distinctiones in libros V Decretalium, ad v. "Cum ex iniuncto"* (1498); Thomas Aquinas, *Summa Theologica, secunda secundae, q.xxiii, a.ii,* which extols charity, the means by which God quickens the soul. There are other, erroneous, citations to works of Aquinas as well.

45. Hostinensus, *Summa, Liber I De Consuetudine;* and Johannes Andreae, *Summa, De Consuetudine;* Thomas Aquinas, *Summa, prima secunde q.xci a.iii.*

Question seven—the final question—leaves the actions of the Brethren behind and turns instead to those of men like von Soest. As outlined by canon law (VI 5.2.8), the task of the inquisitor is to investigate and expunge heresy, but the decree of Pope Gregory XI, directed to the archbishops of Cologne, Treves, and Mainz (that is, *Ex iniuncto* of 1374) makes it clear that the Brethren represent a way of life, a *modus vivendi,* and not a heresy. Thus, the pope had instructed local ordinaries (not inquisitors) to investigate their way of life and to ascertain if any among them be tainted with heresy; an inquisitor exceeds his mandate who intervenes in a matter which does not clearly involve heresy.

So concludes the *consilium* written on behalf of the Brethren by the abbot of Dikningen. In format it is characteristic of the genre. It follows the typical scholastic pattern of argument *contra et pro* and it abounds with citations from recognized authorities. If the abbot's opinion does not bristle with references to Roman law (those references appear more often in the corporate opinion of the Cologne University law faculty to which the abbot also contributed), it is not devoid of them.

Like Panormitanus, the abbot as consultant chose carefully among his supporting authorities. In response to the first question regarding the ban on new orders, for example, he cited *Ratio recta* (which cleared the name of orthodox beguines) but not *Cum de quibusdam* (which almost all the commentators had interpreted as a sweeping condemnation of them all).[46] Academic commentary produced by Innocent IV, Hostiensis, and the ultramontane Henri Bohic is often adduced, but we look in vain for citations to the work which we have studied in preceding chapters—commentary on the law relative to quasi-religious women which, if relevant to the case at hand, was surely too negative to advance it.

Like the auditors of the Roman Rota, the abbot cited the law it-

---

46. In the corporate response of 1398, the faculty felt compelled to mention *Cum de quibusdam*, if only to state that licit societies, as opposed to unapproved religious orders, are permitted by papal decrees such as Gregory XI's *Ex injuncto*, notwithstanding the Clementine legislation, *Cum de quibusdam*. See: Fredericq, *Corpus*, 2:113, p. 177–78.

self, rather than academic commentary, whenever possible. This practice allowed him to give that law his own, rather than the standard, interpretation. For instance, we may recall that in his gloss of *Cum de quibusdam*, Johannes Andreae had cited Innocent III's letter to the Bishop of Metz when condemning lay, particularly female, preaching. Arnold of Dikningen employed that same decretal letter, but he used it to buttress his argument in favor of the reading and translation of Scripture into the vernacular by the laity.[47]

Like the other practicing jurists whose legal opinions we have examined, Arnold of Dikningen acted as an advocate for his client and was at pains to produce a persuasive legal argument by selective citation and creative analysis. In one particular feature, however, the abbot's *consilium* bears little resemblance to the opinions already scrutinized—in his work, references to canon and civil law vie for pride of place with scriptural and theological references, and the latter sometimes achieve it.

Where Panormitanus made a single allusion to Scripture (Psalm 133) in his defense of the *inhumati*, the abbot turned to the Bible at every possible juncture. He cited passages from the Old as well as the New Testament. He marshaled with regularity Thomistic arguments and saintly maxims, which represent another species of moral theology. And although it is tempting to attribute this feature of his work to the author's monastic rather than exclusively juridical formation, doing so would obscure a fundamental truth about all canonical literature, a truth with which we have not yet adequately dealt. Unlike modern lawyers, the canonists drew no hard and fast line between the spheres of law and theology. While some appear to have lost sight of the need to mesh the law of God and man for the good of the soul, this was a desideratum even when dealing with subjects which to our way of thinking have very little to do with salvation. The canon law of prescription, as Richard Helmholz has demonstrated, is an excellent case in point.[48]

---

47. See chapter two for Johannes Andreae's usage.
48. Helmholz, *The Spirit*, pp. 188–89. Note that the meshing of law and theology has merited considerable scholarly attention. See, for example, Stephan Kuttner, "Harmony from Dissonance: An Interpretation of Me-

The developed canon law insisted that before a person who was in possession of property could qualify as *bona fide* possessor of that property, he or she would have to prove that they had acted in good faith when initially acquiring said property. That is, the claimant must have believed that he was the rightful possessor. The Roman law of prescription, upon which the canon law was modeled, had contained no such stipulation. It had admitted the possibility (likelihood?) that someone who had known full well that he had acquired property under suspicious circumstances, with *mala fide*, might still acquire prescriptive right to that property.

The Abbot of Dikningen's blending of law and theology, and his frequent citation of Scripture to justify a decision, do not in any way, then, reflect a less than acute juridical sense. Quite the opposite. Those jurists who had given their opinions about the rights of quasi-religious to inherit property, or to enter into binding contracts, had less need of scriptural and theological supporting texts, since religious orthodoxy had not been an issue in the case.[49] When, as in the case of the *inhumati*, the issue had emerged, even Panormitanus had adduced Psalm 133, along with his favored canonical and Roman law proofs. Arnold of Dikningen had been asked to respond to a question with an obvious moral as well as legal dimension. To fully acquit the Brothers and Sisters of the Common Life, he had to do more than prove that their specific practices and modes of community organization did not violate the canon law—he had to ground their entire way of life in hallowed Christian practice. And how better to do so than by finding scriptural and theological confirmation for it?

---

dieval Canon Law," *The History of Ideas and Doctrines of Canon Law in the Middle Ages,* 2nd ed. (Aldershot: Variorum Reprints, 1992), pp. 1–16; John Van Engen, "From Practical Theology to Divine Law: The Work of the Medieval Canonists," in *Proceedings of the Ninth International Congress of Medieval Canon Law* (Vatican City: Biblioteca Apostolica Vaticana, 1997), pp. 873–96; Yves Congar, *"Un témoignage des désaccords entre canonistes et théologiens,"* in *Études du droit canonique dédiées à Gabriel Le Bras,* 2 vols. (Paris: Sirey, 1965), pp. 861–84; Rudolf Weigand, "Ein Zeugnis für die Lehrunterscheide zwischen Kanonisten und Teologen ausdem 13. Jahrhundert," *Revue du droit canonique* 24 (1974): 63–71.

49. See especially the examples of such cases in chapter five.

In any event, the abbot's approach won the full acceptance of his colleagues. In 1398, when the entire law faculty of the University of Cologne produced a *consilium* in defense of the Brethren, it differed in particulars. Only four, as opposed to seven questions were dealt with. The issue of mendicancy was raised (and immediately put to rest) in the first question, and Roman law citations, especially as regards the distinction between simple societies and *collegia*, occurred with more frequency. However, this *consilium* faithfully reproduced Arnold of Dikningen's arguments as well as his biblical and theological citations.

The abbot's *consilium* and that of the Cologne faculty, taken together with a variety of other supporting documents, helped the Brethren to win a victory. Not only did inquisitorial harassment of the sisters living in Utrecht and Rhenen cease, but in 1401 the bishop of Utrecht, Frederic of Blankenheim, issued a decree approving the *modus vivendi* of the Brothers and Sisters of the Common Life.[50]

By the last half of the fifteenth century, there would be no fewer than sixty sister houses in northwest Germany, and this diffusion outside the Netherlands impressed supporters as the confirmation of Geert Grote's claim to have planted "very many virginal flowers, fields of chaste widows and voluntary poor" on fertile ground.[51] This is not to say that new threats, requiring further legal counter measures, did not emerge within the course of that century.

Writing in the 1450s, Jan Busch, a member of the Windesheim community, described one such threat and the Brethren's reaction to it in considerable detail.[52] The opponent in this instance was a Dominican named Matthew Grabow.[53] Originally from Wismar, in Saxony, Grabow was serving as lector at the Dominican house of

50. Post, *Modern Devotion*, p. 288. The bishop stated that he issued this decree on the basis of preceding legal consultation.

51. Quoted by Post, *Modern Devotion*, p. 269, from letter #58 of Grote to the bishop of Utrecht. For the expansion of the sisters in Germany, see Rehm, *Die Schwestern*, pp. 59–113.

52. Johannes Busch, *Chronicon Windeshemense*, ed. Karl Grube (Halle, 1886, rpt. Farnborough, England, 1968), pp. 172–74.

53. On Grabow and the conflict see: H. Keussen, "Der Dominikaner Matthäus Grabow und die Brüder vom gemeinsamen Leben," in *Mittheilungen aus dem Stadtarchiv Köln* 5 (1887): pp. 29–47; and S. Wachter,

Groningen (in the bishopric of Utrecht) in 1416–17 when he joined
battle against the Brothers of Deventer.[54]

Grabow had written a treatise generally condemning those who
lived in community but who followed no approved rule nor took
permanent vows, and he specifically named the Brothers and Sisters
(whom he called beguines) of the Common Life as an example of
such irregular behavior.[55] As soon as the Deventer brothers heard of
this attack, Busch reports, they procured a copy of the treatise from
a sympathetic local pastor. They then undid the volume, assigned a
number of pages to each brother, and worked through the night to
make their own copy.

This copy was then dispatched to Groningen, where a notary se-
cured Grabow's testimony that he had indeed written the hostile
tract. Next, Grabow was taken by the Brethren to the court of the
bishop of Utrecht, where his work was judged heretical. When the
Dominican appealed to the papacy and was given a chance to defend himself at the Council of Constance (1414–18), the Brethren's
cause was upheld by none other than Jean Gerson, then chancellor
of the University of Paris.[56]

Squarely countering Grabow's proposition that Christian perfection required religious profession, Gerson noted that all are called to
the religion preached by Christ and that all may become perfect
without taking vows of any kind. Grabow's treatise was ordered to
be burned as "erroneous, scandalous, injurious, rash, presumptu-

---

"Matthäus Grabow: ein Gegner der Brüder vom gemeinsamen Leben," in
Festschrift zum 50 jährigen Bestandsjubiläum des Missionshauses St. Gabriel
(Wien: Mödling, 1939), pp. 289–376.

54. Grabow's attack has traditionally and erroneously been seen by
historians as an exclusive assault on the Brothers and Sisters of the Common Life. In reality, tertiaries were among his targets, as the text of his
condemnation clearly asserts: ". . . *quod quidam frater Matheus Grabow contra personas tertii ordinis sancti Francisci de penitentia nuncupatas aliasque de-
votas personas civitatis et diocesis Traiontensis* . . ." Keussen, "Grabow und die
Brüder," pp. 33–47. The beguines were similarly targeted by Grabow's
treatise, as he used the term *beguine* when referring to the sisters.

55. Fredericq, *Corpus*, 2:219.

56. For a summary of Grabow's tract, as well as the text of Jean Gerson's speech, see Mansi, 28:386–94.

ous, offensive to pious ears, heretical, and an incitement to heresy,"
and its author imprisoned until he recanted.

In trying to explain their victory at Constance, R. W. Southern
drew attention to the depth of the Brethren's commitment to a religious life free of binding vows, and to the role of "lawyers who
shared their feelings [and] interpreted the law in their favor".[57] In
their struggle against Mathew Grabow, the brothers and sisters
readily resorted to adjudication, not only because they believed that
their position had validity, but also because they knew that lawyers,
at least certain lawyers, were well-disposed to act as their advocates.
The Brothers and Sisters of the Common Life won a moral as well as
a legal victory at the Council of Constance, but not without the aid
of jurists who had for a long time been routinely exploiting the ambiguity of the canon law in the interest of their quasi-religious
clients.

57. R. W. Southern, *Western Society*, p. 343.

Part III

Assessment and Reassessment

SEVEN

Medieval Lawyers and Modern Scholars

Quasi-religious women in the later Middle Ages had no clear-cut canonical status. While this fact allowed them more freedom than nuns—religious women, strictly speaking—it also made their position within the community of Christians more insecure. Some quasi-religious women, like secular canonesses, had the weight of centuries of tradition to safeguard their way of life. Others, like tertiaries, had the benefit of overt papal approval of their *modus vivendi*. Still others, like beguines and the Sisters of the Common Life, lacked both and were therefore particularly vulnerable to fluctuations in ecclesiastical policy. For these women especially, the manner in which the decrees of popes and councils embodied church policy could have crucial ramifications.

Cum de quibusdam is one of the best known of these decrees and, as we have seen, academic canonists characteristically interpreted it as a blanket condemnation of all beguines. Although mentioning the decree's saving clause that exempted "faithful women living uprightly in their own lodgings" from condemnation, only one commentator, Albericus Metensis, interpreted that clause in such a way as to distinguish orthodox from heretical beguines.[1]

1. As quoted in D. Maffei, "Alberico di Metz e il suo Apparato sulle

Relying on second-hand reports and received authorities, the glossators depicted all beguines as suspect. They were women of "a pernicious sort," little better than prostitutes, women who compromised their reputations by their laxity. They were "wolves in sheep's clothing" deceiving others by feigning holiness and so sinning twice: once by appearing to be religious, and once by rejecting the strictures of monastic life. Beguines led others into error and were themselves victims of deception, since they harbored the "insane" belief that they could profitably discuss Scripture and doctrine. They were as gullible and reprehensible as those women of old who had claimed that they could fly through the night on the backs of animals, predict the future, or produce magical cures.

Were we to judge solely on the basis of the commentary generated by *Cum de quibusdam*, we would have to conclude that the canonists staunchly supported the suppression of the beguines as mandated by the decree, and that they would be likely to disapprove of other manifestations of female religiosity that lay outside the neat categories prized by the legal mind. But, since we have read the glosses on the Vienne decree in conjunction with a variety of canonical opinions in which that decree is cited, we know that the reality is much more complex. We have seen that, in practice, the canonists often did not follow the theoretical guidelines established by academic commentary, even when they themselves had written that commentary; and that in arguing cases that featured or were produced for quasi-religious clients, they used instead a wide variety of techniques to circumvent such guidelines.

At times they avoided an unwelcome interpretation of the Vienne decree simply by not citing it. For instance, *Cum de quibusdam* never featured in the discussions of the fourteenth-century Rota judges, who classed the beguine right of patronage as an ecclesiastical privilege, and who averred that "beguines live religiously and

---

Clementine," *BMCL*, ns. vol. 1 (1971): p. 55 n.47. The observation that Albericus was the only commentator to challenge Johannes Andreae's interpretation of *Cum de quibusdam* as a blanket condemnation of all beguines is made by Jacqueline Tarrant, "The Clementine Decrees," p. 303 n.25.

wear a religious habit and hence do not appear to be merely laity."[2] At other times they cited the enactment, but then discreetly avoided any reference to its standard, ordinary interpretation. In his defense of the *inhumati*, Panormitanus adduced *Cum de quibusdam*, but then proceeded to gloss it in light of the mitigating papal pronouncement *Ratio recta*, the result being something very different from the interpretation given it by the *glossa ordinaria*: "*Ratio recta* states that those women known as beguines who live honestly and who do not involve themselves in preaching are to be tolerated." And when the Abbot of Dikningen cited *Cum de quibusdam* he did so only in order to illustrate the errors from which the Brothers and Sisters of the Common Life had been saved!

Of course, the disparity between theory and practice was not always as pronounced as in the foregoing instances; it was not always necessary or even advisable to avoid reference to the gloss. When arguing for the extension of clerical privileges to Franciscan tertiaries, for example, one would not want to ignore the ordinary gloss to *Cum ex eo*, or to *Cum de quibusdam* for that matter. Yet the examples just reviewed demonstrate that a striking disjunction could and did sometimes exist; they show us that a jurist might argue one way in one circumstance and another when the situation required it.

"*Quod non agnoscit glossa non agnoscit curia*": The court accepts an argument only if it can be found in the gloss.[3] Thus ran the medieval maxim. Yet the *iurisperitus* violated that dictum time and again. In lieu of citing academic commentary that might prove injurious to his argument, he chose more congenial supporting texts— from the Roman law perhaps, or from Scripture or theology. Absent a condign gloss by a widely recognized jurist like Johannes Andreae or Petrus de Ancharano, he used those of a lesser figure, say Henri Bohic. These facts argue for an adaptability on the part of canon lawyers that has long been observed in the same era, although on a quite different issue.

---

2. *Decisiones antiquae*, cccxxxii, fol. 88: "*quia posito quod tales begnine sint seculares religiose tamen vivunt et habitum portant religiosum ideo non videntur mere laice.*"
3. As quoted in Helmholz, *The Spirit*, p. 15.

In the dramatic struggles for sovereignty of the late medieval church, canonists argued the case of the conciliarists as forcefully as they pleaded for papal supremacy—Panormitanus and Franciscus Zabarella, who articulated the conciliar position, and Nicholas of Cusa (d. 1464), who successively championed both council and pope, are exemplary.[4] In late medieval disputes about the legal rights and privileges of quasi-religious women, canon lawyers appear equally versatile.

Only further research into the huge volume of fourteenth- and fifteenth-century legal literature will allow us to determine the frequency with which practicing canonists affirmed the intentions of lawmakers by strictly interpreting repressive legislation, and how often they thwarted that intention by glossing such laws in ways that benefited rather than harmed those targeted. Such research, embracing some of the thousands of extant legal manuscripts and printed books (not to mention local archival material), will result in a view of late-medieval religious culture that is even more highly nuanced than that now offered by the best recent scholarship. But, even in the short run, there are insights to be gained from the study of commentaries, *consilia*, and *decisiones*.

As we have seen, the legal literature poses questions and establishes links that complement and often complicate modern research on quasi-religious women. The commentators on *Cum de quibusdam*, for example, generally felt that women implicated by the decree should not be able to hide behind a name. They observed that in different regions beguines might be called *bizzoche, continentes,* or *pinzocarae,* but that at root they were all still beguines, and therefore to be treated as such.[5] But while medieval commentators, like many modern scholars, routinely identified a variety of extraregular

---

4. Brian Tierney, *Foundations of Conciliar Theory* (Cambridge: Cambridge University Press, 1955) provides a survey of late medieval legal and political thought about proper church government and the canonists' contributions to the debates about the limits of papal authority. See Steven Ozment, *The Age of Reform, 1250–1550* (New Haven: Yale University Press, 1980), chapter 4, for highlights on canonical contributions.

5. See chapter two.

women as "beguine-like," they were not blind to distinctions which separated those women referred to in the Clementine decree from others. The canonists found certain similarities among female quasi-religious that were not to be obscured by "vulgar" regional designations, but they maintained that beguines *per se* were an ultramontane phenomenon.

Again and again they repeated that "there are many such [beguines] in Germany" or "beyond the Alps," and the second-hand reports of beguine dress and behavior furthered the impression that the writers were dealing with a group about which they had no direct knowledge. Cardinal Zabarella, for example, lacking first-hand knowledge, included mere hearsay about beguine dress (they wear grey or brown habits, unsuitably ornamented), and about their sex lives (they prove willing surrogates for those "penitents" who vow to abstain from sexual relations with their own spouses).[6] And Petrus Bertrandus was reduced to saying, "I hear that there are many such [beguines] across the Alps but on this side we do not have any so I am unable to provide a suitable example."[7]

Capable of seeing the beguines as part of a broadly-based European movement, without losing sight of beguine uniqueness, the canonists observed geographical and institutional peculiarities that made beguines uniquely Germanic. Accordingly, they linked beguines to an older Germanic semi-religious group: secular canonesses.

Bonifacius Ammannati stated the case with particular clarity, "Before this decree [*Cum de quibusdam*], beguines too, although not approved by the Holy See, were tolerated in the same way that secular canonesses, although not approved, were allowed to continue to exist."[8] Even earlier, Johannes Andreae had pointed up the connection between these two groups when he used the same conciliar

6. Franciscus Zabarella, *Lectura Super Clementinis to Clem. 3.11.1*, (Venice, 1499), p. 138.

7. Petrus Bertrandus, *Apparatus Sexti libri Decretalium cum Clementinis*, Paris BN lat.4085, fol. 154.

8. Bonifacius Ammannati, *Lectura Clementinarum*, Toledo, Biblioteca del Cabildo, Codex 23–1, p. 87v.

canon (C.18 q.2 c.25: *Perniciosam*), to support his comments on the dangerous "in-between" status of both canonesses and beguines.[9] Practicing lawyers followed suit. In *Consilium LV*, for instance, Panormitanus cited the decree *Indemnitatibus* and discussed the status of secular canonesses in relation to beguines; both, as he pointed out, were designated as "certain women who neither renounce property nor make regular profession." And in their *decisio* regarding beguines, the Rota auditors considered Johannes Andreae's comments on secular canonesses (in his gloss of *Dilecta*) entirely germane to their arguments.

Like medieval canonists, nineteenth-century Belgian and German scholars who sought institutional prototypes for the beguines had regularly noted the similarities between canonesses and beguines.[10] Both canonesses and beguines occupied a "third state" somewhere between the laity and regulars; both kinds of women were products of, and confined to, the area which contemporaries referred to as *Allemania*, the Germanic lands of the lower Rhine and present-day Belgium. Nor did traditional church historians and students of the canon law ever lose sight of the shared quasi-religious character of both groups of women.[11]

Although this interpretation has been out of vogue for some time, eclipsed by historiography that more precisely registered social, economic, and chronological disparities between canonesses and beguines, at least one noted scholar has recently suggested that it be revived.[12] Arguing persuasively that "the conditions that gave rise to the beguines in the thirteenth century may have been pres-

9. See Johannes Andreae, *Glos. ord.* to *Clem. 3.10.2 ad v. canonicae seculares*, in *Corpus iuris canonici* (Venice, 1584), p. 216, as examined in chapter one, for Johannes' treatment of canonesses, and refer to *Glos. ord.* to *Clem.* for his use of legislation related to secular canonesses in his commentary on beguines.

10. For a survey of such scholarship, see Joanna Ziegler, "The Curtis Beguinages," pp. 37–50.

11. Thus, Ristuccia, *Quasi-Religious Societies,* and Stanton, *De Societatibus,* list canonesses and beguines as exemplary since both groups exhibit only some of the features of regular observance.

12. Joanna Ziegler, "Secular Canonesses." See also Jo Ann McNamara, *Sisters in Arms,* p. 206.

ent in the region [Germanic territories] long before then, at least since the eleventh century, when the secularization of the institution of the secular canoness had clearly taken place," Joanna Ziegler's call for the reexamination of the relationship between secular canonesses and beguines would certainly have made sense to late medieval commentators.[13]

If modern historians have hesitated to pursue the question of secular canonesses as antecedent to beguines, they have thoroughly corroborated the significance of another distinction drawn by medieval glossators. As Johannes Andreae, and virtually every academic commentator who followed him, insisted, beguines were not to be confused with female tertiaries. Since both groups of women lacked the *tria substantialia* of religious life, Johannes allowed that sisters of the Third Order of St. Francis might be taken for beguines, but that in this instance it was more than just a difference in name that set the two groups apart.

Tertiaries lived a quasi-religious *modus vivendi* which had been approved by the papacy. Papal sanction, in the form of a rule of life granted by Nicholas IV, established a juridical distinction that neither Johannes nor any subsequent commentator was disposed to overlook. Even when glossing a law like *Cum ex eo*, which implicated some tertiaries in the heretical errors of the *fraticelli*, the canonists favored an interpretation that simply disassociated those heretical tertiaries from the genuine article. Repeatedly and without exception, the academic commentators refused to let female members of the Third Order be enveloped by condemnatory legislation aimed at beguines, and a good number of them were fully prepared to afford tertiaries ecclesiastical status as well.

Fourteenth- and fifteenth-century *consilia* show us that this theoretical stance had practical ramifications; as principals in contests over property and privilege, taxation and testamentary bequests, tertiaries appear as an accepted and even prized part of late medieval society. Modern scholarship demonstrates that beguines were quick to recognize and anxious to share this legitimate status, and

13. Ibid., p. 131.

that they did so by capitalizing on the technical distinction that the academic jurists had drawn between tertiaries and beguines.

After the publication of the Vienne decrees, beguines and their counterparts throughout Europe followed the letter, if not the spirit, of the canon law. Beguines in the Rhineland and the eastern Low Countries began to adopt the rule of the Third Order of St. Francis beginning about 1317, and by the mid-fourteenth century this survival strategy had been employed by many who lived outside of the protective precincts of large *curtis* beguinages.[14] In Italy, *bizzoche* communities became tertiary convents as a means of avoiding the obligation of cloister and as a way of continuing their semi-religious life.[15] And a similar pragmatism encouraged many Sisters of the Common Life (who, as we have seen, were frequently classed as beguines even in legal opinions written in their defense) to accept the Third Order rule in order to escape episcopal and civil investigation.[16]

Finally, it seems clear that when read in conjunction with other types of primary sources, late medieval canonical literature can supply an alternative perspective on a variety of issues that continue to trouble historians of quasi-religious women. Because the canonists' perspective is a legal one, their work can shed light on questions that emerge from, but remain incompletely explained by, narrative or literary sources. One such example is particularly cogent.

Social historians have observed that beguines were consistently

14. Walter Simons, "The Beguine Movement," p. 99 n.126, reads "The expansion of the Third Order of St. Francis can be easily followed from the Rhenish lands into the East of the Low Countries around 1317–1319 reaching the West by the mid-fourteenth century." See also Moorman, *Franciscan Order*, p. 421, and McDonnell, *Beguines*, pp. 547–53, who note the situation in the Netherlands as well as the affiliation of beguines in France with Dominican tertiaries. Dayton Philips, *Beguines in Medieval Strasburg*, p. 221 comments on the variety of arrangements for supervision of beguines who adopted a Third Order rule.

15. Sensi, "Anchoresses and Penitents," pp. 64–69.

16. Post, *The Modern Devotion*, pp. 270–72; Koorn, "Women without Vows," especially p. 138 and p. 143. See also the example of the sisters in the diocese of Utrecht: Hildo van Engen, "The canonical status of the tertiaries of the Utrecht Chapter."

referred to in wills and in pious bequests as "poor" and "pitiable," whereas in reality the women in question were often far from indigent.[17] These anomalous designations have been explained variously, as rhetorical flourishes designed to increase gift-giving for example, but never as having a legal rather than literary resonance. Yet, as we have seen, when the canonists referred to beguines and other quasi-religious women as "miserable" or "pitiable", they meant that those women belonged in the judicial category of *miserabiles personae*, that is, those individuals who, by right of a perceived but by no means exclusively economic disadvantage, were entitled to have their pleas heard in ecclesiastical rather than secular courts.[18] Even a provincial notary, employed to draw up a last will and testament, might have been mindful of this technical usage.

"The most striking feature of the fifteenth-century European church," writes church historian John Van Engen, "was its forbearance with a complex variety of institutional and personal expressions that its sixteenth-century heirs would not allow."[19] A new generation of scholars whose work focuses on the history of religious women have provided support for this characterization of the late medieval period as a whole. They have unearthed evidence for the existence of a broad spectrum of formal and informal communities of religious women in the fourteenth and fifteenth centuries—many of which were not supposed to have survived, or escaped, hierarchical censure![20] Indeed, it might be said that the closer we get

17. Penelope Galloway, "'Discreet and Devout Maidens': Women's Involvement in Beguine Communities in Northern France, 1200–1500," in *Medieval Women in their Communities*, ed. Diane Watt (Toronto: University of Toronto Press, 1997), pp. 92–115. Letha Bohringer, "Urban economics and semi-religious life in Cologne 13th–15th centuries," paper presented as part of the round table on semi-religious women, International Medieval Congress, Leeds, UK, July 2001, argues that beguines in Cologne were likely to have been well supplied by benefactors, if not always in well-documented ways.

18. See chapter five.

19. John Van Engen, "The Church in the Fifteenth Century," in *Handbook of European History 1400–1600*, ed. Thomas Brady, et al., vol.1 (New York: E. J. Brill, 1995), p. 309.

20. See work like that of Craig Harline and Katherine Gill cited in the Introduction. Gill states, for instance, that "In general, a high degree of

to the actual experience of the *mulier religiosa* of the later Middle Ages, the more ambiguous that experience becomes.[21]

It might be said with equal confidence that the closer we get to the work of the late medieval canonists, the less amenable it becomes to clear-cut categorization as well. The more closely we inspect the writings of the men whose job it was to interpret ecclesiastical enactments impinging upon quasi-religious women, the more that work sometimes surprises us by its failure to conform to preconceived ideas and traditions. Future study of this legal literature will repay the researcher who is both familiar with the professional conventions and expectations of late medieval jurists and alert to the countervailing exigencies of circumstance and individual agenda.

---

tolerance for varieties among women's religious communities prevailed in the fourteenth and fifteenth centuries" (p. 198).

21. I paraphrase from the Introduction to *Ambiquous Realities. Women in the Middle Ages and Renaissance,* ed. Carole Levin and Jeanie Watson (Detroit: Wayne State University Press, 1987).

Manuscripts Cited

Baldus de Ubaldis. *Lectura super Clementinis.* Vat. lat. 5925.

Bonifacius Ammannati. *Lectura Clementinarum.* Toledo Biblioteca del Cabildo, Codex 23-1.

Guilelmus de Monte Laudano. *Apparatus in Clementinas,* Paris, BN lat. 14331, fol. 79r–115v. and lat. 16902 fol. 166r–223v.

Jesselin de Cassagnes. *(Zenzelinus) Commentaria super Clementinis.* Paris, BN lat.14331, fol. 116–44.

————. *Commentaria super Extravagantes Johannis XXII.* Paris, BN lat. 14331, fol. 147–78v.

Juan Alfonso de Mella. *Decisiones reverendi patris domini Johannis de Mella.* Vat. lat. 2665, fol. 236.

Paulus de Liazariis. *Lectura super Clementinis,* Paris, BN lat. 4136 and Paris, BN lat. 4102, fol. 50.

Petrus Bertrandus. *Apparatus Sexti libri Decretalium cum Clementinis.* Paris, BN lat. 4085, fol. 154.

Stephanus Hugonetti. *Apparatus in Clementinis.* Philadelphia: University of Pennsylvania Library. MS Lat. 95.

————. *Apparatus super constitutionibus Concilii Viennensis.* Philadelphia: University of Pennsylvania Library. MS Lat. 95.

Bibliography

Primary Sources

Antonius de Butrio. *Super prima primi . . . Decretalium commentarii.* Venetiis: Apud Iuntas, 1578.

Aquinas, Thomas, *Summa Theologica.* Blackfriars ed. New York: McGraw Hill, 1964–81.

Baldus de Ubaldis. *Consiliorum, sive responsorum.* Venetiis, 1575; rpt. Turin: Bottega d'Erasmo, 1970.

Bernard of Clairvaux. *Bernard of Clairvaux, Selected Works.* Translated by G. R. Evans. New York: Paulist Press, 1987.

———. *Opera Omnia.* Edited by Jean Leclerq, C. H. Talbot, and M. Rochais. 8 vols. Rome: Editiones Cisterciensis, 1957–77.

Bullarium Romanum. 25 vols. Turin, 1857–72.

Busch, Johannes. *Chronicon Windeshemense.* Edited by Karl Grube. Halle, 1886; rpt. Farnborough, England: Gregg International, 1968.

Consilia Johannis Calderini et Gasparis Calderini. Rome: Adam Rot, 1472.

Corpus documentorum inquisitionis haereticae pravitatis Neerlandicae. Edited by P. Fredericq. 3 vols. Ghent: J. Vuylsteke, 1889–1906.

Corpus iuris canonici cum glossis. Venice, 1584.

Corpus iuris canonici. Edited by Emil Friedberg. 2 vols. Leipzig: B. Tauchnitz, 1879–81; rpt. Graz: Akademische Druck-u. Verlagsanstalt, 1959.

Corpus iuris civilis. Edited by Paul Krueger, Theodor Mommsen, Rudolf Schoell, and Wilhelm Kroll. 3 vols. Berlin: Weidmann, 1872–95.

De gestis concilii basilensis. Translated by Denys Hay and W. K. Smith. Oxford: Clarendon Press, 1967.

Decisiones antiquae et novae rotae romanae, a variis auctoribus collectae et editae. Rome, 1483. Hain # 6049.

Decisiones capellae Tholosanae. Toulouse, 1560.

Decisiones rote nove et antique cum additionibus casibus dubiis et regulis cancellarie apostolice, diligentissime ememendate. Lyon, 1507.

Decrees of the Ecumenical Councils. Edited by Norman Tanner, S.J. 2 vols. Washington, DC: Sheed and Ward, 1990.

Digest of Justinian. Latin text edited by Theodor Mommsen and Paul Krueger. English translation edited by Alan Watson. 4 vols. Philadelphia: University of Pennsylvania Press, 1985.

Extravagantes Johannis XXII. Edited by Jacqueline Tarrant. In *Monumenta Iuris Canonici,* Series B: *Corpus Collectionum,* vol. 6. Vatican City: *Biblioteca Apostolica Vaticana,* 1983.

Federico Petrucci. *Consilia sive mavis Responsa.* Venetiis: Apud Joannem Antonium Bertanum, 1576.

Franciscus Zabarella. *Clementis Quinti Constitutiones.* Basel: Joannes Amorbachius, 1511.

————. *Lectura super Clementinis.* Venice, 1499.

Gerson, Jean. *Oeuvres Complètes.* Introduction, text, and notes by Msgr. Glorieux. Vol. II, Paris: Desclée & Cie, 1960.

Gratian. *The Treatise on Laws (Decretum DD.1–20).* Translated by Augustine Thompson. Studies in Medieval and Early Modern Canon Law, vol. 2. Washington, DC: The Catholic University of America Press, 1993.

Grote, Geert. "Resolutions and Intentions, But Not Vows." In *Devotio Moderna, Basic Writings.* Translated and edited by John van Engen. New York: Paulist Press, 1988.

Hefele, K. J. von. *Histoire des conciles d'après les documents originaux.* Edited by H. Leclercq. 11 vols. in 22. Paris: Letouzey et Ané, 1907–52.

Hostiensis (Henry of Susa, Henricus de Segusio). *In Primun Decretalium librum Commentaria.* Venice: Apud Iuntas, 1581; rpt. Turin: Bottega d'Erasmo, 1965.

————. *Summa aurea.* Venice, 1574.

Jesselin de Cassagnes (Zenzelinus). *Glossa ordinaria.* In *Corpus iuris canonici.* 4 vols. Venice, 1584.

Johannes Andreae. *Constitutiones Clementis Quinti.* Venice, 1572.

————. *Glossa Ordinaria ad* Clementinis. In *Corpus iuris canonici.* 4 vols. Venice, 1584.

————. *In primum-quintum decretalilum librum novella comentaria.* 5 vols. in 4. Venice: Franciscum Franciscium, Senensem, 1581.

————. *Additiones ad Speculum Iudicale.* Strasbourg, n.d.

Johannes Calderinus. *Consilia.* Venice: Bernardinus Benalius, 1497.

Johannes de Imola. *In Clementinis.* Venice: Andreas Toressanus, de Asula, 1492–93.

Lapus Tactus. *Super Libro Sexto decretalium et Clementinus.* Rome, 1589.

Ludovicus Pontanus. *Consilia et allegations.* Venice: Bonetus Locatellus, 1500.

————. *Consilia vie responsa.* Venice: Horatii Mandosii, 1568.

Panormitanus (Niccolo de Tudeschi). *Consilia.* Lyon: Siber, 1500. Hain # 7187.

————. *Consilia cum tabula Ludovici Bolognini.* Strasburg: Heinrich Eggestein, 1474.

————. *Lectura in Clementinas.* Venice, 1490.

————. *Lectura super primo-quarto et quinto Decretalium.* Lyon: Jehan Petit, 1521–22.

Petrus de Ancharano. *Lectura super Clementinas.* Venice, 1493.

Sanctorum conciliorum nova et amplissima collecto. Edited by Giovanni Domenico Mansi. 31 vols. Florence-Venice, 1759–98.

Secondary Sources

Anderson, Bonnie, and Judith Zinsser. *A History of Their Own.* Vol. 1. New York: Harper and Row, 1988.

Ascheri, Mario, et al. eds. *Legal Consulting in the Civil Law Tradition.* Berkeley: The University of California Press, 1999.

Atkinson, Clarissa. "'Precious Balsam in a Fragile Glass': The Ideology of Virginity in the Later Middle Ages." *Journal of Family History* 8 (1983): 131–43.

Baldwin, John W. "Critics of the Legal Profession: Peter Chanter and His Circle." In *Proceedings of the Second International Congress of Medieval Canon Law.* Edited by Stephan Kuttner and J. Joseph Ryan. Vatican City: Biblioteca Apostolica Vaticana, 1965, 249–59.

Baumgärtner, Ingrid, ed. *Consilia im spätenmittelalter: Zum historischen Aussagewert einer Quellengattung. Studi/Schriften des Deutschen Studienzentrums in Venedig.* Bd. 13 Sigmaringen: Thorbecke, 1995.

Bechtold, Joan. "St. Birgitta: The Disjunction Between Women and Ecclesiastical Male Power." In *Equally in God's Image.* Edited by Julia Bolton Holloway, Constance S. Wright, and Joan Bechtold. New York: Peter Lang, 1990, 88–102.

Bellomo, Manlio. *The Common Legal Past of Europe 1000–1800.* Translated by Lydia G. Cochrane. Studies in Medieval and Early Modern Canon Law, vol. 4. Washington, DC: The Catholic University of America Press, 1995.

Berman, Constance. *The Cistercian Evolution. The Invention of a Religious Order in Twelfth-Century Europe.* Philadelphia: University of Pennsylvania Press, 2000.

Biller, Peter. "Words and the Medieval Notion of 'Religion'." *Journal of Ecclesiastical History* 36:3 (1985): 351–69.

Blumenfeld-Kosinski, Renate. "Satirical Views of the Beguines in Northern

French Literature." In *New Trends in Feminine Spirituality*. Edited by Juliette Dor, et al. Turnhout: Brepols, 1999, 237–49.

Böhringer, Letha. "Urban economics and semi-religious life in Cologne 13th–15th centuries." Paper delivered at Leeds, UK: International Medieval Congress, July 2001.

Bornstein, Daniel, and Roberto Rusconi, eds. *Women and Religion in Medieval and Renaissance Italy*. Chicago: University of Chicago Press, 1996.

Brenon, Anne. "The Voice of the Good Woman: An Essay on the Pastoral and Sacerdotal Role of Women in the Cathar Church." In *Women Preachers and Prophets Through Two Millenia of Christianity*, edited by Beverly Mayne Kienzle and Pamela J. Walker. Berkeley: University of California Press, 1998, 114–33.

Bruin, C. de, et al. *Geert Grote en de moderne devotie*. Zutphen: Walburg Press, 1984.

Brundage, James A. "The Calumny Oath and Ethical Ideals of Canonical Advocates." In *Proceedings of the Ninth International Congress of Medieval Canon Law*. Monumenta iuris canonici. Series C, subsidia. Vol. 10. Vatican City: Biblioteca Apostolica Vaticana, 1992.

———. "The Ethics of the Legal Profession: Medieval Canonists and Their Clients." *The Jurist* 33:3 (1973): 237–48.

———. *Law, Sex and Christian Society in Medieval Europe*. Chicago: University of Chicago Press, 1987.

———. "Legal Aid for the Poor and the Professionalization of Law in the Middle Ages." *The Journal of Legal History* 9 (1988): 169–79.

———. "The Medieval Advocate's Profession." *Law and History Review* 6:2 (1988): 439–64.

———. *Medieval Canon Law*. London: Longman, 1995.

———. *Medieval Canon Law and the Crusader*. Madison, WI: University of Wisconsin Press, 1969.

Burr, David. *The Spiritual Franciscans*. Pennsylvania: Pennsylvania State University Press, 2001.

Bynum, Caroline Walker. *Fragmentation and Redemption: Essays on Gender and the Human Body in Medieval Religion*. New York: Zone Books, 1991.

———. *Holy Feast and Holy Fast: The Religious Significance of Food to Medieval Women*. Berkeley: University of California Press, 1987.

Campbell, Gerard, S.J. "Clerical Immunities in France During the Reign of Philip III." *Speculum* 39:3 (1964): 404–24.

Cerchiari, E. *Capellani Papae et apostolicae sedis auditores causarum sacri palatii apostolici*. 4 vols. Roma: Typis Polyglottis Vaticanis, 1919–21.

Cheyette, Fredric, and Marica Colish. "Medieval Europe." In *AHA Guide to Historical Literature*. Edited by Mary Beth Norton, 3rd ed., vol. 1. New York: Oxford University Press, 1995, 617–24.

Cnattingius, Hans. *Studies in the Order of St. Bridget of Sweden*. In *The Crisis in the 1420s, Acta universitatis Stockholmiensis*, vol. 4. Stockholm Studies in History 7. Stockholm: Almquist & Wiksell, 1963.

Congar, Yves. "*Un témoignage des désaccords entre canonistes et théologiens*." In *Études du droit canonique dédiées à Gabriel Le Bras*. Paris: Sirey, 1965, 2: 861–84.

Constable, Giles. *The Reformation of the Twelfth Century.* Cambridge: Cambridge University Press, 1996.

Dolezalek, G. "Reports of the 'Rota' (14th–19th centuries)." In *Judicial Records, Law Reports, and the Growth of Case Law.* Edited by John H. Baker. Berlin: Duncker & Humblot, 1989, 69–99.

———, and K. W. Nörr. "Die Rechtsprechungssammlungen der mittelalterlichen Rota." In *Handbuch der Quellen und Literatur der Neueren Europäischen Privatrechtsgeschichte.* Edited by Helmut Coing. Munich: C. H. Beck, 1973, 851–56.

Dor, Juliette, et al, eds. *New Trends in Feminine Spirituality: The Holy Women of Liège and their Impact.* Turnhout: Brepols, 1999.

Downs, John E. *The Concept of Clerical Immunity.* Washington, DC: The Catholic University of America Press, 1941.

Elliott, Dyan. *Spiritual Marriage: Sexual Abstinence in Medieval Wedlock.* Princeton, NJ: Princeton University Press, 1993.

Elm, Kaspar. "Die Brüderschaft vom gemeinsamen Leben: eine geistliche Lebensform zwischen Kloster und Welt, Mittelalter und Neuzeit." *Ons geestelijk erf* 59 (1985), 470–74.

———. "Vita regularis sine regula: Bedeutung, Rechtsstellung und Selbstverstänis des mittelalterlichen und frühneuzeitlichen Semireligiosentums." In *Häresie und vorzeitige Reformation im Spätmittelalter,* edited by F. Smahel. München: R. Oldenbourg, 1998, 239–73.

Epiney-Burgard, Georgette. *Gérard Grote (1340–84) et les débuts de la dévotion moderne.* Wiesbaden: F. Steiner, 1970; rpt. Turnhout: Brepols, 1998.

Foote, David. "How the Past Becomes a Rumor: The Notarialization of Historical Consciousness in Medieval Orvieto." *Speculum* 75 (October 2000), 794.

Galea, Kate. "Unhappy Choices: Factors that Contributed to the Decline and Condemnation of the Beguines." *Vox Benedictina* 10 (1993): 56–73.

Galloway, Penelope. "'Discreet and Devout Maidens': Women's Involvement in Beguine Communities in Northern France, 1200–1500." In *Medieval Women in their Communities.* Edited by Diane Watt. Toronto: University of Toronto Press, 1997, 92–115.

Génestal, R. *Le Privilegium Fori.* Vol. 1. Paris: E. Leroux, 1921.

Gill, Katherine. "Open Monasteries in Late Medieval Italy." In *The Crannied Wall: Women, Religion and the Arts in Early Modern Europe.* Edited by Craig A. Monson. Ann Arbor, MI: University of Michigan Press, 1992, 15–47.

———. "Scandala: Controversies Concerning *Clausura* and Women's Religious Communities in Late Medieval Italy." In *Christendom and Its Discontents.* Edited by Scott Waugh and Peter Diehl. Cambridge: Cambridge University Press, 1996, 177–203.

Gilles, M. Henri. "Les Auditeurs de la Rote au Temps de Clement VII et Benoit XIII (1378–1417). Notes Biographiques." *Mélanges d'archéologie et d'histoire publiés par l'École française de Rome* 67 (1955): 321–37.

Grundmann, Herbert. *Religiöse Bewegungen im Mittelalter.* Berlin: E. Ebering, 1935. Translated by Steven Rowan as *Religious Movements of the Middle Ages.* Notre Dame, IN: University of Notre Dame Press, 1995.

Guarnieri, Romana. "Beghinismo d'oltralpe e bizzochismo italiano tra il secolo XIV e il secolo XV." In *La Beata Angelina Da Montegiove e il Movimento del Terz'Ordine Regolare Francescano Femminile*. Edited by R. Pazzelli and M. Sensi. Rome: TOR, 1984.

Guillemain, Bernard. "Les tribunaux de la cour pontificale d'Avignon." In *Cahiers de Fanjeaux, Collection d'Histoire religieuse du Languedoc aux XIIe et XIVe siècles*. Vol. 29. Toulouse: Editions Privat, 1994.

Hanawalt, Barbara. "At the Margin of Women's Space in Medieval Europe." In *Matrons and Marginal Women in Medieval Society*, edited by R. Edwards and V. Ziegler. Suffolk & New York: Boydell Press, 1995.

Harline, Craig. "Actives and Contemplatives: The Female Religious of the Low Countries Before and After Trent." *Catholic Historical Review* 81:4 (1995): 541–67.

Haupt, H. "Beitrage zur Geschichte der Sekte vom freisen Geiste und das Beghardentums." *Zeitschrift für Kirchengeschichte*. 7 (1885): 511–31.

Helmholz, R. H. *The Spirit of Classical Canon Law*. Athens, GA: University of Georgia Press, 1996.

Horn, Norbert. "Die legistische Literatur der Kommentatorem und der Ausbreitung des gelehrten Rechts." In *Handbuch der Quellen und Literatur der neueren europäischen Privatrechtsgeschichte*, Vol. 1, *Mittlelalter (1100–1500)*. Edited by Helmut Coing. Munich: C. H. Beck, 1973, 336–40.

Hyma, Albert. *The Christian Renaissance*. Hamden, Conn.: Archon Books, 1965.

Jelsma, Auke. "The Appreciation of Bridget of Sweden (1303–1373) in the 15th Century." In *Women and Men in Spiritual Culture XIV–XVII Centuries*. Edited by E. Schulte van Kessel. The Hague: Netherlands Government Publications Office, 1986, 163–75.

Jussen, Bernhard. *Spiritual Kinship as Social Practice*. Newark, DE: University of Delaware Press, 2000.

Keussen, H. "Der Dominikaner Matthäus Grabow und die Brüder vom gemeinsamen Leben." *Mittheilungen aus dem Stadtarchiv Köln* 5 (1887): 29–47.

Kienzle, Beverly Mayne. "The Prostitute-Preacher: Patterns of Polemic Against Medieval Waldensian Women Preachers." In *Women Preachers and Prophets Through Two Millenia of Christianity*. Edited by Beverly Mayne Kienzle and Pamela J. Walker. Berkeley: University of California Press, 1998, 99–113.

Koorn, Florence. "Women without Vows." In *Women and Men in Spiritual Culture XIV–XVII Centuries*. Edited by E. Schulte van Kessel. The Hague: Netherlands Government Publications Office, 1986, 135–47.

Kors, Alan C., and Edward Peters, eds. *Witchcraft in Europe, 1100–1700: A Documentary History*. Philadelphia: University of Pennsylvania Press, 1972.

Korth, L. "Die ältesten Gutachten über die Brüderschaft des gemeinsamen Lebens." *Mittheilungen aus dem Stadtarchiv Köln* 5 (1887): 1–27.

Kuttner, Stephan. "The Apostillae of Johannes Andreae on the Clementines." In *Études D'Histoire Du Droit Canonique*. Paris: Sirey, 1965.

———. "Harmony from Dissonance: An Interpretation of Medieval Canon

Law." In *The History of Ideas and Doctrines of Canon Law in the Middle Ages.* 2nd edition. Aldershot: Variorum Reprints, 1992.

———. "Professeurs de droit canon à Toulouse." In *L'Église et le droit dans le Midi (XIIIe–XIVe S.).* Cahiers de Fanjeaux. Vol. 29. Toulouse: Editions Privat, 1994.

———. "The Revival of Jurisprudence." In *Renaissance and Renewal in the Twelfth Century.* Edited by Robert Benson and Giles Constable. Cambridge: Cambridge University Press, 1982, 299–323.

Lambert, Malcolm. *Franciscan Poverty.* London: S.P.C.K., 1961.

Landau, Peter. *Ius patronatus: Studien zur Entwicklung des Patronats im Dekretalenrecht und der Kanonistik des 12. und 13. Jahrhunderts, Forschungen zur Kirchlichen Rechtsgeschichte und zum Kirchenrecht Bd. 12.* Köln: Böhlau, 1975.

Landon, Edward. *A Manual of Councils.* Vol. II. Edinburgh: John Grant, 1909.

Leff, Gordon. *Heresy in the Later Middle Ages.* New York: Manchester University Press, 1967.

Lehmijoki-Gardner, Maiju. *Worldly Saints, Social Interaction of Dominican Penitent Women in Italy, 1200–1500.* Helsinki: Suomen Historiallinen Seura, 1999.

Lerner, Robert. *The Heresy of the Free Spirit in the Later Middle Ages.* Berkeley: University of California Press, 1972.

———. Review of *Mort d'une hérésie,* by Jean-Claude Schmitt. *Speculum* 54 (1979): 842–44.

Levin, Carole, and Jeanie Watson. *Ambiguous Realities, Women in the Middle Ages and Renaissance.* Detroit: Wayne State University Press, 1987.

Logan, F. Donald. *Runaway Religious in Medieval England, c. 1240–1540.* Cambridge: Cambridge University Press, 1996.

Lynch, Joseph. *Godparents and Kinship in Early Medieval Europe.* Princeton: Princeton University Press, 1986.

Maffei, D. "Profilo di Bonifacio Ammannati giurista e cardinale." In *Genèse et débuts du grand schisme d'occident.* Edited by Jean Favier, et al. Paris: Editions du Centre national de la recherche scientifique, 1980, 239–51.

Makowski, Elizabeth. *Canon Law and Cloistered Women: Periculoso and its Commentators 1298–1545.* Washington, DC: The Catholic University of America Press, 1997.

———. "The Conjugal Debt and Medieval Canon Law." *Journal of Medieval History* 3 (1977): 99–114.

McDonnell, Ernest W. *The Beguines and Beghards in Medieval Culture.* New Brunswick, NJ: Rutgers University Press, 1954.

McNamara, Jo Ann Kay. *Sisters in Arms.* Cambridge, MA: Harvard University Press, 1996.

Menache, Sophie. *Clement V.* Cambridge: Cambridge University Press, 1998.

Miramon, Charles de. *Les <<donnés>> au Moyen Âge: Une forme de vie religieuse laïque v. 1180–v. 1500.* Paris: Cerf, 1999.

Moorman, John. *A History of the Franciscan Order.* Oxford: Clarendon Press, 1968.

Morris, Bridget. *St. Birgitta of Sweden.* Woodbridge, Suffolk, UK: Boydell Press, 1999.

Neel, Carol. "The Origins of the Beguines." *Signs* 14:2 (1989): 321–41.

Noonan, John T. *Power to Dissolve: Lawyers and Marriages in the Courts of the Roman Curia.* Cambridge: Harvard University Press, 1972.

Nörr, Knut Wolfgang. "Kirche und Konzil bei Nicholas de Tudeschis." *Forschungen zur Kirchlichen Rechtsgeschichte und zum Kirchenrecht* 4. Köln: Böhlau, 1964.

Oliver, Judith. "Devotional Psalters and the Study of Beguine Spirituality, with Reference to Beguines in the Diocese of Liège in the 13th Century." *Vox Benedictina* 9:2 (1992): 199–225.

Ozment, Steven. *The Age of Reform 1250–1550.* New Haven, CT: Yale University Press, 1980.

Pazzaglini, Peter R., and Catherine Hawks. *Consilia: A Bibliography of Holdings in the Library of Congress and Certain Other Collections in the United States.* Washington, DC: The Library of Congress, 1990.

Pennings, Joyce. "Semi-Religious Women in 15th Century Rome." *Mededelingen van het Nederlands Historisch Instituit te Rome* 47:12 (1987): 115–45.

Pennigton, Kenneth. "Baldus de Ubaldis." *Rivista internazionale di diritto commune* 8 (1997): 35–61.

————. "Nicolaus de Tudeschis (Panormitanus)." In *Niccolo Tedeschi (Abbas Panormitanus) e i suoi Commentaria in Decretales.* Rome: Libri di Erice 25, 2000, 9–36.

————. *"Henricus de Segusio (Hostiensis)."* In *Dizionario biografico degli Italiani.* Vol. 42. Rome: Istituto della Enciclopedia Italiana, 1960–2001.

————. *The Prince and the Law 1200–1600.* Berkeley: University of California Press, 1993.

Phillips, Dayton. *Beguines in Medieval Strassburg.* Stanford: Stanford University Press, 1941.

Post, Gaines. *Studies in Medieval Legal Thought: Public Law and the State, 1100–1322.* Princeton: Princeton University Press, 1964.

Post, R. R. *The Modern Devotion.* Leiden: E. J. Brill, 1968.

Power, Eileen. *Medieval English Nunneries.* Cambridge: Cambridge University Press, 1922.

Rehm, Gerhard. *Die Schwestern vom Gemeinsamen Leben im nordwestlichen Deutschland.* Berlin: Duncker & Humblot, 1985.

Reinmann, Gerald J. *The Third Order Secular of St. Francis.* Washington, DC: The Catholic University of America Press, 1928.

Ribbeck, Walter. "Beiträge zur Geschichte der römischen Inquisition in Deutschland während des 14. Und 15. Jahrhunderts." *Zeitschrift für vaterländische Geschichte und Alterthumskunde* XLVI (1888): 129–56.

Ristuccia, Bernard Joseph. *Quasi-Religious Societies.* Washington, DC: The Catholic University of America Press, 1949.

Rossi, Guido. *Consilium sapientis iudiciale.* Milan: A. Giuffrè, 1958.

Rubin, Miri. *Corpus Christi: Eucharist in Late Medieval Culture.* Cambridge: Cambridge University Press, 1992.

Rusconi, Roberto. "Women Religious in Late Medieval Italy: New Sources and Directions." In *Women and Religion in Medieval and Renaissance Italy.*

Edited by Daniel Bornstein and Roberto Rusconi. Chicago: University of Chicago Press, 1996.

Schäfer, K. H. *Die Kanonissenstifter in deutschen Mittelalter.* Stuttgart: F. Enke, 1907; rpt. Amsterdam: P. Schippers, 1965.

Schmitt, Jean-Claude. *Mort d'une hérésie: L'église et les clercs face aux béguines et aux beghards du Rhin supérieur du XIVe au XVe siècle. Civilisations et sociétés.* Vvol. 56. Paris: Mouton, 1978.

Schulenburg, Jane. *Forgetful of Their Sex.* Chicago: University of Chicago Press, 1998.

Sensi, Mario. "Anchoresses and Penitents in Thirteenth- and Fourteenth-Century Umbria." In *Women and Religion in Medieval and Renaissance Italy.* Edited by Daniel Bornstein and Roberto Rusconi. Chicago: University of Chicago Press, 1996, 56–83.

Simons, Walter. "The Beguine Movement in the Southern Low Countries: A Reassessment." *Bulletin de l'Institut Historique Belge de Rome* 59 (1989): 63–105.

———. *Cities of Ladies: Beguine Communities in the Medieval Low Countries, 1200–1565.* Philadelphia: University of Pennsylvania Press, 2001.

Smith, J. A. Clarence. *Medieval Law Teachers and Writers.* Ottawa: University of Ottawa Press, 1975.

Southern, R. W. *Western Society and the Church in the Middle Ages.* Baltimore: Penguin, 1970.

Stanton, W. A. *De Societatibus, Sive Virorum sive Mulierum in Communi Viventium Sine Votis.* Halifaxiae: Apud Custodiam Libariam Maioris Seminarii A Sanctissimo Corde B.M.V., 1936.

Swanson, Robert N. *Religion and Devotion in Europe, c. 1215–c. 1515.* Cambridge: Cambridge University Press, 1995.

Tanner, Norman. *The Church in Late Medieval Norwich.* Toronto: Pontifical Institute of Mediaeval Studies, 1984.

Tarrant, Jacqueline. "The Clementine Decrees on the Beguines: Conciliar and Papal Versions." *Archivum historiae pontificae* 12 (1974): 300.

———. "The Life and Works of Jesselin de Cassagnes," *BMCL* 9 (1979): 37–64.

Tierney, Brian. "Canon Law and Church Institutions in the Late Middle Ages." In *Proceedings of the Seventh International Congress of Medieval Canon Law.* Edited by Peter Linehan. Vatican City: Biblioteca Apostolica Vaticana, 1988, 49–69.

———. *Foundations of the Conciliar Theory.* Cambridge: Cambridge University Press, 1955.

———. *Medieval Poor Law. A Sketch of Canonical Theory and its Application in England.* Berkeley: University of California Press, 1959.

Ullmann, Walter. "The Recognition of St. Bridget's Rule by Martin V." *Revue Bénédictine*, 3–4 (1957): 190–201.

Van Engen, Hildo. "The Canonical Status of the Tertiaries of the Utrecht Chapter." Paper delivered at Leeds, UK: International Medieval Congress, July 2001.

Van Engen, John. "The Church in the Fifteenth Century." In *Handbook of Eu-

ropean History 1400–1600. Edited by Thomas Brady, et al. Vol. 1. New York: E. J. Brill, 1995.

———. "Friar Johannes Nyder on Laypeople Living as Religious in the World." In *Vita Religiosa im Mittelalter, Festschrift für Kaspar Elm zum 70. Geburtstag.* Edited by F. Felten and N. Jaspert. Berlin: Duncker & Humblot, 1999.

———. "From Practical Theology to Divine Law: The Work of the Medieval Canonists." In *Proceedings of the Ninth International Congress of Medieval Canon Law.* Vatican City: Biblioteca Apostolica Vaticana, 1997, 873–96.

———. "The Future of Medieval Church History." *Church History* 71 (2002): 492–522.

———, ed. *Devotio Moderna, Basic Writings.* New York: Paulist Press, 1988.

van Zijl, Theodore. *Gerard Groote, Ascetic and Reformer 1340–1384.* Washington, DC: The Catholic University of America Press, 1963.

Vauchez, André. *The Laity in the Middle Ages.* Translated by Margery Schneider. Notre Dame: University of Notre Dame Press, 1993. Translation of the 1987 French edition.

Wachter, S. "Matthäus Grabow ein Gegner der Brüder vom gemeinsamen Leben." In *Festschrift zum 50 jährigen Bestandsjubiläum des Missionshauses St. Gabriel.* Wien: Mödling, 1939, pp. 289–376.

Watanabe, Morimichi. *Concord and Reform: Nicholas of Cusa and Medieval Political and Legal Thought in the Fifteeth Century.* Edited by Thomas Izbicki and Gerald Christianson. Burlington, VT: Ashgate, 2001.

Weigand, Rudolf. "Ein Zeugnis für die Lehrunterscheide zwischen Kanonisten und Teologen ausdem 13. Jahrhundert." *Revue de droit canonique* 24 (1974): 63–71.

Wemple, Suzanne Fonay. "Monastic Life of Women from the Merovingians to the Ottonians." In *Hrotsvit of Gandersheim: Rara Avis in Saxonia?* Edited by Katharina M. Wilson. Ann Arbor, MI: MARC Publishing, 1987, 35–54.

———. *Women in Frankish Society: Marriage and the Cloister 500 to 900.* Philadelphia: University of Pennsylvania Press, 1981.

Winroth, Anders. *The Making of Gratian's Decretum.* Cambridge: Cambridge University Press, 2000.

Yunck, John A. "The Venal Tongue: Lawyers and the Medieval Satirists." *American Bar Association Journal* 46 (1960): 267–70.

Zacour, Norman. *Jews and Saracens in the Consilia of Oldradus de Ponte.* Toronto: University of Toronto Press, 1990.

———. "Stephanus Hugoneti and His 'Apparatus' on the Clementines." *Traditio* 17 (1961): 527–30.

Ziegler, Joanna. "The *Curtis* Beguinages in the Southern Low Countries: Interpretation and Historiography." *Bulletin van het Belgisch Historisch Instituut te Rome/Bulletin de l'Institut Historique Belge de Rome* 57 (1987): 31–70.

———. *Sculpture of Compassion: The Pieta and the Beguines in the Southern Low Countries, 1300–1600.* Brussels: Institut historique belge de Rome, 1992.

———. "Secular Canonesses as Antecedent of the Beguines in the Low Countries: An Introduction to Some Older Views." *Studies in Medieval and Renaissance History* 13 (1991): 117–135.

Index

abbesses, 5, 7, 11–17, 46
academic commentary, xxxi–xxxii,
   8–9, 131, 140–42; on beguines,
   108–13; *consilia* compared to, 50,
   81–84, 88; on secular canonesses,
   102–3
Acts (Bible): 4:32, 126
Ad audientiam (Gregory XI), 120–21
Ad nostrum (Clementine V), 4, 25–
   26, 31
Albericus Metensis: *Cum de quibusdam,* commentary on, 36–38,
   42–43, 47, 103, 139
Alexander III, Pope, 49
Allemania, 144
alms collectors, 29, 99. *See also* mendicants
Ambrose, Saint, 35
Ammannanti, Bonifacius, 100; *Attendentes,* commentary on, 21; *Cum
   de quibusdam,* commentary on, 21,
   41–45, 47, 66, 143; *Cum ex eo,*
   commentary on, 57, 60
anchoress, xxxi. *See also* quasi-religious women
ancilla Dei. See pious women

Andreae, Johannes. *See* Johannes
   Andreae
Antonius de Butrio, 45n64, 63, 75;
   Nullus, commentary on, 80,
   83–84
Apostillae (Johannes Andreae), 49
apostolic life *(vita apostolica),*
   xxvi–xxvii
Apparatus (Albericus), 36–38
Apparatus in Clementinis (Johannes de
   Imola), 20
Apparatus on the Clementines (Jo-
   hannes Andreae), 10–11
approbare/approbatam, 9, 17, 20, 39.
   See also papal approval
Aquinas, St. Thomas. *See* Thomas
   Aquinas
Arnold of Dikningen, 125–33,
   141
asceticism, xxii, 46n65, 80
Assisi (Italy), 98, 100
Attendentes, 7–9, 11–12, 21–22. *See
   also individual authors' commentaries
   on*
auditors, 104–5, 110–13, 144. *See also*
   jurists

161

"A Pernicious Sort of Woman" was designed and composed in Meridien by
Kachergis Book Design, Pittsboro, North Carolina; and printed
on sixty-pound Natures Natural and bound by
Thomson-Shore, Inc.